Praise for *Weed Empire*

"Under Adam's leadership, MedMen contributed more to MPP's marijuana reform efforts than all other cannabis companies combined, driving change across America from New York to Nevada. In an industry crowded with wannabes and one-dimensional thinkers, *Weed Empire* is an in-depth look at how Adam simply outperformed other leaders, mastering investments, operations, and cannabis itself. His influence on legalization and the industry's evolution remains unmatched."

—Rob Kampia, Founder and former Executive Director (1995–2017),
Marijuana Policy Project

"*Weed Empire* is a riveting narrative about the wild rise and dramatic fall of one of the cannabis industry's most remarkable companies. Adam Bierman delivers an edge-of-your-seat narrative that reads like a high-stakes thriller, propelling you through every twist and turn as you wonder what could possibly happen next. With its cinematic pacing and unfiltered perspective, it is a must-read for anyone curious about the roller-coaster world of legal weed."

—Shawn Gold, Founder, Pilgrim Soul Creative

"A must-read for all visionaries, entrepreneurs, and rule breakers. Adam isn't just a brilliant innovator but a superb storyteller. The journey he takes you on is as audacious as it is entertaining, and this book will leave you inspired to build, break rules, and create change."

—Dan Murray-Serter, Host, *Secret Leaders* podcast, and Cofounder, Heights

"I love Adam's *why* and the way he tells his story. He speaks the truth and now that I know the whole journey, I admire even more everything he's created and achieved."

—Joe Grande, Broadcaster and Radio Personality

"In 2014, when I took on the campaign for medical cannabis in New York, I knew the challenge was as much about reshaping public perception as it was about changing policy. Part of this fight was to reframe how people thought about cannabis—a battle that would require fearless, bold leaders. When I met Adam Bierman, I knew he was one of them: instinctively bold, brash, maybe a little crazy, but exactly the type of gladiator this movement needed. *Weed Empire* captures the pivotal moves in this fight, including the historic ribbon cutting on 5th Avenue—a defining moment in cannabis history."

—Diane Savino, former New York State Senator

"Fueling the explosive growth of the American cannabis industry, Adam Bierman broke new ground as a pioneer, securing capital and public market access where none had existed before. His vision and tenacity helped turn cannabis into a legitimate asset class."

—David Subotic, Advisor and CEO, DAS Capital

"Adam Bierman's harrowing tale of sacrifice, desperation, survival, and resilience humanizes the journey of a pioneer willing to die on his sword a million times to live his dream. *Weed Empire* gives readers insight into the tensions and trade-offs of a hopeful partner and family man as he navigates the complex and ruthless terrain of what it takes to build a unicorn in today's start-up culture."

—Emily Kwok, Material Artist

"Few have the privilege of witnessing history firsthand. I could have never imagined that I would live to see the day when marijuana is mainstream, but Adam Bierman did and built a billion-dollar business around it. MedMen's demise holds lessons too, but its lasting impact—good, bad, and ugly, is undeniable. *Weed Empire* is a thrilling and intimate ride through a modern day Gold Rush, told by one of its earliest and most influential prospectors."

—Daniel Yi, former Head of PR and Communications, MedMen

"Reading Adam's early journey is like flipping on a light switch in an industry long shrouded in secrecy. Love it or hate it, his 'Apple store' dispensary model forever changed the cannabis landscape, and its effects are ever-present in places like my home state of Florida today. At a time when advocacy groups avoided the issue, MedMen stood with Harborside as cornerstones in the evolution of CannaMoms—the first federally approved nonprofit of its kind. Harborside and MedMen represent the yin and yang of US cannabis, each driven by a shared vision to bring the industry out of the shadows. Despite its meteoric rise, Med-Men sank without Adam's leadership, his story serving as both a cautionary tale and a testament to transformative vision."

—Moriah Barnhart, Patient and Caregiver Advocate;
Founding Partner and CEO, CannaMoms;
and Cofounder and Executive Director; WISE Florida

WEED
EMPIRE

WEED
EMPIRE

WEED EMPIRE

How I Battled Gangsters, Investment Banks,
and the Department of Justice
to Build the Cannabis Industry in America

ADAM BIERMAN

Matt Holt Books
An Imprint of BenBella Books, Inc.
Dallas, TX

Matt Holt is an imprint of BenBella Books, Inc.
8080 N. Central Expressway
Suite 1700
Dallas, TX 75206
benbellabooks.com
Send feedback to feedback@benbellabooks.com

BenBella and *Matt Holt* are federally registered trademarks.

Printed in the United States of America
10 9 8 7 6 5 4 3 2 1

Library of Congress Control Number: 2024050110
ISBN 9781637746370 (hardcover)
ISBN 9781637746387 (electronic)

Editing by Katie Dickman
Copyediting by Michael Fedison
Proofreading by Becky Maines and Cape Cod Compositors, Inc.
Text design and composition by Jordan Koluch
Cover design by Brigid Pearson
Cover photo by Angela Derasmo
Cover image © Adobe Stock / mr_marcom (smoke)
Printed by Lake Book Manufacturing

For Laura

To Laura, my life partner, my ride or die and rock of our family.
Thank you for supporting me through the craziness and helping me become
the man I am today. Love you to the moon.

Author's Note

While I've made every effort to portray events and conversations accurately, my story reflects my perspective, which may differ from those of others. Some names and identifying details have been changed for privacy and security reasons, and some moments have been condensed (for clarity). It's an honor to share my story with you, and I hope it inspires you to pursue your happiest tomorrow.

Contents

Foreword | xv
Prologue | xvii

BOOK 1 | 1

BOOK 2 | 105

BOOK 3 | 199

Epilogue | 295
Acknowledgments | 297

Foreword

This story is personal for me. I remember the night. I was in college and supposed to fly back home, but of all things, I missed my flight. But when I arrived the next day, I learned that my cousins and my uncle had been arrested for smoking weed. They were in his van, listening to eight-track music, and *bam*—the cops got them.

It could have been me. If I didn't miss that flight, I would have been right there with them. They had the arrest on their records, had to live it, and a fight broke out in the family. I always thought it was unnecessary.

Since I started in politics, I've been open to the decriminalization of cannabis, to save other families from the kind of rupture mine went through. But let me tell you—it's no easy task. How do you take something that's been illegal, part of an underground economy, and turn it into a legitimate, regulated industry?

When I was president of the Los Angeles City Council in 2015, I first met Adam. He was a mover and a shaker, a guy that was the tip of the spear of that movement. He surged into my life like a lightning bolt—intense, deliberate, and impossible to ignore.

At first, I thought Adam was another young and cocky hotshot. But unlike so many leaders who are consumed by their own egos, Adam proved to be a great listener, an avid learner, and he leveled up masterfully as MedMen grew.

The first time I walked into the MedMen office, it felt surreal. It was sleek, modern, like walking into a tech startup—Facebook, Google, you name it. Young people with laptops, whiteboards filled with ideas, and talk of taking the company public. A weed company going public? That was unheard of back then. But Adam had a vision—he was determined to change the narrative around cannabis.

Adam was relentless too. He was always there, texting, calling, pushing his agenda. Sometimes, it takes a business to trigger societal and cultural changes, and the government agencies and policy makers just have to catch up and follow. MedMen made it clear that "stoners" were everyday people, transforming the optics of an industry from sketchy, underground dealers to acceptability and something legit.

Being a pioneer, though, comes with its lumps. Adam's genius—and maybe his blind spot—was his ability to move fast, to push forward at a breakneck pace, even when there wasn't much of a safety net. He took MedMen from a small dispensary in Venice to a public company worth over a billion dollars. I had a front-row seat to witness the meteoric rise and spectacular birth of an industry, only to later see how the forces of human nature can conspire to bring down even the best of intentions.

It takes a special kind of grit—to start a company from nothing, grow it to a billion-dollar valuation, and then walk away with grace. That grit is what this story is all about. Adam's determination changed the narrative, the culture, and the laws around cannabis. Now, instead of kids dealing weed on the corner or hustling for gangs, they can earn a paycheck with health benefits working at a store, protected by a union. Or they can even open their own business.

Adam's story is about more than just weed. It's about limits, and how we challenge and break them. That attitude should be all of our new normal.

Herb Wesson
Former Los Angeles City Council President
and California Assembly Speaker

Prologue

Here I am, alone at last, high up in my suite at the Four Seasons in Manhattan. It's the night before everything changes—the eve before my company opens on the Canadian stock exchange. Tomorrow, I'll step onto the frenetic pulse of Wall Street, our stock ready to trade at the morning bell. It's the culmination of my life's work in a single, climactic moment, and one that will finally put to rest any financial worries for me and my family. The startup I created has been valued at $1.65 billion. My stock alone will be worth about $300 million.

I've turned off my phone. It's 8:30 PM and past my bedtime—I need to recover and prepare for another whirlwind day tomorrow. Lying back on the crisp sheets of the king-sized bed and staring out onto the skyline of midtown, the air is indeed thin up here. I find myself breathing shallowly, overwhelmed by the weight. I had set out to mainstream marijuana. I had helped to create a new asset class and industry. My dream was to remove marijuana's stigma and invite everyone to enjoy the benefits. The vision was that college kids, Chardonnay moms, and even my ninety-year-old grandmother Harriet could buy a joint, smoke a vape, and go through life happier. And on this night, as so much of this dream has come true, I feel accountable for it all.

Personally, I am in charge. A company that I started from scratch now has over 1,000 employees all dependent on me, along with legislators we supported in campaigns, legalization advocates we financed, and hundreds of others who supported us along the way to this achievement: the first ever American cannabis unicorn now going public on a stock exchange.

Next to me, Laura, my steadfast wife, who always puts up with too much, is deep asleep. My mother, Mindy, who had flown in with us to share this historic moment, is in the next room over, caring for Mateo and

Ari, our two little boys. Given the stakes, I needed to sleep and focus. No margin for error.

Conspicuously missing is Rick, my father, my hero, my lifelong best friend, my first inspiration in business, and the lone force who laid the foundations of my ambition with his tough love. I never thought of inviting him. How could I, given everything he has done to us? Yet, our estrangement feels wrong at a moment like this. What good is victory without reconciliation?

———

Time for a joint. On the nightstand are my cannabis essentials: a half ounce of Durban Poison, my favorite strain and pure sativa. Hailing from South Africa, its focused buzz always delivers—in the MedMen stores, we call Durban the "espresso" of weed. I go to work using my Banana Bros. grinder and roller, which we also sell at our MedMen stores. Across the country, we carry thousands of SKUs, serving as a hub of innovation and consumerism. Back in 2016, *LA Weekly* called us "The Apple of Weed."

As I light up using a MedMen signature red BIC lighter, my suite fills with the sweetest haze. No worries. The Four Seasons staff, long familiar with my habits, have placed a commercial-grade air purifier outside my door, a nod to the changing laws and attitudes across the country, and the perks of a new kind of CEO in 2018.

With each pull of my joint, the memories flood back—moments from the shadowy corners of my past, a journey from the gun-packing jungles of the streets to the buttoned-up bankers of Wall Street. To get here, I had to write the rules while learning the lessons. There was no playbook to read, no documentary to watch on building a legal business in an illegal industry. I had to make as many decisions per day as possible, learn from the good and bad choices, then wake up the next day, ready to be better. While we were building out America's first national cannabis company, I had also become a spokesperson for the legalization of weed. And whether I was on television or in a board room, my job above all else was to create belief. A belief that we were all witnessing the end of the federal government's prohibition on marijuana and cannabis emerging as the world's most exciting new asset class.

Tomorrow, everything changes. Tomorrow, once that morning bell rings, I will have achieved the impossible. Tomorrow, I will fulfill my childhood dream of becoming the CEO of a publicly traded company. And yes, this public company sells weed. I had developed and evolved past my father and his demons.

I smoke and think and remember where it all began. Not with investment bankers, or with weed at all, but a poker game.

BOOK 1

BOOK 1

HOW NOT TO PLAY POCKET KINGS

I was perpetually broke. I dropped out of college after three years and three schools. I had started a sports agency that then became a marketing company, but only poker consistently paid the bills. I had been chasing the entrepreneur's dream since I was young, running fantasy basketball leagues, giving baseball lessons to kids, bartending at parties, and eventually putting on all-ages concerts for teenagers. I wasn't built to exist inside a system; even as a kid, I knew I would have to create my own. I hadn't chosen the easy path, although it never felt like I had a choice.

I was 25 years old and on a bad run, having just had the car repo man snatch my Nissan 350Z for failure to make my payments on the heels of getting evicted from our apartment. It was "our" apartment because I was living with the love of my life, Laura, and thankfully had her to help cosign the lease.

I had met her through my old friend Nate. I knew him in high school, and he was going to UCLA and living in an apartment off campus with other seniors. I was hanging out with him at his place one night and saw one of his roommates duck into her bedroom.

You couldn't miss her. She had raven dark hair like Snow White, skin as white as alabaster, and electric blue eyes.

"Who is that?" I asked Nate.

"Don't worry about her," he said. "She wouldn't be into you."

A few days later, I called the apartment. Nobody answered, the communal answering machine taking over.

"Uh, this message is not for Nate . . . it's for Laura. When you get home, can you give me a call? I'm going to a Super Bowl party this weekend and wanted to know if you want to come with me and maybe we can hang out after?"

She was in class during the day and working at night at Islands, a burger joint and sports bar. She called me back and we went to the Super Bowl party, a movie after at the Hollywood Grove, then ended up at a late-night diner. I remember the faded jeans she wore and the Burberry scarf around her waist as a belt.

"What do you want out of your life?" she asked me, sipping on black tea and forking into a slice of strawberry rhubarb pie.

Talking with her was so easy. I found myself feeling open and vulnerable—both uncommon if not unheard of for me. I spoke about my desire to provide for my own family and have a chance to raise kids my own way, the way I wished that I had been raised.

"Give my kids exposure to a better life than I've had," I said.

It was only a first date, and yet the conversation never stopped. The college seniors around us were in a daze, partying their lives away, and we were both focused, chased by haunted pasts and determined to achieve a semblance of stability in the chaos around us. We couldn't stop looking at each other, an eye contact so fierce it was as if we were reconnecting from a different lifetime.

But my lack of earning power was destroying the romance. After Laura and I got evicted, we moved into my parents' one-bedroom apartment. There, along with the modest living conditions, it would be impossible for me to hide our issues from her. A brilliant lawyer and entrepreneur, my father was also a gambling addict in denial, and by the time I finished high school, we had lived in a dozen cities, moving from one eviction to the next.

I was just itching to get us out of their place. My idea for a marketing agency had promise. I had teamed up with Andrew Modlin, a wunderkind designer five years younger than me. I would close the clients on a concept and genius Andrew would smoke a joint, put his headphones on, and create the logo, retail build-out, and website. We started with Kreation Kafe in Beverly Hills, one of the first fresh press juice spots, and got some attention. David Subotic and his wife, Tanja, were entrepreneurs who had an office across the street. They liked Kreation so much, they hired us to create Go Greek Yogurt, their own franchise concept. The agency had promise, but wasn't producing enough for me to stay on full time. Poker was always there. I had been playing cards as my main source of income since I officially dropped out of college.

On most days when Laura had class, I would drop her off so I could use her car and 20 minutes later find myself pulling into the parking lot of what had become my office building: the Bicycle Casino. Affectionately dubbed "the Bike" by us gamblers for its own unrefined charm, it was here amid the aroma of cheap Chinese lo mein and industrial-strength carpet cleaner where I felt most at home. The Bike welcomed the outcasts, the shit-talkers, the everyday grinders and gamblers—my people.

We started the game around noon. That morning, I had extracted every last dollar from my sock drawer, a wad of nearly $2,500, binding them neatly with a rubber band. I tucked the bundle into my front pocket and stepped into the unforgiving glow of the fluorescent lights. Here, retirees with sunken eyes and hopeful smiles clutched their chips and cheap cocktails, young hustlers clad in hoodies and sunglasses tried to make a quick buck, and middle-aged regulars drained their 401(k)s.

Deeper inside, the casino's pulse quickened. The clatter of poker chips— the clinks, the shuffles, the strategic tosses—melded into a continuous, rhythmic din. Dealers, with the efficiency of air traffic controllers, orchestrated the games of Texas Hold'em with a practiced, detached precision.

As I settled into my seat at the poker table, a familiar rush enveloped me. The chips were cool and heavy in my hands, each one a chance to change it all and get to the next level in life. To my right, Steve the Pool Guy, a retired contractor wearing a black velvet tracksuit, was making small talk with Amir, the game's host.

"So now I need to find a new divorce lawyer," Steve said.

"Sons of bitches," Amir said.

A few hours into this game I was even in chips, when fortune dealt me a sweet hand. Pocket kings. I tripled the raise.

———

From my earliest memories, the clack of casino chips and the whisper of cards gliding across the felt were more familiar than lullabies. My father, Rick, was my teacher, my guide. Though a lawyer by profession, he was a gambler at heart and used his sharp intellect to count cards at blackjack. My father's knack for numbers and personal charm led to a scholarship at Washington University for undergrad and law school, which kept him in St. Louis, where his side of the family is from. After graduating top of his class, he selected from his choice of enviable jobs and landed in Arizona of all places. The allure of big nights in Las Vegas proved too much for him to ignore. On weekends in the 1980s, he would fly to Sin City to count cards at Caesars Palace. Sometime after I was born, he stopped practicing law. I never got the real story.

My dad was never going to grind his way to a senior partnership at a prestigious law firm. His early hero had been Meyer Lansky, the infamous financial brain behind the Italian-American mafia from the 1940s through the 1960s. Just a small, sly Jewish guy from an immigrant neighborhood, Lansky managed to earn a fortune, wield power with a whisper, and never got caught. Lansky achieved all this using his deadliest weapon: his wits.

Dad was captivated by the "live by your own rules" ethos that the mafia embodied. He wasn't a part of that world, but he admired the defiant independence it stood for, shaping his life around that mentality.

After he got disbarred and stopped practicing law, my dad had the vision to start a business school. Launched with the cash from a paper bag handed to him by a New Jersey wiseguy, my dad was among those who started the first wave of professional business schools in the United States. At that time, the federal government was providing loans to Americans who wanted to attend a professional school. My dad was among the first to capitalize on the opportunity to pair aspiring professionals with government money. When the FBI showed up, he must have been doing well, because we lived in a country mansion on acres of woodlands in Potomac, just outside Washington, DC, located on a private cul-de-sac with a river behind us and endless forests crawling with squirrels and filled with deer.

In the late 1990s, various investigations scrutinized the administration and management of professional schools receiving federal funding. These loans included monthly student stipends, leading many to enroll solely to access the cash without attending classes. My dad was likely more interested in cashing tuition checks than monitoring classroom attendance. The feds didn't appreciate the wasted funds, so they shut down the school and, with it, our life on Big Piney Way.

"They're all just assholes," Mindy, my mom, would say. Her defense of my dad's decisions and the life we led as a result was always willfully, ignorantly articulated.

"Remember, we are all together and that's what matters," she'd say, echoing Dad's mantra, looking at me and Lauren and Michael, my younger sister and brother. "It's the five of us, and the rest is all bullshit."

As a kid, my dad was my hero, even after FBI agents knocked on our door and we hurriedly moved across the country to California. We left Maryland and moved the farthest we could on the map without flying over an ocean: San Diego. Dad launched a fruit stand. I felt embarrassed when the wealthy parents of my friends dropped by to purchase oranges and melons and I'd have to bag them up and carry them to their cars. I hated the shame of poverty, or at least not having the same lifestyle as my friends, and so when Dad started talking about get-rich schemes, I paid attention.

First, he tried to turn me into a professional blackjack player. I learned to count cards before I could drive. While other students in my class were reading *The Great Gatsby* and other classics, Dad quizzed me on playing blackjack.

"What's the count?" he'd ask on our father-son trips to Vegas, flipping over cards on the airplane's seat tray, pushing me to keep track of the weight of the deck (how many big cards were left versus the little cards) while deciding to stand, hit, split, or double based on having memorized the blackjack strategy chart.

Along with cards, he picked an aggressive career track for me. Harvard for undergrad and Harvard Law to follow. As a backup career, I was trained to play baseball for the family team: the St. Louis Cardinals. Since I started in Little League, we established a routine that lasted for nearly a decade: "A hundred ground balls, every day," he said, cribbing that training method from Ozzie Smith, the Cardinals' Hall of Fame shortstop and his all-time favorite player.

Sophomore year, I stole the key to my high school baseball field. Dad made a copy, giving us full access to the field whenever we wanted. Upon arrival we would play catch and then automatically take our starting positions, him at home plate, standing in the batter's box with our bucket of balls, and me at the infield grass cut-off in front of the shortstop position, on my knees. By removing my feet from the process, I was forced to rely on only my hands to field these ground balls. My dad used to watch Ozzie do this before games, and it was now part of our routine.

Not easy balls either. With my knees in the dirt, he'd let the bat rip, cracking into the ball. My palms were always bruised and sore from the speed of the balls crashing into my mitt, but during games I could always move in on batters. I was never afraid. My hands were fast enough to earn a college scholarship for baseball—not to an Ivy League school like Harvard, but a ride to Brandeis.

"Shoot for the moon, land in the stars," he'd say.

I admired his intensity. He woke up every morning at 5 AM, and soon so did I.

"If you want to be great, you can't be like everyone else," he said.

———

Dad's move to poker was instinctual. He turned on the television one afternoon and stumbled upon the very first televised poker event for which producers used a lipstick camera to reveal the players' cards. It was the World Poker Tour, a makeshift poker league that was televising its events on the Travel Channel, of all places.

My dad just knew. Even if there were only a few hundred people that day from across the country that had tuned in mid-week to watch a poker tournament on an obscure cable network, he knew. He understood that giving viewers at home the ability to see a player's cards as they are dealt and then watch them play through the hand as if it were their own would make for irresistible programming and create a new legion of poker players. On a lark, Dad called the poker room at the Bellagio and asked to speak with Howard Lederer, a prominent poker veteran and the winner of that World Poker Tour event my dad had watched. The poker room manager actually put the call through to Howard, and Dad pitched him on a business that would highlight Howard as a welcoming face for the next generation of poker players.

Dad then flew to Vegas, met with Howard, and discovered that he was working on an online poker site called Full Tilt Poker. They became partners, launching a series of "Professor of Poker" instructional DVDs and Poker Fantasy Camps with the intention of funneling traffic to the Full Tilt Poker site. The partnership was a success, as was the site, which would become one of the largest in the world.

He was finally earning enough to live with some stability, cultivating a sense of peace in him that was foreign to me. I remember the house he rented overlooking the ocean in Laguna Niguel, in Southern California, where he would have breakfast with Mom on the patio, looking so confident and proud of himself.

He was resilient, content, and on a tear until prosecutors from the Department of Justice swept in, initiating a crackdown on their operations. The site was shut down as part of a federal sweep—Black Friday, they called it—that targeted the largest online poker platforms operating in the United States, including Full Tilt Poker, PokerStars, and Absolute Poker, freezing player accounts and halting operations across the entire online poker industry. My entire life, Dad had warned me about pissing off the feds, and that's exactly what this upstart, renegade, online poker industry had done. I was determined not to repeat the mistakes I'd seen unravel our family.

———

Back at the table, I peeped at my cards. Pair of kings—pocket kings. Sweet hand. In Texas Hold'em, the only superior starting hand is pocket aces. With the power of the kings, I made my move, the strategy clear and textbook: re-raise the bet to thin out the field and isolate the hand, ideally to one-on-one, where the kings could reign supreme.

To my left, Steve the Pool Guy contemplated briefly before folding. Other players tightened up, sensing the shift in stakes, but there were three of us still in the hand for the flop. As the dealer fanned the community cards on the felt, the pot ballooned quickly, first to $500, matching most of my expenses for the month, then swelling to $900.

With each chip I pushed forward, I delved deeper into the hand, the pot climbing to $1,200. Every bet laid bare my resolve, pocket kings in hand, riding the thin edge between triumph and disaster. A nagging voice taunted me from the back of my mind, warning me not to go too far, not to lose, not to blow it all.

Now heads up, my final adversary pushed all-in with a boldness that rattled my confidence. My mind raced—visions of rent payments and empty pockets flickering before my eyes, the fear of returning home a loser. I felt scared, too hesitant to look my pocket kings in the eyes.

So I folded.

As my opponent raked in the pile of chips, I turned to Steve. His tracksuit seemed a touch less shabby under the dim lights, his wine almost too dignified in its fancy glass.

I revealed my folded hand to him.

"Kid, if you're going to play kings like that, you've got no business at this table," he said.

SLEEPING WITH THE RABBIT

I headed home—well, our temporary home, sleeping in the living room area in my parents' modest Marina del Rey apartment and calling it our bedroom—a truly fuck-me bitter moment, given the shame I felt as a kid every time we had to move because Dad's charm had run out and our landlords had had enough of his stories.

Trust me here. If you ever want to impress your future fiancée, I don't recommend sharing a bathroom with your parents, and especially your eccentric dad, who lords over the place, highlighting everyone's deficiencies (except his own).

"You're a fucking loser," he'd say to me, in response to basically any pushback I would give him on the "life coaching" he would provide.

"You cunt," he'd say to dear old mom, in response to anything she might question. Or if he was just in a fucked-up mood.

When we started dating, I tried to tell Laura that the warm, gooey, unconditional love that she received from her own family was foreign to me. She had grown up in Argentina, in a familial and friendly Latino culture. They hugged and kissed each other. They laughed at each other's jokes. They made small talk for hours. Ahem. Small talk?

Growing up under the thumb of Rick Bierman and enrolled in his Elite School of Hard Knocks, I only knew the cruel and ugly path to survival, and even fielding a hundred ground balls a day—while missing after-school playdates, birthday parties, casual hangs at the mall—was not enough to win me a heartfelt compliment, an "attaboy!", or hug.

He had his reasons for being so cold. Like many immigrant families, my great-grandfather left the family behind and fled the pogroms of Europe to land at Ellis Island and begin looking for work. Having worked as a farmer in Poland, he wandered west and settled in St. Charles, Missouri, where he could practice his trade.

Growing crops was a slow way to earn a living, and my great-grandmother got tired of waiting around for him in Poland and famously hopped a boat herself, along with all their kids, and somehow found her way to Missouri, and her husband. My family has been there ever since, for more than 100 years.

Leonard Bierman, my dad's father, was a salesman. He fixed up antiques and hand-me-down furniture, selling bed frames and chairs from the back of a truck in East St. Louis, now considered one of the most dangerous cities in America. To prepare for work each day, he loaded up a pair of guns, placed them in holsters under each arm, threw on a sport jacket, and didn't come back home until he was drunk.

With their dad spending all day hawking furniture in the slums, my father and his five siblings spent a lot of time alone in the house, learning to fend for themselves and stay clear of the old man when he came stumbling home. And my grandmother wasn't around too much either, working as a sales associate at Macy's and always off to a mah-jongg game. My grandfather must have been stressed because after surviving his first heart attack in his early 40s, he died of his second heart attack at only 48. His premature death put the household, already a haven for chaos, into a state of uncertainty. The role of family patriarch fell to my uncle Alan, the oldest kid and my dad's idol. But tragedy struck again: Alan was killed in a car crash, throwing the family into an even deeper abyss.

Amid this maelstrom, it was now my dad's turn to be the leader. He rose to the occasion, scoring nearly perfect grades in high school and earning a scholarship to college and then law school. He was Mr. Magna Cum Laude, brilliant with numbers and gifted with people.

"Why not?" he'd say, always cold-calling for new prospects or business opportunities. But there was another side to him marked by mood swings, darkness, and a gambling addiction that led to terrible decisions and drained our family's savings accounts and souls.

When I shared my family's history—and there were other stories, almost too dark to share—Laura always felt empathy toward my father.

As an expert in psychology and childhood development, she had empathy for Rick. She understood the connection between his trauma and his actions.

I didn't. He could have made an effort. He never tried. He was the worst roommate in the history of domesticated living.

"What are you doing for extra work?" he'd say to Laura, as if traveling an hour each way to school, working toward her doctorate, and then going into homes to work with children with some of the most severe cases of autism left time for "extra work."

Brave Laura. Humble Laura. Valiant Laura. She was so compassionate and sweet about our nightmare, spending hours after school reading, studying, going to the gym, or just walking around the neighborhood to stay away from their apartment, to keep the oxygen supply fresh, ready for another night in paradise pretending their living room was our bedroom.

I also found myself wandering to stay away, walking around the Marina and the paths that loop around the neighborhood and down to the inlet that feeds the world-famous Venice Canals. Here I could get lost and see the bigger picture. I wasn't alone. I was in a city surrounded by almost 10 million people, too many of them stuck in traffic, all seemingly scraping by, just like me.

As hard as we tried, Laura and I could not avoid my father totally. Sick with a cold and runny nose, a frequent occurrence given her work with kids, Laura was pounding decongestant and burning through boxes of Kleenex. She and I were used to this cycle of sickness in the house. Dad was not.

"What's with the fucking tissues?" Dad said, uncovering a trash can full and snapping. "Tell that filthy bitch to clean up her tissues and trash."

I got up from the couch and grabbed him by the lapels of his golf polo. Then I shoved him against the living room wall with a thud.

"What did you call her?" I prodded. "You call her a fucking bitch? If I have to pick between you and her, I'll always pick her. You will never disrespect her like that again."

I then stormed out of the house. Laura ran off after me, her face looking frozen. We hopped in her car and I sped off. I was gunning it, scaring her further, lost in a fugue of anger and frustration. We had no destination, no place to go, no money to spend. We drove around, aimless. Then Laura made a call.

Her best friend, Aubree, had a spare room. We could crash there, she said, only we would have to share the space with Jersey, their pet rabbit.

The air in the room was thick with a farm-like musk, a blend of Jersey's natural essence, the sawdust she lived in, and my own desperation. I wasn't sleeping much, my mind was spinning planning our next steps, and I often spent the night looking over at Jersey, our black and white spotted companion, ensconced in her cage.

She refused to sleep—scampering, nibbling at her water tank, and flopping around in her own pellets of poop. She'd thump against the cage, surely a ploy to get my attention. With my head on the pillow, I'd open one eye and there she was, nose twitching between the bars and with a look that said, "Tough night, huh, big guy?"

There was something about Jersey's bright, knowing eyes that felt too real. We were both prisoners in our own way, I thought. The difference was that Jersey had no choice. She was an innocent pet, enslaved in the attic. I had gotten myself here, dragging Laura with me. As the nights wore on, I studied Jersey. The little rabbit's life was simple: she pooped and ate, waiting to die. Maybe we were like that? Maybe life was that simple?

Next to me, Laura slumbered away under the covers, her steady breathing a reminder of how calm she can make me feel. Her parents were pushing her to take it slow, and I couldn't blame them. I got it. I wasn't Prince Charming, not right now.

THE BLUE-HAIRED LADY

The next morning, I felt determined to set our course right. I worked out harder than usual, running a little farther, feeling sharp, my senses heightened, ready to tackle the world.

"Just get in the room and it's over," I muttered to myself, using a mantra that I developed in college.

We got into the car and I tossed the Hartmann, a caramel leather briefcase—my father's hand-me-down from the '70s—into the back seat of Laura's car. The Hartmann had seen countless exchanges, more than its lifetime warranty ever promised. No sentimental value attached, just utilitarian, classic Dad. It wasn't my style, but today it felt like an extension of my armor, a declaration of intent. With it, I pictured myself commanding a boardroom table, while doing it my way, just like Sinatra. Inside the briefcase lay my arsenal—a yellow notebook and a trusty pen, the salesman's tool kit.

Still, I was so embarrassed by this setup. Los Angeles is a beast of a city that demands wheels, and here I was, navigating this concrete jungle, wasting precious hours and gas to drop Laura off at school so I could use her car throughout the day. It was a ludicrous loop—all because I couldn't keep up with the payments, just like Dad. Was he right about me when he said, "You're a fucking loser"? Or was he just projecting? Or were we both stuck?

The silence in the car was heavy as Laura and I pulled up to Alliant International University, her school. Dressed for class, she was the embodiment of ambition and grace. Soon, she would graduate and go on to earn her doctorate in clinical psychology. I wondered then how someone so smart, altruistic, and risk-averse could stand by someone like me. Her superpower was delivering warm, unyielding support—concepts alien to me. In my family, affection was seen as a sign of vulnerability, hence a weakness, and something to be exploited.

We fought over the silliest things.

"You can't wear sweatpants to Rosh Hashanah dinner," she'd chide me, before heading off to a holiday dinner with her folks.

"Why not?" I'd say, sticking to my guns. "If we're going to sit around making small talk, we might as well be comfortable."

The small talk, the aimless chatter, was a new concept to me. Time was always money to the Biermans. Why waste it?

We settled on jeans.

As I drove away that morning, watching Laura stride across campus and so confidently toward her future, I was torn. No matter which way I could steer us out of this financial mess, she was bound to get hurt. It was the price of being with someone that was wired like me—ruthless, relentless, a product of my father's genius and his flaws. The path I was on was unforgiving, and I knew no other way.

―――――――

Cruising down Sunset Boulevard to my lone meeting of the day, I was swallowed by the street's pulse—it's a living, breathing artery of glitz, glam, and the quintessential collection of LA's finest grime. Here, dreams are both forged and shattered under the relentless glare of neon ambition. Sunset serves as a kaleidoscope of LA's spirit—high-end boutiques brush shoulders with storied venues like the Whisky a Go Go, where The Doors and Led Zeppelin once played. Celebrities casually sip on overpriced lattes, while a stone's throw away, a hopeful street artist peddles his life's work. The sidewalks are strewn with the ambitions and disappointments of those who tread them, each aspiring star or washed-up veteran playing their part in LA's endless drama.

Shielding my eyes behind sunglasses, I scanned the signs for the address of the Sunset Super Shop, whose owner had reached out to us for marketing services. Lost in this urban labyrinth, my thoughts, too, were lost on my ticking financial bomb. After blowing much of my poker bankroll at the Bike, I was operating upside down and had no path to next month's payments. Driving around Sunset, I wondered: *What am I even doing here? Chasing pennies at some obscure weed dispensary?*

Pulling into the strip mall parking lot, I retrieved my dad's old briefcase from the back seat. The sight of its worn leather kindled a spark of inspiration. A glance at the car's half-full gas tank solidified my resolve. Now I finally knew where to go. Las Vegas was only a few hours across the desert. If I could double my funds, I could float through another month.

I hadn't spoken to my dad since the Tissue Incident, but when it came to conflict or emotions, avoidance was our way of coping—no apologies, no discussions. We simply moved on, ignoring the past. So, when I dialed his number and he answered, I jumped straight into my dilemma, acting as if nothing had ever happened.

"Hey, Dad, what do you think about this?" I began, laying out the dire math without mentioning our estrangement. "I've got maybe $3,000 left, and it's all going to be gone—first week of the month . . . plus stuff I need to pay for now . . . And no money coming in."

My words tumbled out, a rambling stream of nerves and panic.

"Do I just sit here and wait to run out?" I continued. "Or do I get in the car, drive to Vegas, and play the Five-Ten game at Caesars?"

The new poker room at Caesars had proven to be a mini gold mine, swarming with tourists happy to lose their money. Plus, the floor manager was liberal with comped rooms. I could be at the tables by nightfall. I could even ditch this weed shop meeting.

"Maybe I win," I mused aloud. "Maybe I cover next month's expenses. Maybe it buys me more time . . ."

Dad was silent on the other end. This was part of his Godfather-esque manner. Then he delivered his succinct verdict with a punch.

"What else are you going to do?" he said gruffly. "You can't just sit around. Get in the car. Go."

He was right. If I lost it all, I'd find a way to make it back. But first, I needed to find the Sunset Super Shop and have my meeting. I was already there and had nothing to lose to commit the next hour of my life to hearing what these drug dealers had to say. Then it was Vegas or bust.

Among a smattering of other establishments—a rental car outpost, a dusty travel agency, a Thai massage parlor, and a Persian ice cream shop—the Sunset Super Shop was tucked away, marked only by the universal symbol for a marijuana dispensary: a green cross.

I walked up to the door, skeptical. I wasn't against weed. As part of a rebellious middle school phase, I smoked every day. But that was a long time ago, and in no way a part of my life at this point. The whole dispensary setup felt like a sham, a hippie charade to peddle weed under the guise of medical necessity—a ploy from the Birkenstock-wearing brigade I'd always scoffed at.

The vibes were spooky as I approached the anonymous storefront. No sign bore its name, just tinted windows. The door, fortified and uninviting, required a buzz-in. As I pressed the intercom, a wave of paranoia washed over me. Was I being watched? If so, by whom?

"I should just head to Vegas," I muttered under my breath, entertaining the thought of turning back.

Then the door clicked open.

"You must be Adam," said the woman, stepping out from the darkness.

Her skin was as pale as porcelain. Her hair was electric blue, cut short and spiked high with gel—a modern-day Elvira. She extended a hand. Her touch was delicate, like a queen, and soon she had pulled me into the dim, dungeon-like shop.

As I looked around, the place looked like the set of last night's party. Cheap rattan chairs circled a chintzy glass table. A worn blue pleather couch was parked in the corner. A curtain, which Elvira promptly swept aside, veiled the inner sanctum of this odd little shop.

The back room unfurled like a scene from a Prohibition-era joint. Instead of bootleg liquor, the shelves were lined with medicine jars. Each was filled with a different marijuana strain that looked otherworldly. This wasn't the schwag I smoked as a teenager. These buds were impeccable, crystalline, sprouting red hairs like tiny flames. Elvira pulled me deeper into the store, introducing me to her partner, her stepson. He could have been the doppelgänger for Scooby-Doo's Shaggy. Slouched in his chair, he barely acknowledged me, his attention glued to his smartphone.

"He's the brains," Elvira proclaimed as we all soon found ourselves sitting across from each other at another glass table. I settled into my sales routine, comfortably shedding my jacket as I opened the old briefcase.

"So, tell me about your clientele," I ventured, fishing for insights into their business operations.

"Mostly young guys, all guys," Elvira responded crisply, her tone suggesting a well-versed script.

"And your daily customer count?" I prodded further.

"A hundred, maybe more on a good day."

I leaned in. "And the revenue? Monthly?"

"Three hundred thousand," she replied.

I paused, processing the information. "Annually?"

"No, each month," she corrected.

I masked my shock poorly. How was this unassuming dump raking in $300K a month? And in . . . cash? I did the quick math. That was $3.6 million a year! The blue-haired lady and her dopey stepson were sitting on an actual gold mine. As I thanked them and retreated to my car, the figures haunted me. I had only $3,000 to my name. They generated more than three times that in a day. Why was I going to Vegas, risking my bankroll? Was there a solution for me somewhere inside this world I had just discovered?

———

The drive back was a blur, my thoughts already spinning with the possibilities of a big score. For the first time, I began to notice the scattered presence of individual dispensaries across the city—each a small, unremarkable storefront marked only by a green cross. Their windows were either blacked out or nonexistent, giving nothing away. Were all these nondescript shops generating that kind of cash? How big, and how real, was this opportunity?

I needed more intel. I called Andrew Modlin, by now my business partner. He was younger and deeply entrenched in stoner culture.

"Is it actually possible for a weed dispensary to pull in over $300K a month in cash?" I asked him, skepticism threading my tone.

"No duh," he replied nonchalantly.

"Did you just 'no duh' me?"

"My friend manages one; she makes way more than that," he said.

As I drove down Sunset, I envisioned those green crosses marking spots of immense opportunity. The natural questions emerged. And the largest looming was why it didn't seem like anyone was trying to optimize anything. It seemed like a shadow economy, thriving unseen, the secrets known only to those on the inside.

The next steps seemed so obvious to me. Why not mainstream these stores with real marketing and a thoughtful retail experience? Why not make them feel normal? The thought of the blue-haired lady's shop made me want to take a shower, but what if they brightened the place up, slapped on some fresh paint, and hung up a vibrant sign? What if they removed that prohibitive black tint from the windows? If medical weed was legal, why should buying it make you feel like a criminal?

The possibilities began to stack up. With a full rebranding, maybe we could help her franchise? License out her brand? Expand her own product lines to other shops? The blue-haired lady and her dazed and confused stepson could become icons of LA's marijuana scene.

Then it struck me, a lightning bolt of capitalist ambition. Why hand over this lucrative blueprint to someone else? Why not spearhead this weed empire myself? Vegas could wait. I went home instead to study up on cannabis.

THE WEED LAWYER

I needed an entry point, an expert. And the man to see was Stewart Richlin, Esq., weed lawyer.

He had been a loudmouth for the legalization movement since the late 1960s. Online, I found photos of him in tie-dyes and long hair, but when we chatted on the phone, he was all business.

"Bring the retainer," he said.

The price: $4,000.

"Bring it in cash," he added.

I rolled up to the address he gave me in Hollywood. I was thrown off. This wasn't some high-rise office with a doorman and a sleek, modern lobby. He worked out of a townhouse on Melrose, the headquarters of his 420 Law Office (what else, of course?). I parked in its driveway as if I were visiting a friend's grandmother.

I approached the front door, a sense of unease creeping up my spine. My finger hovered over the doorbell, the bulge of cash in my pocket feeling more like a burden than reassurance. I rang the bell. Silence followed. No footsteps, no voices. Doubt gnawed at me as I checked the address again. Melrose—this had to be it, but the nagging thought of a con job lingered. Was this the final act of a well-orchestrated scam?

As I was about to turn on my heel and write off this whole venture, the sound of the door creaking open halted me. A woman's voice cut through the silence.

"Hi, Adam," she said, and my eyes turned quickly to look.

She was a vision from another era—a poodle skirt hugging her frame, short blond hair styled in a throwback fashion, and spiky stilettos that looked like they belonged on a runway in Paris.

"Follow me," she said with a voice older than her years. I ascended the wooden stairs behind her, each step echoing with the click-clack of her heels. At the top of the stairs, she pushed open the door. A heavy whiff of weed and incense hit me like a punch in the face. I took a seat in an imposing leather chair across from a desk the size of Grant's Tomb.

I looked around. Above the desk lay a kaleidoscope display of Tibetan flags. Richlin's lair felt like a museum of cannabis, filled with everything from vintage covers of *High Times* magazines to framed photos of Richlin rubbing shoulders with icons of the weed world, and a prominently displayed, larger-than-life picture of Richlin with Snoop Dogg.

Then he appeared, entering through a side door, the self-proclaimed sage of cannabis legality. He wore a pair of wire-rim glasses perched just so on his nose, and was dressed casually in jeans and a T-shirt. He sat down at his desk, hoisted his sneakered feet on it, and lit up a joint.

"I'm waiting for my partner," I informed him, trying to infuse a bit of professionalism into this surreal tableau. Somewhere out there, Andrew was MIA.

"Your time is your time," he said, with a nonchalant wave of his hand, as if we were paying him by the minute.

"Do you have the retainer?" he asked.

I fished out my wad of cash, the bills feeling like dead weight in my hands. He took it and started to count each note with the meticulousness of a seasoned bookie.

Once he finished counting, he pushed a stack of papers in my direction. It was a pile of legalese more than an inch thick, and it looked slightly less official than a Kinko's printout.

"I'm giving you this binder," he announced, and leafed through the photocopied pages, each one with sections marked in yellow highlighter.

"So you live in California?" he asked, almost rhetorically.

"Yeah."

"California passed Proposition 215 in 1996," he began, his voice taking on the tone of a professor lecturing a freshman class. "And the way that it works is there is protection legally now for medical marijuana patients within the state who have recommendations from doctors who are licensed."

He continued, talking like a machine.

"Those patients have the ability to share their cannabis in the event that they grow excess and other patients don't have the ability for whatever reason to grow their own."

As he spoke, I pieced together this puzzle—California's rules were set up as a cooperative, a club of sorts. A nonprofit where farmers and patients could share weed, a communal garden of green relief.

"As you can see here in this highlight, this section clearly states that any patient wanting to access a network or dispensary must sign these forms to provide consent," he droned on.

Inside the packet, I saw all the forms and templates our customers—scratch that, our patients—would need to sign. I got that part. Compliance, no problem. But it all felt fishy.

"What kind of license does this business have?" I probed, looking for some solid ground in this legal quagmire.

"Well, there are no licenses in Los Angeles per se," he replied, waving his hand dismissively. "But what will happen is you'll take all of these documents, and . . ." He paused dramatically, lifting a finger as if he were about to reveal the secret of the universe. "In the event that you can find a location," he continued, "I will go ahead and I will file the necessary paperwork. You will be operating a retail business and sharing cannabis with patients under the protection of the nonprofit mutual benefit corporation I will set up for you."

In the event that you can find a location . . .

Ah, there was the rub.

"Just so I'm crystal clear on where the line is," I pressed on. "That medical marijuana collective does not have a license to buy or sell marijuana?"

"No. It is a nonprofit mutual benefit corporation."

Great. More jargon, I thought.

"So how does the collective make any money?" I asked.

"Operators are able to be compensated for their time and energy running the collective," he reassured. "Again, I will file all those forms with the state once you have an address."

My time was nearly up.

"Okay, Stu, so I call you once I have an address, but am I at least protected enough with this paperwork, and without that license?"

"Well, yeah, that's why I'm here," he said, a hint of impatience creeping into his voice.

As I sat there, absorbing this barrage of information, I realized I was now the proud owner of a $4,000 stack of papers drenched in yellow highlighter that offered no legal protection to anything.

"I'll call you once I have a location," I said, grabbing the binder, heaving it under my arm, and heading off to find a spot.

THEY EVEN SHOT THE DOG

I t took a few months, but between poker winnings and income from the fees we were earning through the marketing agency, I had managed to save enough to afford an apartment in Marina Del Rey, next to my parents of all places. After grocery shopping at the local farmers market one day, Laura and I were headed home when the universe seemingly sent me a message.

Stopped at a traffic light, something caught my eye—the police. Patrol cars, unmarked vehicles, and an imposing SWAT truck surrounded a dispensary called Ironworks Collective. I watched in disbelief as law enforcement, guns drawn, swarmed the building. Some officers stormed inside, while others cordoned off the area with crime scene tape. As I drove away, my mind raced—what had I just witnessed? What had Ironworks done to warrant this? And more important, could the stack of papers Stu Richlin had given me protect me from a federal raid like this?

While reviewing Stu's materials the next day, I saw the news report. Those agents and SWAT team members were from the Drug Enforcement Administration, and they had raided Ironworks and another dispensary, confiscating their cash, stash, and plants. The reports detailed a chaotic scene: shattered glass, doors forced open, and, most disturbingly, a watchdog that had been shot in the line of duty.

One of the dispensary owners was arrested and was now facing criminal charges and prison time. Mandatory minimums were part of the federal law, and they existed regardless of the "paperwork" Stu had provided me under the protection of California. This was a problem that would not go away. Despite California's attempt to protect dispensary owners, marijuana was federally classified as a Schedule I narcotic, explicitly illegal.

During my morning runs, my meditation hour, I processed the puzzle pieces. The local laws provided a veil of protection, but it was thin and could be torn away at any moment by the feds. This opportunity was a minefield, but I just kept becoming more convinced that on the other side was a promised land. I would have to navigate this complex landscape wisely, threading the needle between opportunity and overreach, between making history and becoming a cautionary tale.

———

I studied up. While Laura was studying to get her doctorate in psychology, I was earning my master's degree in weed history. Hunched over my laptop, I began to deep dive into the world of cannabis. This wasn't just a plant. Cannabis was a historical juggernaut, a witness to human evolution, culture, and conflict. I wasn't just skimming; I was digging deep, unearthing the roots of this ancient herb.

I discovered a story from ancient China, 3,000 years ago, about an emperor supposedly named Shennong who prescribed marijuana tea for a myriad of ailments—from gout to malaria and even poor memory.

The trail led me to India, where cannabis, called *ganja* in Sanskrit, took on spiritual significance. It is mentioned in the holy script called the Atharva Veda as one of five sacred plants. I was fascinated by how it was deeply ingrained in religious rituals, used in ceremonies to commune with the divine. The plant wasn't just a crop; it was a gateway to the gods.

Then, Viking explorers, it turns out, used hemp fibers to make durable ropes and sails to cross the high seas. I could almost visualize these brave warriors, in their primitive boats, their ships rigged with cannabis.

I delved into Europe's relationship with cannabis, discovering how there the plant was also cultivated for its fibers and then used to make clothing and even paper. The American chapter unfolded next. The early twentieth century saw a cultural shift. Cannabis crossed into the United States, primarily brought over the border by Mexican immigrants, and began to grow in popularity among jazz musicians and artists throughout the country. I chuckled, reading the letters of Louis Armstrong, the godfather of jazz and big band, who was a stoner.

"It really puzzles me to see marijuana connected with narcotics . . .

dope and all that crap," Armstrong once wrote to his manager. "It's a thousand times better than whiskey—it's an assistant—a friend."

Muggles. Gage. Mary Warner. As jazz spread from the nightclubs of New Orleans to the North, musicians mainstreamed marijuana, singing and waxing poetic about the benefits of loosening up and feeling more fluid. I was snapping my fingers, listening to a catchy tune from Cab Calloway, who during the Great Depression released the song "Reefer Man," a playful take on the effects of weed.

The more popular weed became, the more controversial it grew. Directly after the end of Prohibition, when the federal government lifted their national ban on alcohol, federal agents targeted marijuana. Delving into this history felt like watching a movie, witnessing the pudgy racist bureaucrat (Harry Anslinger) start his crusade against cannabis, holding his hearings in Congress like fellow racist Joe McCarthy (Anslinger's good friend).

"Marijuana is the most violence-causing drug in the history of mankind," Anslinger proclaimed during hearings. It could not have been scripted more perfectly. "Most marijuana smokers are Negroes, Hispanics, Filipinos, and entertainers. Their Satanic music, jazz, and swing result from marijuana use."

Satan's music, eh?

"This marijuana causes white women to seek sexual relations with Negroes, entertainers, and . . . others," he claimed.

The forces for criminalizing weed, I was learning, were far from medical. They were political.

———

My first mission was to snag a location. After responding to all the ads I could find online, mostly Craigslist, I was nowhere.

"Not interested in that use," one landlord sniffed, as if the mere thought of our green cross and the parade of "patients" was enough to soil his property.

"Isn't that illegal?" another questioned, skepticism dripping from every word.

I pitched them my whole spiel—Stu's blessing, our bundle of legal magic, our mainstream appeal—but nobody wanted the patients. Weed, I was learning, had a terrible image in the public eye. Rent to a glorified drug dealer? Not happening.

Plan B: I hit the streets. I was like a detective on wheels, riding around on my beach cruiser, eyes peeled for rental signs, on the lookout for that one landlord who'd join me in my green dream.

Then, there it was on Lincoln Boulevard. A rental sign winked at me from a second-floor window. I was on the phone in a flash.

"Meet me there tomorrow afternoon," the voice on the other end said. An in-person meeting? This was my turf, my stage. I recited my mantra: *Get in the room and it's over.*

I rolled up early the next day, pumped and ready to charm the pants off this landlord. He was waiting for me outside. He introduced himself as a Navy vet, a retired fighter pilot, and he had the aura of someone's Uncle Bob—Midwestern, complete with the folksy accent.

Uncle Bob and I climbed the stairs and settled onto the bare, carpeted floor of the empty space. No chairs, no tables. We sat cross-legged like a couple of meditating monks.

"Tell me about what you'd like to do here," he said.

I launched into my plan, painting a picture of mainstreaming cannabis.

"It's legitimate," I insisted, thrusting the stack of papers that Richlin had given me toward him.

He wasn't buying it.

"There's one of these right down the street, and they do not appear to me to be legitimate," he said.

Desperate to build a bridge, I played the local kid card.

"I just want you to know, I live right down the street," I said, "and nobody's going to hustle harder to make sure you're paid rent early every month than me." I could hear the corniness in my own voice, the eagerness bordering on desperation.

Uncle Bob nodded, a thoughtful look etched across his face.

"Well, that's great, son," he replied. "I don't judge the dispensaries. Got friends who swear by it. Who am I to judge how people find relief?"

We moved into numbers. Rent was set at $1,500 a month, first and last payment due up front, plus a security deposit. We shook on it, and I was half expecting him to back out any second. But no, Uncle Bob was a man of his word.

I hopped back on my bike, peddling hard, my mind a whirlwind. I had done it—snagged us an address, 756 Washington Boulevard, soon to be the epicenter of my cannabis venture. I thought of the blue-haired lady and her bankroll. Soon, I would have my own. I pulled over and dialed Stu before I could second-guess myself.

"Stu, I've got a spot," I said, tripping over my words in excitement, rattling off about the traffic, the neighborhood.

Stu cut in, all business, laying out my next steps like he was reading from a grocery list.

"I'll file the final paperwork and register it to that address," he said. His tone was flat, sounding so cold and so far away.

"And then we're golden?" I asked.

"And then you're on your own, cowboy."

WELCOME TO THE TREEHOUSE

We had our first meeting in the empty space, imagining the possibilities. Andrew lounged against a wall, looking around. Our new dispensary was a blank canvas. The only furniture our landlord had left us was a dingy couch that looked like it was plucked from a fraternity house basement and had been the recipient of a million farts over the years.

"Guys, listen," Andrew began, his voice a blend of casual surfer dude and sharp-witted artist. "What if we turn that wall"—he pointed with a dramatic flourish—"into a chalkboard?"

I couldn't help but smirk, caught up in the infectious energy of his idea. It was what made Andrew so special. Status quo at a dispensary at the time was a printed menu, maybe placed inside a binder at the counter.

Andrew looked at this tiny space and said, "Let's go get some spray paint—it will be so cool."

We raced off to Home Depot, and a few hours later, we were back painting the wall with chalkboard paint. Each strain, each special offer, would be more than just a product; they would be stories told in elegant, sweeping chalk strokes.

"The website is going to be so next level," Andrew said, imagining our digital game. "There isn't a single good dispensary site."

Now we needed a name, a brand.

"How about 'the Treehouse'?" I suggested, a sanctuary above the noise, away from the day-to-day nonsense of life, a place to escape it all.

Watching Andrew bring the brand to life—converting the space, building the online platform, and creating an environment where buying weed felt comfortable—was a true showcase of his remarkable creative talent. I was partners with a once-in-a-generation visionary.

Five years younger than me, Andrew had grown to feel like a little brother. We were introduced by my mother, who had spent her career as a recruiter and recognized his potential from the moment they first met.

"I just interviewed the most talented person I've ever interviewed," she said. That was a statement—my mother had been studying résumés for over 15 years, and worked for major companies like Target.

"And he's only 20 years old," she went on, demanding I meet him.

I was expecting some cocky art school prodigy. Instead, I was greeted by a painfully shy young man, trying to blend into the walls. His cheeks were scarred with acne, his shaggy brown hair fell over his eyes, and he drowned in an oversized dress shirt. His parents were overachievers, a doctor-lawyer combo, and perhaps it was the pressure they applied that gave him the aura of someone who had never quite fit in. He had a rebellious spirit, but I wasn't sure who he was fighting against.

He did not present well. He was a mumbler, often tripping over his words—social skills were not his specialty. But when he passed me his portfolio, I opened it to the first page, and *bam*! It was like a revelation. Each page was a masterstroke. Visceral, tasteful, clean. His work leaped off the page, his art and designs filled with a voice that was clear, resonant, and emotionally moving. The work was bold, fresh, and it was unlike anything I had ever seen. Collections of contemporary art, fine art, and photography adorned each page, along with recognition, praise, and awards.

I hired him on the spot. He started doing graphic design for my marketing company, but he quickly became an ally. His looseness, his casual nature, was a complement to my rigid and ambitious professional self. It didn't take him long to go from freelancer to business partner.

I had been in a bind. As we got going with our marketing company, I needed $10,000 to pay all the business's bills, and had nobody else to turn to. I called an in-person meeting with Andrew and explained to him that I wanted him to become my business partner in everything we did going forward. He was too talented to share with the rest of the world. But to be my partner, he would need to contribute something.

"How much?" he asked.

"Ten thousand," I said, detailing our debts.

"Well, I was really wanting to buy this tiny sailboat," he said, to which

I retorted that once our business was running full throttle, he could purchase his own marina of tiny sailboats.

"Can you drive me to the bank?" he asked.

And so we hopped in Laura's Honda, and I drove us over to the Bank
of America on Wilshire. I parked out front with the hazards flashing, and
watched him come out a few minutes later with a thick envelope.

"Here," he said, handing me the cash. We then shook hands on the
deal, becoming equal partners on all projects going forward.

Now, over two years later, I watched as Andrew unloaded the mason
jars from the pallet they arrived on, carefully unboxing them on the floor
of our soon-to-be-open dispensary. Every jar felt like a reflection of the
boundless potential before us, and the doors that selling marijuana would
open and the countless opportunities it would create. As we put the final
touches on the space and prepared for opening day, those jars stood ready
to be filled, marking the next step in realizing the vast possibilities ahead
of us.

OUR FIRST STASH

My dad taught me a rule: If you don't know, start asking and don't stop until you find the answer. Now getting a reliable supply of excellent weed? How hard could that be? I hadn't smoked a joint since eighth grade, but I started asking around—first friends, then friends of friends. Eventually, at the Chabad house in Marina del Rey during Yom Kippur services, the holiest day of the year, one of our marketing clients introduced me to his younger brother, Shiloh.

Shiloh looked like Jesus. That day, I learned he had dropped out of Brandeis—the same school as I did—with dreams of cultivating the best weed on Earth. He had gone full hippie, forsaking the medical school path his doctor parents likely envisioned for him, to instead grow his hair long and preach the gospel of cannabis salvation.

"Sure, I'll hook you up," he said, when I explained my predicament.

Problem solved.

"Just bring a couple of empty bags to my place," he said.

On the way, I picked up Laura from her internship. She was about to graduate with her degree in clinical psychology. Dressed professionally in a gray pantsuit, her appearance was neat, her long hair styled perfectly, and her nails manicured short, reflecting her disciplined, goal-oriented nature. I felt guilty even bringing her along, but we were committed now and had the rent and the cost of all those mason jars and the chalkboard paint to cover.

"This is all crazy," she said, referring to Shiloh's offer and the empty Whole Foods paper bags in the back seat of her car.

"It's illegal. We could get arrested."

She'd never smoked, never been around drugs, and, outside of being with me, was generally allergic to risk.

"Honey, it's fine. Please calm down," I reassured her as we pulled up to the building, trying to muster more confidence than I felt.

"What about our apartment?" she said. "It's in my name. I could lose everything—my license, my future."

She was right, but I got angry and defensive.

"We need this, baby," I said. I was trying to convince myself as much as her. "We can't miss out on this chance. If you have any better ideas, I'm all ears."

Upon arriving at Shiloh's place, Laura grabbed my arm.

"What will I tell my mom if you get arrested?"

"Tell her the truth," I responded. "We are *not* going to get arrested."

Shiloh greeted us warmly at the door of his studio apartment.

"Welcome to paradise," he declared.

The apartment was bare except for a dingy couch and a grimy kitchen.

Shiloh opened the door to the bedroom area to reveal an indoor Eden: rows of cannabis plants thriving under intense grow lights.

"This is 'Amethyst Dream,'" Shiloh began, his voice filled with pride as he showed us around. "It's meant to uplift the spirit."

"I had no idea there were all these kinds, and they all look so different," Laura said, genuinely curious.

Shiloh looked thoughtful, his eyes searching the ceiling before answering.

"Life can be painful," he said. "This plant can help ease that pain. Life can seem tough, and this plant can take that edge off, allowing reality to present itself as simple and even joyful."

Shiloh was preaching. I was fascinated. Laura was impressed.

"Look at the trichomes on this bud," he said, referring to the tiny, hairy-like fuzz that grows on weed.

"Look at this purple," he said, inspecting a classic strain from the 1970s that came from DJ Short, whoever that was, tasted like blueberry, and was known for its sweet flavor and upbeat high.

I wanted the Treehouse to have a range of products, to present our patients with the best options. However, stocking a full range of strains would be costly. The going rate for a pound was about $2,500. Without any sales yet, we didn't have any more cash.

Shiloh proposed a solution: a sampler pack of various strains provided to me on consignment. This would put us into business with a range of inventory without any up-front investment.

I handed him the paper bags and watched him pack the strains into baggies with the meticulous precision of a surgeon. He then noted the names and weights in a little notebook. The plan: We'd sell them at the store and then pay Shiloh his share.

"Thank you. This is incredible," Laura said, hugging Shiloh and feeling enamored with his mission of easing pain and bringing joy.

"It makes me feel way more comfortable with all this knowing you're involved," she said. "This really was eye-opening for me."

Driving home, the reality of our venture weighed on us. We were silent, each lost in thought about the implications of having Shiloh's weed in the back seat and the immense potential of what we were starting.

"I'm not going to lie and tell you this doesn't make me really anxious," she said. The stench in the car was so thick it seemed to crawl out of the back seat as it engulfed the car in the dankest odor. Laura was holding her nose, trying not to get a contact high.

In the rearview, I kept an eye out for police cars and slowed down, driving like my grandma Harriet. If we got pulled over, we could get arrested. A broken taillight could take us down. I was driven by the desire to create financial security and an untroubled life for Laura and our future family. Now, thanks to me, we were driving home more vulnerable than ever.

OUR FIRST CUSTOMER

I t was opening day at the Treehouse, and there I was in our new dispensary, pacing back and forth like a caged lion. The place was quiet, too quiet, the kind of silence that makes you want to pull out your hair and scream. Had we made a mistake? In the back room, I watched the clock's hands crawl by, each tick pounding like a hammer.

"Where are they?" I said, wondering when the patients would come.

Our marketing operations were thin. We had no choice. We couldn't advertise—that was illegal—but we had listed our store on Weedmaps, a stoner's shopping guide. And yet, it seemed nobody cared. Another hour passed, and my frustration was growing. I knew nothing about weed—certainly not enough to sell it.

So I had enlisted Chris Bennes, an old baseball buddy and the biggest pothead I knew, to handle the customers. He'd moved up from San Diego for the opening and was sleeping on our couch. He was a fortysomething former college athletic trainer, with that Bruce Willis buzz cut. He wore a fanny pack (long before they were cool again), was in impeccable shape, and smoked out of an old wooden pipe all day long.

I waited in the back room, a boss of nothing. Just as I was about to start a conversation with the window out of desperation, Chris popped his head in, his demeanor as laid-back as ever.

"Hey, Adam, we got our first customer!" he announced.

"Who was it?" I asked.

"A kid from LMU," Chris replied.

A religious school, Loyola Marymount University wasn't far from us, just a mile or so away. I thought it was unusual—or perhaps it made perfect sense—that the first in our door would be from a religious school. Stoner rebels were everywhere.

"What did he buy?" I asked.

"Nothing," Chris said. "I had to turn him away."

My heart sank. I asked what happened.

"He wasn't twenty-one yet," Chris added.

I spun around, incredulous. Not twenty-one? Since when did we care about age? This wasn't some elite club with a strict door policy; it was a dispensary in LA, a city teeming with stoner kids. And buried in the mountain of legal documents that lawyer Stu Richlin had sold us was a guideline about age: legally, you didn't need to be twenty-one to buy weed from a dispensary. Eighteen was old enough as long as you had a doctor's recommendation.

I bolted out the door and sprinted down the street.

"Hey, wait up!" I called out, catching up to him. "I'm so sorry, it's opening day and we still have a lot to figure out. Come on back and we'll take care of you."

He turned around, confused but too polite to decline, and followed me back upstairs. Inside, Chris took over. He was a natural, talking strains and their effects. He was like a weed psychologist, promising a more chill, better future.

Eventually, the kid left, a little brown bag in hand and a lightness to his step. As the day went on, more LMU students came by, along with commuters and pedestrians who noticed the sign and made their way upstairs to check us out. As I locked up after our opening day, the thrill of success buzzing through me, a daunting realization settled in. This venture was more than a business; it was a tightrope walk over a legal and ethical abyss. But somehow, now that we were in it, my nerves were overtaken by a giddy feeling of sharing Shiloh's magical buds with our first customers.

I couldn't shake the desire for more. I started to realize there was an unexpected side effect to selling weed. It seemed to loosen everyone up, making the weight of the day feel a little lighter. Maybe, just maybe, it even helped break down the unspoken hypocrisies we all lived with, bringing a sense of honesty into our interactions and daily life.

The theory turned out to be true. Each day, more students from LMU began showing up at the Treehouse, quickly becoming a steady stream of clientele. But it wasn't just the students—the professors were my customers too, regularly visiting to tap into the benefits cannabis offered.

I called Shiloh to thank him. I had learned to never underestimate the draw of good weed—it transcends boundaries, slicing through societal facades, and can draw the most unexpected customers.

After the first month in business, I remember driving over to Islands, the burger joint where Laura had worked when we first met, before she'd quit in full-time pursuit of her degree in clinical psychology. Now, she had picked up a few shifts for some extra cash. I arrived about an hour before I was supposed to pick her up, sliding into a booth in her section and waiting for her to notice me. She was surprised and delighted to see me and I told her I was bored and hungry and wanted to be around her. I sat in the booth, munched on fries, slurped down an iced tea, and waited for her to deliver the bill at the end of her shift. I stuffed $3,000 inside the leather folder.

Her eyes lit up and she laughed. She sat down next to me, shoving the money into her tip pocket.

"Honey, this is all from the store?" she asked. "That's crazy!"

THE HOCKEY BAGS ARE IN MY TRUNK

I was a workingman now. But the routine wasn't pretty. I woke up at the crack of dawn to exercise and hopped on my beach cruiser, pedaling down Lincoln Boulevard. Opening the shop each day had become my ritual. I walked up those stairs, flicked on the lights, and checked the inventory to ensure everything was just so. When closing time came, it was the same routine in reverse: lights off, doors locked, and a quiet satisfaction that mingled with bone-deep exhaustion. Every waking moment was dedicated to keeping this dream alive, ensuring Chris got paid, the patients were happy, the cash continued to flow, and learning about a world only a niche group of criminally minded people knew about.

The gangs, drug dealers, and other dispensary owners did not seem to care about more people knowing about their businesses, let alone "retail branding." Competition could always emerge, but I just didn't see anyone treating one of these businesses as if it had a permanent future. Not when the feds, on a whim, could take your business away. I also could see customers being pulled to a store that acted like buying and selling marijuana was "normal." This was my opening and, if I was right, there was money to be made. Just like my dad used to say: Why not?

I understood that despite all those highlighted sections in the stack of documents that lawyer Stu Richlin had sold me months ago, my role at the Treehouse would be sketchy. I couldn't afford to become the next Ironworks. What if the agents from the Drug Enforcement Administration, feeling bored one day, decided to raid our dispensary? I understood I would be placing myself in the crosshairs of both law enforcement and my new competition: street gangs like the Crips and Bloods, the Mexican Mafia, the Hells Angels, and the dozens of other crews that thrived on the illegal sale of weed.

One afternoon, as I sat at our desk in the back room thumbing through the legal documents, I stumbled upon the clause about firearms and dispensaries. Stu had highlighted a typed recommendation: A nonprofit mutual benefit corporation is encouraged to avoid the presence of firearms anywhere in or around their premises. When a gun is present during a drug crime, the prison sentences for offenders skyrocket. But how could we protect ourselves against gun-toting gangbangers? As I peered out the window, watching the traffic on Lincoln Boulevard, a persistent sense of paranoia took hold. Someone was bound to come for us. I had to be prepared. And without the law to protect us, I knew that I would soon have to take matters in my own hands.

One day as I was sitting in the back office wondering how we could turn the business into a legal one, I was interrupted by a knock at the door. Chris's knuckles were rapping against the wood.

"We have a problem," he announced as I looked up.

"What's up?"

"We're almost out," he said, nodding toward our chic mason jars, which were getting perilously low.

"Don't worry," I assured him quickly. "I'll figure it out."

Supply was an issue. We couldn't just pop down to the local Weed-Mart for a restock. As the door shut behind Chris, I was left fretting about our dwindling supplies. Shiloh, our friendly wunderkind grower and primary supplier, had recently been promoted. His talent for cultivation had attracted investors who gave him his own farm to run up in Lake County. He'd moved up north to the Emerald Triangle, the country's cradle for cannabis, and I hadn't heard from him since. It was time to find new sources for products for the Treehouse.

Then another knock came, this time more urgent.

"Someone wants to see you," Chris said when I opened the door.

"Who is it?"

"Don't know." Chris shrugged. "Some guy in the parking lot out back. Says it's important."

This was it, I thought, as I marched down the stairs, expecting to confront a cop or a thug. But instead, I was greeted by a figure who looked like he'd stepped straight out of Woodstock—long hair, tie-dye shirt, dreadlocks.

His name was Sky.

"Hi, friend," he said, in a mellow drawl. "I've been meaning to stop by. I'd love to show you some of my work."

He motioned to the trunk of his Jeep. He unzipped a hockey bag to reveal one-pound bags of neatly packed Skunk, Purple Haze, and Blue Dream.

"How much?" I asked, peering inside.

"$2,000 a unit," Sky replied.

We were desperate. I knew the math; we needed a reliable supplier and fast. But could I trust Sky? He could easily be a DEA informant, or part of some setup to rob us.

"Let me think about it," I said cautiously, starting to turn away.

"You can have it on consignment," Sky called after me.

Consignment? That meant no up-front costs and less financial risk. Looking back at the Treehouse, I knew our inventory issues were critical.

"All right, we'll take it," I said.

As I lugged the hockey bags inside, the reality of what I'd just done hit me. I'd solved an immediate business problem, sure. Our startup would continue to be stocked. But I'd also stepped deeper into the murky waters of the drug trade, buying far more than the Treehouse had the capacity to sell.

Yes, we weren't alone in bending the rules, but a felony was still a felony. And the more weight I was carrying, the more we were a target for the gangbangers whose careers were made from stealing cash and inventory from newbies like me.

Riding home that evening, the city a blur from the seat of my beach cruiser, I felt like I was pedaling toward an ocean pier at night. My backpack was heavy with the weight of my snap decisions—a stash of contraband and wraps of cash. The lines between right and wrong, between legal and illegal, blurred just like the laws that were supposed to govern us.

Arriving home, I was greeted by the familiar comfort of our new apartment, though that comfort felt elusive due to the storm swirling inside me. Laura sat on the couch, talking softly to her mom on the phone, her voice a soothing hum in the background.

"Dinner at my mom's this Friday," she reminded me, but her words barely sank in. I was lost in my thoughts, heading to the bedroom to unload a shoebox full of cash and change my clothes.

"He's doing marketing for cannabis companies," she explained to her mom—not wanting to lie but not quite ready to tell the whole truth. "Just like the Greek yogurt projects," she added, giving it a gloss of legitimacy.

"Hi, Irma," I said over Laura's shoulder as I walked into the kitchen.

Laura hung up and turned to me, now furious.

"Ana is coming over tomorrow," she said, referring to the housekeeper that had been with her family for years.

"So? It's all out on the porch in hockey bags," I said. Within these bags, I had placed the product in tightly knotted turkey bags, but apparently it wasn't enough to keep the stench from taking over the apartment.

"This entire place reeks of weed," she said.

"Well, just tell her the truth, then," I said.

Instead, Laura heaved the bags up and left the apartment, scurrying into the garage and hiding them in the trunk of her car.

"I can't keep doing this," she declared back in the apartment, her voice echoing off the apartment walls. She marched off to the bedroom and slammed the door.

MEETING THE DOCTOR'S LIEUTENANT

Sky was not alone. Every day, working at the Treehouse drew me deeper into the shadowy underworld of the California cannabis trade, meeting characters that schooled me in the nuances of the weed business. The headquarters for the industry, of course, was the Emerald Triangle, the grower's paradise in Northern California. Like the winemakers throughout France, or the lab biologists at MIT, the passion behind these legacy growers led to the modern evolution of the plant. From these farms, the best product was distributed across the country. The routes were well known and controlled by the most powerful forces. To the north, the Hells Angels allegedly smuggled the weed into Canada and traded it for cocaine, which they then smuggled back into the States. To the east, filled shipping trucks hit the major cities, making the big stops in Chicago and later New York.

The most important and largest market is of course California itself, a state worth an estimated $8 billion annually in illicit sales around that time. Shipments made their way through Interstate 5, stopping in San Francisco and later Los Angeles and San Diego, powered by an established network of freelance operators that had, for years, moved product for farms.

Take Joey, for instance. He'd been shuttling product from the Emerald Triangle for decades. His face was as weathered as an old leather jacket, with eyes that looked like they had seen a little too much. He'd shuffle in with a battered hockey bag, his voice a gravel road, raspy from years of smoking and whispers.

"I need to get these OGs off my hands," he said. "I'll make you a deal if you take all 10 units."

There were all kinds of reasons a guy like Joey would be desperate to make a deal even on consignment. His reasons were not my business, but improving my margins certainly was.

Then there was Sasha. She was sleek, her methods refined. Her designer tote never contained anything so crude as a hockey bag's contents; instead, she dealt her goods with the flair of a couturier.

Scotty, in contrast, played the part of the laid-back surfer with his penny loafers and Hawaiian shirts and blond ponytail that flowed like a golden stream.

"I'm happy to meet you tonight at the bar to talk about business opportunities," he would text.

He was into everything from weed to pills to counterfeit hats and clothing. I would hear him out, always focused on the weed side of his world, but fascinated as I feigned interest in all the rest.

Soon, the business grew. Each week, we were taking in $20,000 in sales, all cash transactions. I was making enough to lease a Toyota Prius to drive to work, and it was clear to me that our small-time operation could not keep up with our demand. We needed more product, and at lower prices, to increase our margins. We were already buying in bulk, but our business needed as much traditional retail planning as was possible. Up to that point, I was reacting to what was brought to my doorstep, and handling street-level dealers was cumbersome and risky. It was time to create our own supply chain.

Scotty made the first big connection. He introduced me to Jackie, a respected veteran in the game, who had paid his dues, including a federal prison stint. Our first meeting took place at Freebirds Burritos, one of my spots close to the dispensary on Lincoln, a laughably casual setting for a discussion that would determine the trajectory of my enterprise. Standing in line ordering burritos like we were friends out after a party, Jackie looked like he had come from the golf course, with a collared shirt, massive Rolex, and Chinese tattoos crawling up his neck.

"Congrats," he said.

"On what?" I wondered.

"You've made it this far."

His laughter was infectious and, for a moment, I joined in, allowing myself to release a spurt of steam from the nerve-packed pressure cooker I'd become.

"I may be able to help you ascend the ladder in this game," he said.

We agreed to terms that would catapult my business. With Jackie, I now had a steady supply of high-grade product at a manageable cost. Our margins exploded, along with our profits. But the more I was saving on product, and the better I was getting at this business, the deeper I was diving into criminal waters.

Driving back to my apartment complex, lost in thought about logistics and strategies, I nearly collided with a Mercedes pulling into our lot. I looked over. It was Jackie. The irony wasn't lost on either of us and we both simultaneously rolled down our windows and busted out laughing; here was my supplier, my new advisor, and he was now also my neighbor.

Unbeknownst to me, we had been living in the same apartment complex. At that moment, I saw a glimpse of my future in him. If I stayed on my current path, I could achieve the stability he had. Despite his reputation and earnings, he wasn't living extravagantly in a mansion by the beach, blowing his cash. Instead, he chose a modest two-bedroom apartment, where he was raising his family and providing for his three young daughters. His life was a paradox—stable and grounded, yet built on dealing drugs. What stood out to me most: his intelligence. Jackie was far more than just a gangbanger, and this depth gave me hope for my own path forward.

AMONG THE DOCTOR'S HENCHMEN

s the weeks turned into months, I spent more time with Jackie, learning the more intricate parts of the business and its players. I also met his family, his young daughters. We were growing close, and he could see my potential. He also introduced me to his inner circle.

"Time to meet the Duke," he said one day as I got in his car.

We drove downtown. Duke's warehouse was fortress-like, with high fences and security cameras at every turn. Inside, the space was vast, filled with row upon row of cannabis in various stages of packaging. Duke himself was an imposing figure, his burly frame matched by a booming voice that echoed off the concrete walls.

The relationship was straightforward. Duke would supply me with high-quality cannabis at a discount, trusting that I would maintain the discretion and reliability required for such a partnership.

As he spoke, I noticed that Jackie and Duke had referred often to the Doctor, surely their boss. He was an elusive figure, rumored to be the linchpin in a sophisticated operation that used shipping companies to move weed across the states. His identity was a closely guarded secret, known only to those deeply embedded in the network.

Leaving Duke's warehouse, the weight of the evening's agreements settled on me. I was now in with them, and thus under the thumb of the Doctor too. I owed it all to my neighbor Jackie. He opened a door I could never close, leading me through a supply chain of risk and opportunity. As I parked outside my apartment, the reality of my situation was clear. I was no longer just a dispensary owner; I was on my way to becoming a significant node in a massive drug distribution network, climbing the ranks of an empire ruled by shadowy figures like the Doctor.

Stepping into my apartment, I realized that I was now playing in a world where mistakes were not just costly, but constantly becoming more dangerous. Every level up meant I had to be that much more in it to stay ahead and maybe even to stay alive. The game had changed, and so had I.

I needed protection. I asked around about security for hire. Scotty, my Hawaiian-shirt-clad connector, had a lead and set up the meeting. Under the darkness of night, I left the apartment, Laura asleep and blissfully unaware. This had become my life, and living outside the protection of the law means protecting yourself.

We met at The Whaler, a dive bar in Venice Beach infamous for its mediocre fries, watered-down drinks, and drug deals amid the patrons. We chose a dimly lit table outside, the ocean's murmur mingling with distant laughter and clinking glasses.

Rags was built like a fullback. He had a rap sheet, a gun, and he worked off the books.

"I just need the work," he said.

Rags was a strategic hire. As a lifetime Crip, he wasn't just personal muscle. He was part of a storied institution that had deep roots in Los Angeles's complex social fabric. They were intricately woven into the narrative of LA's drug trade. They were sophisticated, almost corporate, in their logistics and reach.

Our arrangement was simple.

"I'll pay you $200 each time you come out with me," I explained, laying out the terms of our deal. "Could be half an hour; could be four hours."

Reliability and readiness were crucial.

"If I text, you gotta be ready. I need you there," I stressed.

He gave a nod.

"I'm down for whatever," he said.

MR. BRAZIL AND THE BACKPACK OF CASH

S oon, I was now spending time with Duke, and he became my point of contact. He was reliable and resourceful. He always delivered what he said, when he said, and for the best price that I could find. Sometimes he forced me—as everyone did—to take on more product than I wanted. But there were margins in wholesale, and I didn't have much of a choice.

He also had his own network, always looking for an opportunity.

"There's someone I want you to meet," he said one day. "A guy I know from Brazil, looking to invest. Maybe sell the Treehouse?"

I didn't believe him. The possibility of selling the Treehouse had never crossed my mind. I was too wrapped up in the daily grind to consider an exit. Yet, here it was, a potential opportunity to cash out with a profit. Or perhaps a trap, rife with risks unknown?

The following day, giddy with the prospect of selling my first weed business within a year of opening, I drove to Panera Bread, one of my common meeting spots, to meet Mr. Brazil, Duke's prospective buyer. The yeasty smell of hot bread and roasted coffee was floating through the windows.

I spotted him immediately. Bryan sat outside at a café table, chain-smoking cigarettes, looking every part the Brazilian beach bum who had strolled off Venice Beach. He wore a white linen shirt and linen pants and was putting out the butt of a thin cigarette.

"Ola, nice to meet you," Bryan greeted, his English tinged with a Portuguese rhythm, practical and straightforward.

"Likewise," I replied, settling across from him. The clatter of dishes and the murmur of conversations around us felt distant, secondary to the gravity of our meeting.

I pretended to be casual, trying to sound more confident than I felt.

"So, what are you thinking?" I began.

"I'm interested," he said, telling me that he ran bars and nightclubs back in Brazil. He liked the idea of all-cash businesses.

"The Treehouse is our baby," I went on, telling him how hard we had all worked and suffered to get the business up and running.

"What price would you accept?" he asked.

"I've thought about it—the run rate, the investment—and probably the lowest price we would take is $500,000."

He squirmed in his café chair.

"I don't think we can afford a half million," he said, running his fingers through his hair.

"What's the maximum you can spend?" I asked.

"Probably $250,000," he said.

I got up to leave.

"I'm afraid that just won't make sense for me," I said, thanked him for his time.

"I understand," he said. "It's a big decision. But think about it—this is clean for you, and I'm ready to move. That's the most I can do though."

Driving back toward the Treehouse, I felt confident that I had played the hand correctly. Sooner or later, Bryan would come back to me and increase his offer. I had no idea how to put a number on our business. I was making it all up, but I knew that based on my experience in negotiations, and that timeless wisdom from my dad ("be willing to walk away"), Bryan would be crawling back. Quickly, a sense of panic washed over me. What if I was wrong? Had I just turned down $250,000? Only recently, I was sharing a room with a pet rabbit.

Arriving at the Treehouse, I sprinted up the stairs and zipped past Chris, heading straight to the desk behind the weed counter, opened my laptop, and wrote: "Bryan, Good to meet you. Upon further consideration, we will accept your offer of $250,000. Let me know when we can discuss next steps. Congratulations!"

———

I expected a back-alley transfer of cash and keys, but Bryan wanted to meet at the Washington Mutual Bank in Hollywood.

"Gotta withdraw the cash," he told me. It was a red flag. If he was a cash business guy, why were we going to a bank? Shouldn't all his cash be in his safe or under his mattress?

It sounded simple, but my gut was tying itself in knots. Was it a setup? My mind played out every gangster movie scenario.

Rags picked me up and we sat in the parking lot and waited. Mr. Brazil was inside the Washington Mutual, waiting for the bills to come out from the vault. Finally, he stepped out and waved me inside.

I grabbed the hockey bag and walked across the pavement, Rags trailing me, a loaded Glock tucked inside his waistband.

Inside, the bank was cool and sterile. I could feel the weight of every gaze as we walked in, Rags and me—an unlikely duo in this polished setting. My hockey bag felt too big and awkward, conspicuously empty as I lugged it along. It was going to be filled soon, with the kind of cash that changes lives. At least mine. At least that was the plan.

And then it happened—the money came out. But it wasn't the dramatic cache of bills I had imagined swimming around in. Instead, the $250,000 was small enough to fit into a backpack.

There was no contract or paperwork to sign for this transaction. Dispensaries, under the law, could not be bought or sold. I simply handed Bryan the keys to the Treehouse, then Rags and I walked out with the hockey bag, a symbol of a deal done, another chapter closed. As we left the bank, I peered around the parking lot, looking for signs of an ambush. No Brazilian gangbangers. No federal agents. Nothing.

Back home, Laura was waiting. We divided the cash, which was packed up in clean $10,000 wraps. One for us, one for Andrew. One for us, one for Andrew. We all felt like millionaires.

To celebrate this milestone, we decided to do something special for my folks. It was time to give back, in the most Adam way possible.

Before heading to their place, Laura and I made a detour to Costco, eyeing the perfect gift for them. We wandered the aisles until we found it: the biggest flat-screen that could fit in their apartment.

Armed with the TV, we arrived at my parents' apartment. Their surprise was palpable, their gratitude even more so.

"So what's next?" Dad asked.

"Too early to say, but we're going to try to buy more dispensaries down in Orange County," I said, teasing our expansion plans.

Dad put his hand on my shoulder.

"I can't think of a better way to use that money," he said.

Setting up the television, he shared a piece of his own history, a glimpse into his past successes.

"When I made my first money, I bought furniture for a brand-new home we were building," he reminisced. "What a fucking waste."

With all that cash, I also made another shopping trip. My brother-in-law introduced me to his friend Tal, a diamond dealer, and we met at his office in the diamond district in downtown Los Angeles. Here, among the sparkling beauties, he showed me the biggest diamond for the money I had. I had found a setting earlier, and he put it all together.

Later that day, I tucked the ring into my pocket and put goodies for a picnic—sandwiches, cornichon, a bottle of wine—into a basket. Once Laura got home, I grabbed the basket and we walked over to Mother's Beach, a sandy inlet in Marina del Rey. The sun was falling, and I was nervous and couldn't quite get the words out.

"So, obviously, I love you, and I am going to love you forever, so . . . you're going to marry me or what?" I asked, almost too afraid to give her the option.

Laura planned the wedding, and for a brief moment, my life felt normal. That Sunday morning at the California Yacht Club, our families came together from all over the country. The sun was bright, the air filled with laughter and love, and everything felt peaceful. But even amidst the clinking glasses and joints Andrew passed around, I couldn't fully pause and take it all in. I was there, but part of me was still elsewhere—lost in the game of work.

After the meal, when the party was in full swing, the microphone was handed to me. Guests were dancing, drinking, and enjoying the moment, but I awkwardly told them they didn't have to stay longer than they wanted.

"Why did you say that?" Laura asked, her voice gentle but confused.

"I don't know," I replied. "I just didn't want anyone to feel compelled to stay."

"Were you talking to them, or yourself?" she asked.

———

We flew to the Riviera Maya, in Mexico, for our honeymoon. We booked a flight and package stay through Costco Travel—and checked into the Royal Hideaway Hotel, an all-inclusive retreat that was our first real vacation together. As we walked along the beach, the soft white sand beneath our feet, Laura's laughter blended seamlessly with the soft lapping of the Caribbean waves. In the beach cabana, sipping a Sprite and scooping up guacamole, her smile radiated a peace I hadn't ever seen.

"I'm so proud of you," she said, reaching out and holding my arm.

I struggled to relax, as I saw that Duke was blowing up my phone, calling every five minutes. Before I left, I had placed an order with Duke for $40,000 worth of product. He was bringing it down from the Emerald Triangle, from a farmer that was among the Doctor's closest allies. And then, gazing out into the Caribbean, a text message buzzed silently in my pocket.

It was Duke.

"Bad news, bro," he wrote.

"?" I wrote back.

"We got robbed last night," he wrote. "They took everything."

GROWING THE EMPIRE

Rags was waiting for us at the airport. He now had the keys to my car—a lifelong gang member now turned my family confidant and escort. We drove off in silence, the low hum of the highway a stark contrast to the chaos of my thoughts after the robbery. Had I just lost $40,000 in product? Was the story even real? If it wasn't, was someone trying to set me up? If so, who? I knew the product had come from a farmer close to the Doctor, whoever he was. Was he now trying to shake me down? Was this part of my initiation into the higher stakes of the weed game?

We dropped off Laura and unloaded the suitcases at home in the Marina, and then headed across town to Hollywood and Vine, where Duke kept his apartment and stash house, to talk to him and learn about the robbery.

Rags kept his eyes fixed on the road, his voice deep and even.

"Duke's too smart," he said. "He sold your shit to someone else, or he never had it."

I wanted to confront him first. We pulled up to the building, the decrepit, run-down complex doing nothing to ease the knot in my stomach. Rags parked the car in a shadowed spot across the street.

"Ready?" he asked, a serious look on his face. He then removed his gun, checked the magazine, and slid it back into his waistband.

I nodded, taking a deep breath to organize my thoughts and eliminate this annoyance that was nagging at me. *What was Duke up to? Who was behind him? Focus. Breathe.*

"Let's go," I said, as we walked up the stairs.

Rags pounded on the door, and soon I could hear the sound of dead bolts unlocking. Duke looked surprised to see us, his eyes flicking nervously behind me and Rags before settling back on my face.

"Adam, hey, what's up? I wasn't expecting you," he stammered, blocking the doorway slightly.

"Are you okay?" I said, pushing past him into the apartment. "We wanted to make sure you and your girlfriend are okay."

Duke's apartment was clean, almost sterile. Nothing looked ruffled. I checked the door locks, the walls. I couldn't see any sign of a violent break-in. His face was clean too. No marks on his hands, no black eyes. He would have never, ever, allowed these robbers to steal our stash—not without a fight.

Over on the couch, his girlfriend was there, watching a movie.

"Are you okay?" I asked her.

She looked at Duke and she nodded at me.

"Great," I said and hugged him. "Have a great night."

Rags and I looked at each other and excused ourselves. Walking back to the car, any doubts we had were cleared up.

"Fucking liar," Rags said.

"Fucking liar," I said, and knew something was afoot. As Rags drove me home, the weight of the situation settled heavily on me. I wasn't the victim of a botched robbery.

I got into the weed business to make a living. The legal murkiness had been an opportunity for me, and with nothing to lose, I embraced the challenge. I now found myself descending deeper into the darkest corners of the drug trade and committed to being the gangster this kind of job required.

The next morning, I drove down to Orange County to check on our latest project: a pair of new dispensaries that Andrew and I had recently purchased. For opportunities, I had been searching on BizBen.com, a site where businesses are placed for sale. I typed in "cannabis collective for sale" and a few listings popped up, mostly across Southern California. Immediately, I clicked on the following ad.

"Medical Cannabis Dispensary—Garden Grove, 200+ patients per day."

I made an appointment to meet the broker down in Irvine. The office was located inside a strip mall filled with lawyers, doctors, shrinks—all professional types. I opened the office door and thought I was in a bank. There, in some makeshift room with a fold-out table as the centerpiece, I met Danny, who sized me up from behind his glasses.

"I have clients ready to sell for less than a few months' revenue. Tell me what you're looking for."

Danny's stores for sale and their revenues were making me salivate, but we didn't have enough to purchase those places. Our windfall from the Treehouse sale was intact (minus my parents' new TV and some great sushi) but it wasn't going to be enough. We needed partners. That's when I thought of Craig and Cameron Wald, a father-son duo itching to dive into the dispensary business. They had reached out to me, interested in buying the Treehouse, only a few weeks after we sold it to Bryan. I had put them off then, saying we had already sold, but promising to report back with the next lucrative opportunity.

Later that day, I called Craig Wald, the father.

"So I found something, two stores actually," I told him, and relayed all the details about Danny's Orange County locations.

"If you want to come in as partners, let me negotiate for the best deal possible," I said.

"We are still looking for the right first deal to get into the business. If you found it down in Orange County, we would be in!" he said.

I looped back to Danny.

"Any follow-up thoughts?" he asked.

"Yeah, I've spoken with my partners," I said, "and if it's all the same, we'd like to take over both the Garden Grove and Santa Ana stores you showed me."

"Perfect. Come back to the office tomorrow," he said, "and I can introduce you to my client."

Back in the little office, Danny introduced me to Tao, who might as well have been Danny's brother. He was young, Chinese American, and businesslike. We finally agreed on a sale price—$250K, for both dispensaries—and soon I was back with Rags, $250,000 in my backpack and raring to open my next two dispensaries.

The first, in Santa Ana, we called Santa Ana Daily Deals. The second, down in Garden Grove, I named the Golden Nug, after my family's passion for casinos in Las Vegas.

The Golden Nug location was disgusting inside. No windows. Concrete walls. Ugly, fluorescent lights. Once, it had been used as the sales floor of a used car dealership. The ceilings were massive, 18 feet tall.

"Wow, this place is huge inside," I said, walking in to meet Andrew and check out his plans for the build-out.

He was already there, hands tucked in the pockets of his short shorts, strolling around in high-top Nikes.

"What do you think?" I said, as he made another lap around the space.

He was silent—surveying the walls, his eyes darting at the floor, up at the ceiling.

"Well," he said in his stoner drawl, looking away from me. "You know, I went to Joshua Tree over the weekend and . . . did some mushrooms and thought about the space and . . . well . . . I think the concept is all . . . it's all about not waiting in a line."

I was confused.

"All right, what do you mean?" I asked.

"Just build it in the middle here," he said.

"What do you mean, in the middle here?"

"I just want to build it in the middle."

He started in circles, at the very center of the space.

"I don't want anyone to be walking up into a straight line. It's about . . . not having to be in a straight line."

"Okay, tell me more," I said, desperate for specifics.

"Let's put the budtenders and the product in the middle," he said, "and the customers will never feel like they are stuck waiting in line."

I was blown away.

"Wow, I love it. That's super fucking smart," I said. "How do we do it?"

"I'll do it," he said, no specifics, and walked off in circles.

Just talking about the layout got me fired up for opening day.

"Andrew is so fucking smart," I said, calling Laura as soon as I got outside. "He's literally designing this thing to be unlimited."

"I'm so happy for you, honey," she said. "Do you think you'll be home for dinner tonight?"

As we were talking, my phone started ringing. I looked down to see it was Duke. Fucking liar.

"Okay, Laura, what were you saying?"

"When are you coming home?" she said, though I couldn't hear. Duke was calling me again, blowing up my phone.

I switched lines, took a deep breath.

"Bro, we got a problem," Duke said.

"I'm going into a meeting; can I call you after?" I asked.

He wasn't listening.

"Whitney wants his 40 grand," he said.

"I'm not sure I follow you."

"Because you never paid Whitney. You owe him $40,000."

"What? I never got any product. I don't understand."

"But he sold it to you, and the Doctor isn't happy."

"Duke, I'm not going to play games on this shit," I said. "If someone has an issue, please give them my number and ask them to call me."

I dropped my voice into a hushed tone, a calming purr that I had learned from binge-watching *The Godfather* with my father.

"I sympathize. I am happy to continue to do more business with you," I said. "But I can't pay for something I never received."

"You don't know who you are dealing with," he said. "As a friend, I am telling you."

SHOWDOWN AT THE PANDA EXPRESS

I was in Home Depot, picking up light bulbs and extension cords for the Golden Nug and Santa Ana Daily Deals when I got a call and looked down to see the caller's area code: 707. Humboldt County. Emerald Triangle. Cannabis Capital. Must be Whitney. I had never met him. But from his voice, he sounded like an old-school farmer, and his vocabulary suggested he had worked intentionally on becoming an articulate businessman.

"Adam, we really need to get paid," he said.

"I respect your position," I said, "but I've got to be straight with you. I never laid eyes on that product. I can't pay for something I never received. I can't pay for air."

"That's not how this works," he said. "You made a deal. We sent your stuff. You've got to honor it."

"I want to do business with you; I really do," I went on. "But I can't pay for 20 units that I have never seen. It's simply not happening."

Whitney started to raise his voice, his tone now flashing to anger.

"Pay us the fucking money," he screamed.

I reminded myself to stay calm, get even calmer if that was possible.

"Let me be very direct with you," I said, now back in the Corleone tone. "I am not paying for product I never received. I'm not avoiding your calls, which obviously would be the easiest path. I would want nothing more than to put together a deal right now to make money together. But I'm not paying for something I did not receive."

"You're playing a dangerous game here," he said.

"I don't know what else I can possibly share with you at this time," I said. "Like I said, I'm here and available."

"I'm going to have someone call you to work this out," he said.

"Great. Perfect. I look forward to that discussion," I said, and hung up the phone.

Driving home, I knew that I had triggered a war with one of the Doctor's top growers, and thus, with the Doctor himself.

A day later, I was at a carpet shop downtown, picking up the rolls that Andrew ordered for the Golden Nug, when I got a call from an unknown number.

"You Adam?" the voice asked.

"Yep," I said.

"Friend of Whitney. We need to talk."

"Great to meet you," I said. "He told me you would be calling. How can I help you?"

"We need to meet to discuss this issue."

"Absolutely. I can meet anytime this week. Just let me know which day is best for you."

"I'm coming down from NorCal," he said, and so we made a plan to meet late that week in the most public place I could think of: the food court at the Villa Marina Marketplace in Marina del Rey.

Before I went over, I picked up Rags. In the car, I went over the plan.

"Success is for this person to understand I won't be scared into paying him, and for us all to move on," I said.

"I got you, bro," Rags said.

We arrived early, taking a seat in front of Panda Express, the Chinese fast-food joint. I then instructed Rags to sit at the table behind me, pretending to read a newspaper.

I spotted the messenger instantly. Black baseball cap. Black jeans and boots. Tattoo sleeve on his arm. Dusty brown hair.

He introduced himself as Eric and sat down in front of me.

"Adam, this is not how we expected things to go down," he said. "We need to sort this out."

"I'm confused," I said. "I never received anything to pay for."

"But that's not how it works. Once you made the deal with Duke, that was your product. It's not our responsibility he got robbed."

"It's not mine either. And I told your boss this the other day."

We were haggling in the gray areas of an illicit industry. No product insurance to protect goods. No courts to appeal to.

"This isn't something you walk away from," Eric said. His face reddened, his facade of control slipping. Surely, he had his orders. He stood up in front of me, fists clenched.

Watching and listening from the table behind me, Rags rose from his seat. He then leaped over me and punched Eric in the face. The blow landed with such a wallop that Eric's chair toppled backward, screeching against the floor. His baseball cap flew from his head, and his body crashed against the glass wall outside the Panda Express. I then watched him roll down the glass, sliding into a semiconscious lump. The sound of impact—imagine a condor slamming into a glass window at full speed—was so loud that those in line waiting to order their combo platters turned and looked at this inert man on the ground.

He was bleeding. I watched the crimson streaming from his nose and mouth drip onto the sterile tiles of the food court floor. An elderly lady sitting nearby grabbed a napkin from her table and handed it to Eric, who was now starting to twitch back to life and writhe in pain on the ground.

Rags was already gone, having calmly disappeared into the parking lot, where our car was parked. I calmly stayed in my chair, waiting for Eric to get to his feet, wobbly and dazed.

"Why did you do that?" he asked, struggling to form the words.

From my chair, I stared coldly into his eyes and said: "Did you think you were going to show up at a meeting and threaten me?"

He put his baseball cap back on, and pulled the napkin from his face.

"I'll be back—you're fucked," he said, and scuttled off.

Back at my house, Rags was in pain, holding his hand.

"You okay?" I asked.

"I'm good, man. Fucking broke my hand, I think," he said.

He was upset.

"What's wrong with me? I'm getting old." He wanted to smoke a joint on my couch. I would have rolled it for him, though I didn't know how—I hadn't smoked in decades and hadn't yet come to appreciate how it could help people live happier, healthier lives. That understanding would come later, eventually turning me into a daily smoker myself. For now, I watched him roll it with his good hand, all the while picturing Eric bloody at the mall, crashing against the Panda Express window, and wondering what story he was spinning to his bosses.

When Laura came home from school, it was dark. Normally, I had dinner on the table waiting for her. A rigatoni bake with vegetables from the farmers market was my go-to dish, or chicken quesadillas. Tonight, I had picked up takeout from our favorite, In-N-Out Burger, and we sat at the kitchen counter with our double doubles, fries, and iced tea.

"So, how was your day?" she asked.

I couldn't hear her. I felt catatonic. I kept thinking of Eric's hat flying and the blood on the food court floor.

"So, I have some news," she went on, as I was distracted thinking about the Doctor and wondering how violent his goons were. They could be outside now, waiting for me to leave, following me to the parking lot. I had crossed a new point of no return, awaiting a response from a lord of the cannabis space. Surely, there had to be retribution coming my way. But what?

Now, Laura was shouting at me.

"Adam, aren't you paying attention?" she implored. "I'm pregnant."

MEETING THE HELLS ANGELS

A week later, I found myself back in Orange County, checking in on the progress of the Golden Nug. It was Friday afternoon, and we were set to open shop on Monday morning. After Rags had knocked out Whitney's messenger, sent to intimidate me into paying money I didn't owe, I had been on high alert, expecting retaliation. But instead, I was able to breathe a long sigh of relief after Jackie informed me that Whitney had run to the Doctor in an attempt to initiate retaliation and capture the $40,000, only for the Doctor to laugh him out of the room.

"He thinks you did the right thing," Jackie said, referring to the Doctor. It was a clear sign that I had passed another test in the gangster world.

With the Whitney episode behind me I was satisfied with business being as boring as possible for a while. As I pushed open the front door to what would be the Golden Nug, Andrew was walking around in circles, as if in a trance. Boxes were thrown everywhere, the floor a mess of supplies. At the center of the store, a series of glass jewelry display cases were displayed in a large square, like the perfume counters in a department store. All were empty—stocking the weed was my department.

I walked up to Andrew and asked, "How is it coming?"

"It's coming," he said.

"What does that mean?" I pushed, always wanting specifics.

"It's all happening, man."

"Ready by Monday?"

"It won't be perfect," he stammered.

"Perfect enough to open?"

"Yeah, well," he said, not answering the question.

I walked outside, back into the parking lot, and I noticed a sign. It was not ours, and it was promoting a flash sale for weed. I followed the arrow and marched over to the door of a little office. I knocked. No response. It was early in the morning, the neighborhood still asleep. I knocked, and knocked again, banging my knuckles harder, furious. It opened, and I was now looking up at a hefty man with an unruly beard and a black leather vest.

"Hi there," I greeted him, keeping my voice neutral. "I'm your neighbor. I own the place next door. Could we chat about your sign?"

He motioned for me to follow him, the thud of his motorcycle boots trailing on the floor. He opened a door into an office as tight as an elevator. It smelled of tobacco, old whiskey, and bad ideas.

"This neighborhood is ours," he said.

"I understand," I said. "I'm not looking for any trouble, but I am going to operate my dispensary."

He scoffed, leading me back into the main area, while gesturing up to the ceiling. I followed his gaze, landing on a hefty metal gate—like a medieval door that turned the tiny space into a jail cell.

"Listen, little man, when we have issues, we don't call the cops," he said. "I push a button and that gate locks this place down until me and my brothers are finished."

This place belonged to the Hells Angels, the notorious, Harley-riding crime syndicate who ran a drug-dealing network across the United States and into Canada and probably beyond.

"Thanks for your time," I said, and left. The morning light seemed harsher, the air chillier—a harbinger of more violence to come.

Often, I left our apartment at night. Rags waited in the car as we went to pick up stacks of cash, turkey bags of weed, and suffer through the bluffing, posturing, and tough-guy routine that was common in the drug trade. Rags and I would pass through In-N-Out Burger, fueling up for the drives through Los Angeles and all the waiting around. I'll never forget those drives taking us to the furthest crevices of a city that seemingly sprawls forever. The encounters on those late nights were eclectic, surprising, sometimes unnerving, but never dull. I remember one night we were in the slums of North Hollywood. Rags and I were sitting in a dingy apartment living room, waiting for a payment to arrive from Vegas. I found myself deep in conversation with a call girl turned weed broker, discussing her plans to go to grad school.

After handling the evening's work, I would tiptoe back into our apartment, trying not to wake Laura, who was radiant and nearing the end of her pregnancy, her belly beautifully rounding as she prepared to give birth.

I remember the day that Mateo was born. In the hospital, I had gotten a text from Scotty. He had goods to deliver. He met me in the hospital parking lot, flipping open his trunk. Like I had done so many times before, I reached in and lugged the hockey bag over to my car, opened my trunk, and dropped it in. Upstairs, my family was celebrating one of the greatest moments of life. Downstairs, in the parking lot, I was executing a deal that could net $10,000 and send me to prison.

MY DAD'S GAMBIT

Our apartment was always clean and neat, and now filled with bright, primary-colored toys that a therapist mother would have for her firstborn. With Mateo scooting around, it was a lively space, complete with bouncing balls and diaper stations. My conviction to build a business and provide for my growing family was only strengthening. It didn't matter that I was in the cannabis trade. I could have been in any trade.

"Let's get coffee," was the text I received from my father. No other context. During my next break from Mateo play time I responded and said I could meet later that afternoon. We met at the Coffee Bean & Tea Leaf near our apartment. I knew the meeting was not casual or just a chance for Dad to check up on me. He always had a script, a plan for every conversation. He'd ask a few questions and let you talk, sit there nodding along, then wait for a pause in the conversation—his moment to pounce and take center stage.

Today was no different.

"Okay, Adam, here's the deal," he began, his voice assuming that familiar authoritative tone. "Me and Mom need $2 million to retire. Simple as that. And I've got a plan."

I took a gulp from my almond milk tea latte and nodded along.

"I can grow plants, Adam. Always have been able to. So, I'm going to grow marijuana."

I raised an eyebrow. Dad in the weed business, like me?

"Got this guy. He's got a strain—calls it Blue Poison," he went on. "It's our answer."

I couldn't help but let out a chuckle, my latte nearly coming out of my nose. Rick Bierman, my dad, the family patriarch, sitting across from me in his golf shirt in Marina Del Rey, growing his own bootleg strain of Blue Poison?

He laid out his plan with the precision of a field general. It started with location. He'd found a space in the San Fernando Valley, a secret warehouse. Now, logistics. Dad had put an ad on Craigslist, interviewed a bunch of "master growers," and settled on one. The details were classic Rick—a mix of overconfidence and naivety.

"Two years, Adam, and we're set. No more work for Mom."

He'd already started, he said, and he wanted my help. As I listened, I felt a mix of bewilderment and pride. Pride because my old man had chosen to step into my world. In a way, this was his perverse way of complimenting me, to honor my success by following in my footsteps and not the other way around. Bewilderment because, well, it made no sense. Dad knew nothing about the process of growing consumer weed, nor the forces behind it. This criminal world was very real and my dad of all people knew that, yet here he was putting himself at major risk. If he pissed off the wrong person or failed to make a payment, he could get himself hurt or killed. My dad was a live grenade, notorious for paying late or not at all.

I felt the need to stay close, to protect him. I knew it was all so wrong but I had to keep an eye on his operation before he got in too far and took us all down with him.

I drove up with Jackie.

"If he can produce it, and it's any good, I can sell every last ounce of it," he said, liking the idea of a supply source that was only a half hour drive from our apartments, and not up in the Emerald Triangle.

We pulled into the warehouse complex, and I realized Dad's first mistake. His secret grow was not much of a secret at all. He had taken up residence in a typical industrial center, with a smattering of carpenters, loading dock workers, and other laborers all around us. It was only a matter of time before someone would stumble on his grow, shake him down or rat him out, or both. Getting out of our car, I could see other workers nearby, watching and wondering.

"There's my boy!" Dad exclaimed, waiting for us outside and ushering us into the space.

The interior was spare and in poor condition. An electrical panel here, a row of lighting here, using this power source over there (all completely exposed and sprawled about).

Dad started the tour with the pride of a new father. "These are the babies; these are the gold," he declared, gesturing grandly at the rows of plants.

Jackie eyed the setup with a critical gaze.

"Rick, how exactly are you managing the post-harvest stuff, the curing process?" he asked, his tone diplomatic yet probing.

Dad launched into a detailed explanation, but it was clear he was out of his depth. His master grower with the fabled Blue Poison was also nowhere to be seen.

"It's just like growing any other plant," he said.

Jackie looked my way, and I knew it would take more than optimism to salvage this operation. Dad was breaking the law, and unlikely to develop any commercially viable product. His plants were already in a sorry state, clearly a subpar attempt.

"Rick, I love the passion, but growing top-quality weed is an art," Jackie said gently. "I'm happy to help even if I have to bring some friends here to get the final product to this A-level quality."

Dad bristled at the suggestion.

"I've been growing plants my whole life!" he said. "Don't tell me about those legacy growers with their magic formulas."

It was then that I stepped in, trying to bridge the gap between Dad's stubbornness and Jackie's expertise.

"Dad, let's think this through. Maybe we need a bit more help here. What if Jackie knows someone who can consult?"

Dad sighed, a mixture of frustration and resignation in his eyes. "Fine, but I'm telling you, we're close," he said. "We just need a little tweak here and there."

The meeting ended with Dad making a pitch to us: Invest. Front him the money that he would need to survive until the place was cash flowing for a piece of the action. He was now a cannabis startup too.

"We'll think about it, Dad," I said.

———

Back at home, Laura was doing exercises on a giant ball.

"Your dad called," she said.

"Oh, really? I was just with him. What did he say?"

"He told me to tell you to support his business, and go partners with him. And I had to convince you of this."

I rolled my eyes, kissed her forehead, and passed out.

THE CHINESE STREET GANG HUSTLE

On opening day, the Golden Nug was electric. Our neon sign finally arrived—a glittering throwback to old Vegas. Once the doors opened, a flock of customers flooded in. The foot traffic was unreal. "Do you have the Sticky Icky OG?" one asked, then another.

"We don't, but we can look to find it for you," I'd say. "But we also have these other amazing OGs. Here, let me show you."

It was peculiar. So many customers, so many questions. But it was all a ruse, we soon learned, and painfully. The crowds were an illusion, straw men and women paid by Danny and Tao to give the appearance of customers. These customers were part of a clever text message system, we found out, and hired by the sellers to inflate the store's popularity and asking price. We'd been duped.

To discuss the business, I met our partners, Craig and Cameron Wald, for an early lunch at El Cholo, the buzzy Mexican joint on Santa Monica Boulevard. It was supposed to be just another meeting, but as I sat across from father and son, crunching on chips and salsa while waiting for our main course, the atmosphere took a sharp turn.

My interactions with them had always been straightforward, frequent updates through texts with Craig and occasional in-person briefings when Cameron visited our locations. Andrew wasn't as communicative with them, which hadn't seemed an issue. Until now.

"Andrew . . . he's not helpful," Craig said. "The deal we cut with you, we're not gonna keep that going forward. We appreciate your efforts, truly, but Andrew's contributions don't justify a 50-50 split."

I paused, the salty crunch of the chips suddenly sounding overly loud in the quiet tension of the booth.

"Okay, Craig," I responded, trying to keep my composure and my voice even. "It's a 50-50 deal. Andrew's my partner. If you two don't want to be partners anymore, that's fine with me, but that was our deal."

Craig's reply was firm.

"It's not going to continue this way. We have to figure something else out."

"There's nothing to figure out, Craig. That was our deal. We don't have to do more stores together, but where are you taking this?"

"We'll take this wherever we need to, and we need to cut a new deal," he said.

At that moment, I felt utterly alone and betrayed. My every fucking penny was in those stores. Every ounce of energy was in those stores. What did he mean cut a new deal?

Without another word, I stood up, the sound of sliding out of the booth cutting through the muted conversations of the restaurant. I didn't wait for my crab enchiladas to arrive; I didn't look back.

I thought the bad feelings would all blow over. I went to work at the Golden Nug the next day, and the security guard would not let me in. The Walds had told him they'd bought Andrew and me out, and they had the connection to the security firm, and had gotten to them first. We had nothing. No contract. No dispensaries.

––––––

In the street, the Walds had violated an unwritten law and needed to pay the price. I considered my options, and knew how the gangsters I was dealing with would have handled it. I kept the lines of communication, along with my options, open. Over a series of calls with Craig Wald, it became painfully clear: I was boxed in. Running stores without licenses, I lacked legal protections and couldn't leverage the courts. In my search for solutions, I turned to a streetwise attorney, Nigel Burns, a sharp legal mind and boxing manager downtown who could possibly help me navigate this mess.

I liked Nigel's style from our first phone conversation. He was born in Ireland and couldn't shed his accent. He drank more than one beer with lunch and didn't appear to be afraid of much.

"Let me take care of them," he said.

I was torn, ready to unleash my own street justice on the Walds, but after meeting Nigel and hearing him out, I decided to hold back and give him a chance.

MEET THE NEW CANNABIS "CONSULTANT"

Scrolling through BizBen, after the success I had finding Danny, an idea started to spark in the back of my mind. Expertise. I had battled through the nonsense—navigating regulations, landlords, retail setups, and sourcing weed. Why not turn all that hard-earned knowledge into a profitable venture?

That night, with my head buzzing, I typed out an ad to post on BizBen.com: "$50,000 for Turnkey Marijuana Dispensary Setup." The offer was bold. We'd handle everything—finding locations, negotiating leases, managing the build-out, and guiding clients through the legal maze. It was a ticket for those eager to enter the industry without getting their hands dirty, something I'd had to do countless times before.

The excitement was palpable. The Cannabis Consultancy—a one-stop shop. I wasn't just selling cannabis anymore; I was selling the dream of building a dispensary from the ground up. It was a move straight out of Stu Richlin's playbook, but with my own spin. This wasn't about paperwork; it was about offering a master class on turning an idea into a profitable business. It was also a way to diversify my income in a field where I was quickly becoming an expert.

———

The morning light filtered through the blinds. I was up with the sun, that familiar itch of anticipation tingling in my feet. I shuffled to my laptop—my finger hovered over the mouse, a moment of hesitation. What if it was all just a pipe dream?

I opened my inbox, and—jackpot! Email notifications flooded my screen from people from all corners of the country, each one looking to collect their piece of the Green Rush and wanting my help to do it.

"It's over!" I hollered, reading notes from growers, aficionados, opportunists—a whole spectrum of green-thumbed dreamers.

One email caught my eye: "Ready to Invest in Your Expertise."

I opened it. The message was from an entrepreneur in Arizona who had his own grow house and was looking to increase his annual take-home by adding a dispensary to his operations. He wasn't alone. There were queries from a retired couple in Santa Barbara County looking to turn their farm into a cannabis haven, the husband of a Hollywood producer, and a string of others, each with their own story.

I'd struck a chord. The emails kept coming, each another validation, a sign that grinding it out in the trenches wasn't for nothing. As I answered each one, a new sense of pride swelled.

———

I went office hunting for our new consultancy and ended up in Century City. I found a cramped pair of cubicles tucked into the corner of a massive, expensive-looking office building where Regus had leased an entire floor with their business sub-leasing small spaces to entrepreneurs like me. In the lobby, security guards stood watch behind a desk, controlling access to restricted elevators. Upstairs, we had access to a sprawling conference room where I could meet clients and hold court.

With my momentum stalled from the Walds having booted me from our stores and still decompressing from the angst created by the Whitney conflict, the consultancy quickly took on greater importance. I placed more ads for our services, and soon a colorful mix of characters began walking through the door, each one eager to open their own dispensary and carve out a place in the rapidly growing cannabis industry.

I remember "Cowboy Jim." He was a grizzled and veteran grower from Mendocino. He ambled in, his boots echoing on the polished floor, a stark contrast to the suits and ties gliding around us in wing tips and loafers. He had calloused hands and a gaze as sharp as a hawk's. In the boardroom, he unfurled maps of his land, his eyes alight with visions of transforming his once-clandestine operation into a booming legal enterprise. He was there to pounce on an opportunity to sell his product direct-to-consumer. If he could add a dispensary to his operations, it would supercharge his profits.

Soon, our shared conference room became a revolving door of dreams—some wild, some calculated, but all united by a belief in the Green Rush, the power of the plant, the conviction that it was only a matter of time before it was all mainstream and legal. Much like Prohibition, the race was on for our clients to get in early, snag a license, and reap the fortunes. Andrew and I named our consultancy Modman, a play on our last names; later, we tweaked it to MedMen, a direct nod to the cannabis plant, like medicine men bringing weed to the people. It also didn't hurt that the name felt like a play on *Mad Men*, the hit television show. We thought of ourselves as the rebels and vanguard at once, and soon we were signing up clients from across the country, including salt-of-the-earth businessmen like Matt Philbin, who was looking to break into the business in the critical cannabis battleground state of Massachusetts. He hired us to prepare the applications for him and invited me on an all-expense-paid trip to pitch his business to local legislators in his hometown outside of Boston.

In preparation for the trip, it was time to don a new armor, and so I found myself driving downtown to meet Ido, an old Israeli friend, who ran a suit shop.

The boutique was a blend of old-world charm and modern hustle, much like its owner, who greeted me with a bear hug and a knowing smile.

"You see, a suit is not just clothing," he told me. "It's a statement. It tells the world who you are before you even open your mouth."

He introduced me to Gilberto, the head tailor, a craftsman from Mexico with a gentle demeanor and an eye for detail. As he kneeled around me, lingering around my ankles, taking my measurements, I felt like one of the dons from a wiseguy film, only dressed as a corporate tycoon.

Standing in front of the mirror, trying on the suit he'd chosen for me, I soon saw a different me. The reflection staring back wasn't just that of a cannabis entrepreneur; it was the face of a different weed—corporate weed—a concept so alien that even I didn't know what it meant, only that it would be up to me to create and define it.

A few days later, I went to pick the suit up. Wearing it, I felt more confident with every step, ready to face the unknown. Looking in the rearview mirror, I saw a different person. I could see the traces of Gordon Gekko and the corporate heroes of my childhood. I saw the person that my dad had groomed me to be.

THE BOSTON CONNECTION

The hum of the plane's engines was comforting, a calming soundtrack to the turbulence of my thoughts. As I settled into my seat on the flight to Boston, I was dressed in my costume, playing the part. It felt weird wearing the suit, playing the corporate role. But like an actor, I was fully in character, traveling from the sun-soaked, gun-slinging, gang-patrolled streets of Los Angeles to the historic, patriotic, cobble-stoned streets of Boston.

At the time, very few states had approved local laws for medical marijuana operators. But Massachusetts was doing something unprecedented. They were the first state to create a merit-based oligopoly, and were planning to issue the first set of state licenses—all legally approved—to grow and sell. The race was on to snatch these licenses, and to win you would need to demonstrate access to compliant properties, proof of funds, and operational capabilities, and not have a rap sheet. In witnessing what Massachusetts had created, I very quickly concluded that every state would follow this new model. If I was right, we could swoop in and bolster applications with business plans and experience. States would be requiring what we were in the unique position to provide.

I hadn't been back to Boston since I dropped out of college. On the plane, I gazed out the window, watching the sprawling cityscape of Los Angeles shrink away. I couldn't help but chuckle at the irony. Only recently, I was riding around with a hundred pounds of weed in my trunk and living a life in the shadows. Now I was jetting off (all expenses paid) to the cradle of American liberty and the birthplace of American virtues. This was blue blood country, a Puritan stronghold on the Eastern Seaboard, the land of prep schools, rep ties, and family trees that ran back to the *Mayflower*.

———

A layer of light snow covered the tarmac, and the skies were gray and unforgiving. I had forgotten to bring a coat and shivered uncontrollably as I walked out of the Logan Airport terminal.

My client was waiting. Matt Philbin was unmistakable in his plaid shirt and khakis, a blend of rugged Irish charm and polished businessman.

"Adam Bierman?" he called out in a Boston accent as thick as clam chowder.

We hopped into his late model Ford truck and drove off to lunch at his favorite red sauce joint in Little Italy. I could see a hint of a tough past in his eyes. He was a man who straddled worlds too—blue-collar in spirit but living a life draped in luxury. I could imagine the top-end whiskey and scotch bottles at his house, the symbols of status folks who come from nothing crave.

At the restaurant, we found our way to the back booths. Matt was fired up. He spoke of the impending legalization like it was the gold rush, and he was damn sure he wasn't going to be left panning for scraps.

"I've paid my dues, you know," he said. "I've got an opportunity down in Revere to get a piece for me out of this weed rush."

He was like me. He did not smoke weed, but he made his career and came to local power running the kind of cash businesses that dominate the street, like motels, apartments, and parking lots. Cannabis was the next logical step. His plan was to use his political connections, snag a coveted license, and open the doors to his own dispensary.

"I've got the perfect spot in Revere," he said, talking about a nearby village named for Paul Revere, the Revolutionary War hero.

The only thing in his way: the local and state applications. To give himself the best chance at success, he had stacked his team strategically with business and political big shots and power brokers who could open doors and create a pathway to Matt's green dream.

"I've even got the former sheriff," he said, digging into his plan like a high school football coach.

He had a busy 48 hours planned for us.

"Tomorrow, we present in front of the city council," he went on.

I was the wing man, the operator, the weed guy with experience.

"I need you to sell it," he said. "Show them you know the business like nobody else, that you are the guy."

I was twirling my spaghetti arrabbiata.

"I got this, Matt," I said.

He laughed and the boom filled the small restaurant.

"That's what I like to hear!"

I was in sales mode, telling him about all the other services we could provide, too, like managing the stores and organizing the supply chain.

"Let's see how you do tomorrow, kid," he said, and asked for the check. Despite the energy, I was only a pawn in his game.

He dropped me off at a local motel he owned to rest up before our big presentation. As we parted, he put his bear paw hands on my shoulders, digging his heavy fingers into my scapula, and looked at me cold.

"Don't fuck this up," he said.

———

The next afternoon, Matt, the local sheriff, others, and myself stepped onto the front steps of Revere's city hall. American flags billowed above us, and I imagined a marching band, cheerleaders, drum sticks, and timpanis.

Inside, I followed Matt around like a puppy, greeting his old friends. He had a talent for owning the room, shaking hands, and making strong eye contact.

In front of us, a panel of local officials sat like a tribunal of judges. In the corner, I saw a stenographer take her seat, ready to take statements and notes. It was like a courthouse trial and I was here to represent a local businessman and share my insights on the future of a new industry. Just like that, I had gone from outlaw to upstanding, shady to expert.

Soon, he was up and our turn to present was on.

"Ladies and gentlemen, you all know me," he said, "and so you also know that I have not smoked a joint ever in my life."

He got a few laughs.

"I also don't know the business, which is why I am thrilled to introduce you to the guy who does, our resident young guru on our team, our Mr. Marijuana and colleague from Los Angeles."

I cleared my throat and did my best to deliver an Oscar-worthy performance.

"There is a big wave coming," I said. "And there's only one choice to make. Do you want to ride the wave or get wiped out by it?"

Matt's team had printed out a few posters and diagrams that Andrew had designed before I left LA for the trip. I shuffled across the carpet, pointing to my photos, assembling them in strategic order. I turned over the first photo: a picture of dispensaries in Denver, Colorado.

"There is chaos in Denver. This is what uncontrolled looks like."

I then turned over the next photograph: Our Treehouse. Then another of the Golden Nug. They were real stores, not eyesores.

"This is how we ride the wave," I said. "We have embraced it and look to partner with city officials like yourself to participate in this new cannabis economy; in a responsible and safe fashion."

I continued my spiel, talking about how we had transformed the idea of a dispensary into an experience, how we catered to not just stoners, but professionals, retirees, those LMU students and teachers.

"This wave is coming," I said. "And when it comes to Revere, we must control it, make it safe, set the standard."

The room buzzed with a mix of curiosity and skepticism. I felt like I was introducing color TV to folks who had only ever seen the world in scratchy black and white. Then came the questions.

"How do you ensure it doesn't get into the wrong hands?"

"We use software at the front door that tracks our patients through their purchase."

"What about the message it sends to our kids?"

"That if a doctor recommends someone a plant for their medicine, they should be able to access it? I would hope we are telling our kids they should advocate for their health and well-being."

"What about smoking and driving?"

"We aren't a bar. People aren't getting intoxicated then driving home. People are buying their medicine in a sealed container and taking it home."

Matt gave me a hearty pat on the back, and on the plane ride home, I couldn't shake the feeling that maybe I wasn't bluffing anymore.

LIGHTS, CAMERA, ACTION

S oon, our tiny set of cubicles and shared conference room was my new home. I arrived early and stayed late trying to close deals. I hired a small sales team and built a boiler room to bring me qualified leads.

One day my phone rang, slicing through the cacophony. I glanced at the caller ID—MSNBC.

The voice was female. Young, perky.

"Mr. Bierman, this is Jenna from MSNBC," it said. "We're running a segment on the legalization of marijuana and the banking system and would love your insight. Can you be in our studio Thursday afternoon?"

This had to be a prank. MSNBC? National television? Calling me?

"Sure, Jenna, I can make it. Give me the details," I said, my mind already racing through logistics.

As I hung up, the weight of the opportunity began to sink in. I had never been on television before, never even contemplated it. Yet here I was, with a chance to showcase myself in a way I hadn't imagined. This wasn't just about a TV appearance; it was the culmination of all the momentum we had built, every effort pushing toward this moment. I wasn't fully committed to being a corporate suit yet, but this call felt like validation, pointing me in that direction.

Meanwhile, the law was proving to be an ally—as long as the right people were orchestrating things. Nigel Burns, our new lawyer, had worked his magic, securing the return of our $250,000 from the Walds—delivered in garbage bags, no less.

I pulled into the television building and found my way to the studio floor. MSNBC, FOX, and other networks were sharing space, with interview booths where any broadcaster could interview you from their "Los Angeles studio" and the background looked professional.

A producer escorted me into the greenroom, where I popped on my suit jacket. I then was given an earpiece to listen to the national show and taken into a giant studio, where I was plopped in front of a few cameras. A makeup artist soon approached me with powders and brushes. As she worked her magic, transforming me into the polished talking head, the surreal nature of the moment hit me. Here I was, about to go on national TV to talk about my passion.

As I waited for the segment, my phone vibrated—a text from Jackie.

"I have 6 units for you, $1,800 per," it said.

Even as I sat there in the television studio, prepped for a national appearance, the underground world of weed was still beckoning me. I knew where the product could find a home.

The studio assistant's voice broke my thinking.

"Mr. Bierman, you're on in five."

The weight of my choices hung heavy. The risks I'd taken, the lines I'd crossed, all for a shot at something bigger. Sitting under the bright studio lights, waiting for my cue, I realized this was more than a television appearance. It was a test for a man now trapped between worlds, each with its own rules and risks.

The host's voice snapped me back to reality.

"Joining us today is Adam Bierman, a cannabis industry consultant..."

———

Once I got home, Laura was there at the door, jumping into my arms.

"You were amazing!" she said.

I felt a smile creep onto my face. It was time to celebrate—if for only a moment.

I called my dad, perhaps hoping for a rare stamp of approval.

"What the hell were you thinking?" he fumed. "Going on national TV? You've just painted a huge target on your back!"

I thought he'd be proud.

"You've just personally invited every cop and federal agent to start sniffing around our operation. You think they won't trail this back to our grow? To our project?"

His words landed over me like a bucket of cold water. He was right. In my pursuit of legitimacy, I had exposed us to unprecedented scrutiny.

"Sometimes you just don't think things through," he said.

But as I ended the call, his advice did not feel right. Instead of lying low, I needed to do the opposite.

INTO THE GROTTO

Within months, our little office was a swarming hive. All the manic energy that I had used to build up our dispensaries was now put into the consultancy. I paced around, trying to train our new team, and work the phones to sign up new clients. Many of them saw me on television—the best marketing—which triggered subsequent speaking engagements at a smattering of industry conferences that were popping up. The majority of our clients were successful businesspeople, inspired by these new applications that states were offering. I was right about the merit-based applications process, and I was right that there was about to be a domino of legalization leading to new markets.

To navigate this world, I hired Morgan Sokol. She was a razor-sharp policy nut and politically savvy operator. If the states were acting too slowly to legalize weed, I thought, why not jump-start it ourselves?

Soon, Morgan began working the phones, communicating with political operatives, campaign fundraisers, and the politicians themselves.

Andrew was in charge of operations, including the stores and eventually cultivation facilities, the design, the brand, websites, and our own line of products. He hired an assistant, I hired a few salespeople, and we were now a full-on team. To make payroll, I would disappear back to the Bike to play poker. We were often short five or ten thousand, and I would play until I had it.

———

At our consultancy, I paid special attention to calls coming in from Nevada, where the state was in the midst of issuing its first medical marijuana licenses. It was an open secret that the real influence in the desert lay with lobbyists and politically connected lawyers—individuals who could expertly navigate the local and state political networks. These power play-ers were adept at aligning themselves with decision-makers and shaping outcomes. As a result, anyone hoping to secure a coveted license, regard-less of industry, often began their journey by engaging with one of these key influencers. Cannabis would be no different.

I noticed many of our potential clients from Nevada were represented by the same lawyers. Amanda and Derek Connor were determined to build their business around this new industry. And so I reached out to them, thinking we could refer clients to each other.

"My husband and I are transitioning our practice," Amanda said. "It's an exciting time for cannabis as me and Derek are committing 100 percent."

Our conversation was flowing effortlessly, ideas bouncing back and forth, when Amanda chimed in with an invitation.

"Adam, why don't you come down to Vegas next week? We're hosting a roundtable event at the Grotto."

It was an old-timey restaurant in Old Town, away from the Strip.

"You'll get to meet some key players looking to get into the business."

It all felt like fate. With her invitation, I felt a new sense of comfort, and perhaps for the first time in my push thus far, I had reached a poten-tial ally in Connor & Connor, a pair who, like me, had bet their future on cannabis.

———

The Grotto was caked in old-world charm. As I walked in, the scent of garlic knots and simmering tomato sauce filled the air, mingling with the rich ambiance, evoking a time when cigar smoke would have lingered in a haze. The walls were adorned with vintage photos of Vegas in its heyday. Here in the back room were the Connors, fielding questions from an array of characters. I remember a girl with a purple mohawk, an online trader in a tracksuit, and a slew of others. They were forming an association, pooling their resources to hire the Connors, and each individually seeking their own pot of gold at the end of the rainbow.

I got up and made my pitch. I had the messaging down by this point.

"Don't make the same mistakes I have made. Every dollar you generate in your dispensary can be lost," I warned, "without a proper set of systems."

The crowd hung on every word, their eyes lighting up at the prospect of avoiding the pitfalls I had stumbled into.

"Hey, what's the real cost of setting up a dispensary?" asked the girl with the mohawk, her voice booming over the chatter.

"It will cost you all the application-related costs, licensing fees, build-out costs, and initial operating expenses," I said.

"Most importantly," I added, "what nobody can afford is to spend money on a business with no operating plan or operating systems because that would be an investment lost forever."

"What's the ballpark price?" someone asked.

"Years of your life and over a million dollars just to get open," I said.

An online trader, swirling his drink, chimed in, "And what about the competition, man? How do you stand out?"

"You stand out by treating this like a real business," I said. "You stand out by speaking to your patients with confidence, not shame."

As the evening wore on, I could see where the real power was. There were about 20 small-time players, individuals who wanted those licenses but most of whom lacked the bankroll and political connections to make a compelling licensing application that we could submit to the state. And then I met Kathy Gillespie.

She gave me the shivers. Her posture was stiff, her gaze piercing. She exuded a no-nonsense aura like that of a jail guard. She was a woman who had clawed her way to the top in a man's world. She ran one of the big print shops in Vegas, and had deep ties to the union. After my presentation and shaking a few hands, she beelined for me.

"I'm told you're no bullshit," she said. "I am getting one of these licenses and would love to set up a time to meet with you."

As she continued to speak, it was clear that Kathy was in a different place than most of the other tire kickers there. She had a fixed determination and was unworried about the necessary political support.

This could be my big Vegas play, I thought. Nevada was going to issue licenses for the entire supply chain—to grow, manufacture, and retail.

Kathy was certainly going to make a grab for as much of it as possible. We agreed to meet the next day.

———

Kathy's print shop was located on the outskirts of town, between the strip clubs and the warehouses. I arrived at a long chain-link fence and parked in front of the loading docks. Getting out of the taxi, I stared down a pit bull attached to a chain, the dog snarling and dripping with saliva. This was Kathy's domain—functional, unpretentious, and a bit scary. I walked in the door and could hear the hum of printing presses and the heavy smell of ink and dust. At the front desk, I introduced myself to Barbara, a pixieish woman in her fifties, blonde, attractive, sweet.

She was Kathy's wife, she said, and soon Kathy marched in, shaking my hand, and this time nearly yanking my arm out of its socket. I followed her through the shop, dodging stacks of paper, to her back office.

Kathy was so arrogant, I learned, that it was hard to decipher between her actual strengths and her naive delusions. But Kathy was indeed a local power player. We could handle the cannabis operations if she could get us a location and a license.

As we spoke, I noticed her eyeing me suspiciously.

"And what's your angle in all this?" she asked.

"I see a huge opportunity here," I said. "This is Vegas; you have 40 million people coming here per year and over a third of them are coming from California, the global capital of cannabis. It all makes so much sense. If I help secure this license, I would want to be the operating partner for the company."

Kathy nodded, a slight smile playing on her lips.

"I like your honesty. I'll want to check you out a little more, first."

Before formalizing our agreements, Kathy and a few of the others wanted proof of our expertise. They needed no further convincing on the dispensary side of the business. They wanted to get comfortable by seeing a grow that I was managing.

I didn't have access to grows—or dispensaries for that matter. After the MSNBC appearance, I made a clear decision. You can't be half a gangster—there was no middle ground. I realized my future was brighter on the legal side of the business. I severed ties with the unlicensed operations, cutting myself off completely from the illicit weed world in California. I deleted every contact connected to that life from my phone. All that remained was my dad and his failing, gonzo grow in the valley. So I decided to put it on display, calling in a favor to have him open the facility for a tour.

———

I picked Kathy and a few of her allies up from Bob Hope Airport in Burbank, keeping the destination under wraps until the last possible moment. We drove in a small caravan, and the secrecy added a layer of intrigue and importance to the day's agenda.

When we arrived, Dad was there to meet us, his presence a blend of authority and charm. He was ready to play his part, to help his son land a crucial deal.

Rick, full of charisma, guided our guests through the intricate setup of the grow site. We walked through the repurposed industrial warehouse turned indoor marijuana farm.

"This isn't rocket science," Dad explained as we moved from the bright lights of the veg room to the larger, less chaotic ambiance of the flowering room. He was easy, clear to understand, lulling them into a comfort zone with his laid-back Missouri charm.

"Plants are plants," he said. "I've been growing all my life."

He casually dismissed the common lore, showcasing his straightforward, scientific approach instead.

"Please don't tell me about stoner growers and their magic formulas," he scoffed. "You notice here we're using simple salts for nutrients—no magic, just good, honest growing."

The tour wasn't just about impressing them with our facilities or growing prowess—it was about securing trust, and Dad knew exactly how to weave his magic. He played Kathy to a tee, the key decision-maker of the group, connecting over their shared Midwestern roots.

"You were a seed salesman in Iowa, right?" Dad asked as they inspected the nutrient mix, finding common ground in their agricultural lineage. His efforts were transparent but effective, resonating deeply.

Before they left, I pulled Dad aside, giving him a hug, feeling a mix of pride and relief. I knew we had closed the deal with Kathy and her Nevada group.

"You were great," I whispered to him, hoping to hear similar words from him someday.

YES, OUR NEW PARTNER OWNS THE BROTHEL

I t was early. As dawn crept over the Washoe mountain range and twin-kling lights of Reno, the world's biggest little city, I found myself alone on the floor of the Atlantis Casino Reno, where the elderly roam using walkers and oxygen masks, and obese truckers can be found feeding the slots any time of day. I had flown up the night before and just finished my morning routine: shit, water, run, shower, and prepare for battle. At the craps table, my dad's gambling advice for this game lingered: "Find the biggest schmuck at the table, and then bet against him." But this morn-ing, there was no one else at the table—just me and the croupier. Did that mean I was the schmuck?

Outside, I found Cary Richardson, one of our partners, waiting in his formidable Ford pickup truck—a beast with four doors and six tires. He had joined the group as the result of him hiring us to provide consulting for his own applications; over time, we were convinced we were all better off combining, using his connections in the north of the state and Kathy and her team in the south. We sped off, leaving the chintzy glitz of Reno behind. I put on my sunglasses and watched the landscape transform into arid, open country dotted with bands of wild horses. The area was famous for these mustangs, their shaggy coats and untamed beauty a stark con-trast to my strategic, calculated risks.

"Ever been to the Mustang Ranch before?" Cary asked, breaking the silence.

"Nope, first time," I replied, keeping my tone neutral. "Lance Gil-man's quite the character, huh?"

"One of a kind," Cary said with a chuckle. "And now that you know him, if you are ever up here and want a blow job or anything, you have quite the connection."

We passed the sign for Storey County, a place with a history as wild as its mustangs. It was the first county in the country to legalize prostitution. This was a land of pimps and cowboys, both in lifestyle and politics, where the rules were bent, broken, and rewritten.

Lance Gilman was more than just a brothel owner; he was a real estate mogul who, along with his partner, had transformed the barren Nevada desert into the Tahoe Reno Industrial Center (TRIC)—the largest industrial park in the country. He also had political juice. He had run for local office, winning a seat on the county council, and eventually rose to county chairman. With his blessing and letter of recommendation in our state application, I felt we were a shoo-in.

The geographic location was crucial to TRIC's success. Reno is one of the few places in the West—outside of heavily taxed California—where trucks can reach both the Port of Seattle to the north and the Port of Long Beach to the south within a single day. Additionally, Nevada offers a significant advantage with its zero corporate tax policy, making it a highly attractive hub for logistics and industrial operations. When the federal prohibition eventually ends as we predicted, growing weed there would have meant MedMen would save 100% of what would be California taxes while our trucks could in one day achieve the same West Coast reach. But first, I had to win Gilman over.

The door of the brothel creaked open, followed by an alarm bell. The air was heavy with the scent of cheap perfume and anticipation. I caught sight of Lance Gilman in the corner, a big man with a ruddy nose, dwarfed under a giant cowboy hat.

"Well, I need to apologize, Adam, for moving the meeting out here last minute," he said as he guided me past bar tables. "Last night, we got a new girl in and she got so excited onstage when I dropped $100 into her panties that she jumped on me and I came crashing down right over there," he said, pointing toward the stripper pole. "My back is all fucked up and I wasn't going to be able to ride my Harley into town."

In the distance, a younger girl appeared in pajamas, walked our way, pawed her hand on Lance's shoulder, and left.

"I'm going to be honest with you," Lance said. "Most of these girls are here and have issues. They are strung out on drugs or are running from something worse than you can imagine, but that one . . ."

He turned to look her way.

"She just loves to fuck!"

He then started to talk about the industrial park and the blue-chip owners that fled here to the desert.

"Nobody believed in this place before me," he said. "Nobody could fathom the scale. I understand more than anyone working on something that only you can see . . . I get it and I need to understand why I should believe in you."

I dove right in.

"Lance, I'm not here to waste your time," I started. "I understand from Cary that you're meeting with other groups, and that some have offered you millions to support them, albeit after they open for business. But let's be real—those offers are as fake as me claiming I need your support so I can buy and manage the second largest industrial park in the United States, promising to pay you millions once I somehow figure out how to be successful."

My approach grabbed the attention I was aiming for.

"It's utterly ridiculous," I continued, the intensity in my voice rising. "These groups have as much chance in weed as I would competing against you running Reno industrial parks. I also believe one of these groups is led by a prominent personal injury lawyer. If that's true, then let me be clear: We aren't personal injury lawyers; we aren't industrial park developers. We're weed people. This is all we do. And when I tell you we will compensate you to support us, you can count on me to actually deliver. We have the highest likelihood of getting all the appropriate final licenses, capitalizing a business of this scale, and actually opening for operations."

Lance listened intently, nodding along.

"I got into this business in a roundabout way," he said. "It's all about a plan to seize opportunities and being ready to pull it off when you hit go."

"That's exactly what I'm doing right now," I said. "We're creating institutional cannabis. We are going to spend over $20 million on this world-class facility once we are licensed. The future of this industry will start right here inside your industrial park."

"So you brought him up—what do you actually think of Ramon Ruiz?" he asked.

Ruiz was a local attorney, and our main competitor. He'd been a boxer, went back and graduated from law school, got into local politics, and was looking to secure his own cultivation license in Storey County.

"Seems like a nice guy, hell of a story," I said. "But what does he know about the business of cannabis? How much has he learned and how committed to marijuana is he truly?"

I finished my pitch, noting that we were the industry experts, and Kathy, Cary, and our team had all the appropriate local firepower and financial backing to execute our plan statewide.

He stood up, extending his hand my way, which I firmly shook.

"Thank you for your time," Gilman said as our meeting drew to a close. "You've given me a lot to think about."

The next morning, I felt like I was floating on clouds on my way into the office. Outside the front door to the building, my phone buzzed. Cary Richardson's name flashed on the screen.

"I spoke to Lance," Cary said. "He's in. He's giving us the green light for the factory license in Storey County!"

I stopped in my tracks, right there on the curb. My legs gave out, and I found myself sitting on the sidewalk, a grin plastered on my face.

"It's over!" I hollered into the street.

ENTER THE INDIAN DOCTOR

With our bank accounts roller-coasting from client to client, I landed in Chicago for the first annual National Cannabis Industry Association conference, a gathering of the world's growing number of cannabis entrepreneurs. I was on the prowl for clients, allies, and funding.

I was there to give a presentation about the path to licensure, at a time when Illinois was emerging as a hot new market. The state had set a clear outline for regulations and was poised to create another merit-based oligopoly, where a very limited number of applicants that had the financial wherewithal, operational experience, and community connections could earn a golden ticket. The commercial thrill of these programs lay in their exclusivity: the number of licenses was limited, making them immensely valuable. To put it in perspective: Illinois, a state with over 12 million people, would only see 55 cannabis dispensaries operational during this initial period. The race to snatch these licenses was fueling a surge of interest among cannabis entrepreneurs across the country, many of whom were shelling out hundreds of dollars for entry into multi-day events. And yet, despite getting a crash course in this new, exciting business, so few had the resources, political juice, or access to operational expertise to ever stand a chance.

"Unless you can demonstrate to the state of Illinois that you have set aside millions of dollars to launch one of these new businesses in locations you have already secured, all before knowing if you actually won, then you really don't have a chance," I said.

My speech was strategically designed to thin out the crowd. By eliminating the majority, I aimed to siphon off the best equipped, most experienced, and most committed. I didn't make many friends with my icebreaker opening, many viewing me as callous and cold.

"Most of you in this crowd will not end up in the cannabis industry," I said. I wasn't here to be a nice guy. We needed clients and funding. With a venue like this, I could hunt both simultaneously.

"For most in this crowd, this will be a super entertaining, educational experience," I said. "These licenses are only going to the elite business leaders who've invested lifetimes into their communities.

"For those positioned in that way, those that are also humble enough to acknowledge their own complete lack of any operational expertise in the subject matter, there are fortunes to be made."

As I made my way off the stage, I navigated through the crowd, striding down the aisle toward the exit door. Then I noticed a man so out of place among this eclectic crowd. He wore a crisp polo, khakis, and loafers. He introduced himself as Fred Portnoy, president of N Squared Technologies, an investment firm based in Miami. His interest in cannabis was on behalf of his chairman and boss, Dr. Naresh Nagpal, a doctor from India and an entrepreneur in the biomedical field. Portnoy had been sent to Illinois by his boss with the directive of finding the best opportunity inside the mayhem.

We walked over to the hotel bar and ordered a round of iced teas.

"Fred, think about this for a moment," I said. "If you're aiming for exposure to the industry, you're far better off partnering with me than chasing after a single license. The capital you've earmarked for that one license—I can leverage it across the country."

I was learning these business words, picking up the corporate nomenclature.

"Invest in me and then you will have a piece of all these projects across the country," I said. "I have paying clients in multiple markets and those relationships will just continue to grow."

Then, baiting the hook, I went on, "I can't tell you how excited I am about Nevada."

"What about it?" he asked.

"I've been laying the groundwork for a while now, and we have awesome retail locations around the Strip as well as a factory location inside the Tahoe Reno Industrial Park."

Portnoy's eyes lit up, a legit opportunity shining through an illegitimate market. Rare indeed.

"This Tahoe Reno Industrial Park is the biggest in the country for a reason," I went on, name-dropping our neighbors like Google, Panasonic, and Walmart.

"I can't really argue with you, although your ideas are contradictory to our current plan," he said. "I need to talk to Naresh. He will love you. I already know that."

DAD'S GROW GOES BUST

Sitting in the makeshift office at the back of my father's grow house, the stench of weed hung heavy, mixed with the tension of our conversation. Jackie, Andrew, and I were all back, gathered around an old, battered desk cluttered with papers, waiting for the reveal of Dad's second harvest and moment of truth. Had our investment in him, over $100K by then, been a smart move or utter waste?

Always the showman, Rick brought the goods out in a turkey bag—the culmination of his work—and laid it on the desk. I saw the buds were sparse and lackluster, missing the vibrant, dense appearance of top-tier weed. Jackie opened the bag, took a deep breath, and inhaled as if it were his last breath on earth.

"This smells and looks like hay," he said. "I can't sell this."

"We can fix it," Rick piped up, trying to turn the tide and find a victim to pin the poor result on.

"There was a power outage," he said, "and due to some dumb fuck who no longer works here, we missed 24 hours of watering . . ."

But nobody was buying it. Rick was in over his head, determined but lacking the expertise to grow and cure this highly unique plant. We all stood up and walked out, leaving him there to face the situation alone.

"Hey, Dad, I'll call you later," I said.

The car ride back was heavy, until Andrew finally broke the silence.

"I can't be involved with this anymore," Andrew said, not wanting to split the costs of financing it with me anymore.

"I'm out too," Jackie said. "Sorry, Adam."

———

Back at home, I went into the bedroom, closed the door, and dialed his number.

"Hey, Dad," I started, the words thick in my throat. "Andrew and I . . . we've talked about it, and it's just not viable anymore."

As I said these words, I felt like I was walking on cracked ice.

"When you asked me to get involved," I continued, "I said I couldn't have our involvement screw up the family. You promised—good, bad, or ugly—it wouldn't affect us personally. Remember?"

There was a pause, a breath of silence.

"It's just going to be a couple more months, Adam. We'll get it on track," he said.

But the echoes of past promises filled my ears.

Plus, Andrew and Jackie had already backed out.

"Without their support, and without a viable product, I just can't continue to fund this," I said.

I could almost hear his heart sink, a soft exhale on the other end.

"Okay, all right," he said, a sense of resignation in his voice.

As I put the phone down, a sense of dread settled over me. I was relieved to have made the decision, but the fallout loomed large on the horizon. With Dad's volatile history, he was capable of anything.

———

Back in the office, my desk became the front line of the battlefield, one that changed by the hour. The longer we stayed in business, the higher our bills became.

One minute, Laura was calling. Then Andrew appeared in the doorframe, his usually unruffled demeanor now frazzled.

"Adam, the design software subscription was canceled. I need a new card."

"Try this one," I said, hoping it would work and having lost track of which cards I had already maxed out.

As Andrew left, Morgan Sokol, our head of government relations, appeared, and her usual composed self was replaced by a whirlwind of urgency.

"The application fees for the dispensaries aren't going to pay themselves," she said. "Do you have a credit card I can use?"

I closed the door behind her, needing time to think and find a way to juggle all these grenades, each ready to detonate. Silence, please.

Then Fred Portnoy called. He was the investor that could change it all.

"Adam, I'm here at Naresh's house," he said. "He is in the other room. We have been working through this the last few days and he asked me to drive over today so we could focus and finalize our game plan."

I waited for the news.

"We are getting into cannabis," he went on, "and regardless of your deal we are going to proceed with the application in Illinois. The doc has a group of friends and they are all doing it together."

I asked about their interest in investing in MedMen.

"We are interested, but I need a few more days to process it," he said. "We'll get back to you."

———

Waiting for Fred Portnoy's call turned my mind into a pressure cooker. Each ring of the phone, I hoped it was him. Our business was on life support, gasping for the promise of an investment from Fred and Naresh. I called and left messages. I paced the office, paced my living room—each step an attempt to break the frustration and anxiety.

One day I turned and walked out of the office, into the hallway, and down into the stairwell. I sank down onto the cold steps, my head in my hands. The coolness of the concrete seeped through my jeans. Tears welled up, and I started to cry. I was supposed to be the problem solver, the one who fixed things. But this? We were over. And me crying? What the fuck?

The stairwell door opened. Andrew was behind me, his presence marked by an awkward silence. His voice was tentative, almost unsure. I looked up at him, wiping my face with the back of my hand.

"You'll figure it out," he said.

———

A few days later, I tried Fred again. Miraculously, he picked up.

"I'm glad you called me back, Adam," he said. "I've been meaning to connect with you but Naresh has me helping him on a loan he gave to this Indian company whose owner he is friends with. The problem is, there is no real paperwork and it's my job to clean up the mess."

My heart pounded in my chest as I improvised a lie.

"I'm heading to the East Coast on other business," I blurted out, the words tasting of both hope and fear.

Portnoy's voice was casual.

"Whereabouts?"

"New York," I said, a city chosen for its proximity to Fred.

"What are you doing there?" he asked.

"Meeting potential investors primarily," I said. "I thought to reach out in case you are still sincerely interested in investing. If you are, we can meet while I'm out there and work through all the details to see if we can agree on a structure. If not, I completely understand and just wanted to reach out for this one last time."

"We definitely want to pursue this with you, and I need to be in New York soon regardless, so I can coordinate my trip around your plans."

We agreed to meet in New York and work out the details later.

"See you then," I said, and hung up.

It was a lie. There was no reason for me to be in New York, and I could not afford to travel. But all that mattered was closing Fred and Naresh, bringing in the money the business needed to flourish.

I bought a flight on Southwest Airlines for the cheapest fare possible. I then booked a suite at the Trump International Hotel & Tower and prepared for my biggest bluff yet.

SHOWDOWN AT THE TRUMP INTERNATIONAL

I made my way to Central Park, one of New York's most expensive spots, and checked in. The Trump International was a beacon of luxury and prestige. Gazing out at the bustling streets below, Manhattan seemed the ultimate arena for my next major gamble—a city that has birthed and shattered countless dreams, now the backdrop for my potential rise or last shallow breath.

The next morning, I left the hotel in the dark for my morning run, which had been my ritual for years. My war dance. I plugged in my headphones and cued up the same song as usual.

As I tore through the park, blasting Eminem in my ears, I found myself energized, ready to blow all the ideas and thoughts right out of my brain, singing along to the lyrics. I found myself screaming back. *Fuck yes. This was my shot.*

Back at the hotel, I paced back and forth, getting into character for this stunt. The suite had cost me a fortune at over $1K a night, and it was an all-in gamble. I glanced around, noting every extravagant detail around me: the plush living room with its sumptuous sofas, the bedroom with its inviting king-size bed, the state-of-the-art kitchen, and the reason I chose the suite in the first place: a conference room table.

My ruse was all designed to convey a sense of legitimacy, power, and wealthy connections—all of which were, of course, fictions. To stage the act, I gathered all the discarded room service platters from the hallway—leftover eggs Benedict smeared with hollandaise, empty juice glasses, and espresso cups. I carefully arranged them around the room, crafting the illusion of a day so packed with meetings that we couldn't even step out for a meal. The scene was set, ready to provide the perfect backdrop for the pivotal move I was about to make.

I waited for the front desk to call, and soon enough they did. Fred Portnoy was on his way up, and the buzzer outside the suite sounded. I looked in the mirror and removed my suit jacket—too stuffy. I rolled up my sleeves, grabbed the door handle, and glanced at the scattered remains of untouched food, a reminder of the facade I had created. It was all a smoke and mirrors show, a stage set for my greatest performance.

I put my cell phone to my ear, pretending to be on a call, and then opened the door and gestured for Fred to step inside. I went into the other room to finish the fake call, and then emerged a few moments later.

"Wow, Adam, this is quite the place," he said, having taken his seat at the conference table. "I'm staying just down the street, but this . . . this is something else."

Did I hear admiration in his voice? A touch of envy?

I grinned, playing it cool.

"So glad we could make this work," I said, and shook his hand. No matter that Portnoy had been ignoring my calls for weeks, or that investing in a company like ours had so many legal risks and uncertainties that it had never actually been done before.

"So what are the final points we need to work out?" I said, assuming the close.

"Naresh is concerned about the budget and projections. He needs solid numbers."

I nodded, feeling a twinge of panic. My financial acumen in Fred's world was all but nonexistent. Technically, I did not know how to use Excel, but Andrew was on it.

"We have a few new models in the works," I said. "I can send them to you and Naresh when they are done this week."

Portnoy nodded, though he had another concern.

"And what about your partner, Andrew Modlin? Naresh wants to be sure about who he's getting into bed with, business-wise."

I thought of my cofounder, no doubt packing his bong right now.

"If you believe in me, you believe in Andrew," I said. "We are 50-50 partners on everything. He is a genius. He has zero social skills and will never communicate well with you or anyone else for that matter. But he both designs the stores and builds the models. He's a world-class artist and mathematician. We can't have it all."

Portnoy nodded and excused himself to make a call to Nagpal. He stepped out into the hallway, and as hard as I strained to listen in, I could hear only murmurs through the door.

Finally, Portnoy returned.

"I'm empowered to make a deal with you," he said. "But there's a main condition . . ."

I stood emotionless. Inside, I grimaced.

"We'll invest in quarterly tranches, and based on specific benchmarks at first," Portnoy said. "Naresh wants to ensure we make progress and have accountability as we go."

Quarterly tranches? What did that really mean? No problem! This was it! The lifeline I was so desperately seeking.

"Well, that's fine with me, Fred. I'm so glad we figured this out at the last second like this. Can you send over the docs for our lawyers to review?"

It was all a bluff, another poker game, and I had just won the hand. We secured the first-ever private investment of this kind into a cannabis company, a staggering 3.75 million fucking dollars! It was more than just money; it was validation—the turning point. I started writing the press release in my head, knowing it could help legitimize us and open new doors, knighting us as a leader in what could be a brand-new industry.

———

On the way to the airport after the meeting, I picked up the phone to share the news with the one person who I thought would be most thrilled—my dad. But I saw that Nigel had called me a few times earlier in the day.

I dialed his number, the phone barely ringing once before he picked up. Nigel's voice, usually calm and controlled, carried an urgent tone.

"You're not gonna like this," he said. "I've received a rather disturbing letter addressed to you, from your father."

I was stunned.

"What letter? What does it say?"

"He's demanding $20,000," Nigel said. "Says if he doesn't get it, he's going to rat you, Andrew, Jackie, and your other associates out to the feds with information about your grow operation. Not to mince words, he's blackmailing you."

I felt my stomach tighten, knots upon knots.

"What the fucking fuck?" I said. "You have a letter from him, or he threatened to send a letter?"

"I am holding the letter in my hands," he said. "Your dad dropped it off at my office. Want me to read it to you?"

"No," I said. "How serious is this?"

"Serious as it gets," he said, "and you understand the people ramifications way better than me. I'm just referencing the potential legal shitstorm."

My dad was supposed to help me. And here I was, with my own young family, and he was threatening to send me to prison.

"What do you want to do?" Nigel said. "How do you want to handle this?"

BOOK 2

BOOK 2

BUILDING THE BASE

I came home that night on edge, carrying the weight of a day that went from triumph to turmoil in the span of a phone call.

"Hi, baby," I said to Laura as I kissed her, without breaking stride, slumping down beside her on the couch, defeated.

"What's wrong?" she said, moving closer to me.

"My dad is trying to extort us for $20K," I started, the weight of the words feeling surreal even as they left my mouth. By then, Laura and I had long moved past the stage of tiptoeing around delicate subjects.

"20K? For what?!" she asked.

"He sent Nigel a crazy letter and said if we don't pay, he's going to call the feds on us."

This was the first time the reality of my family dynamics truly unnerved me. Growing up, and well into my twenties, I never saw my father as anything but larger than life. I clung to the superhuman aspects of his character: his relentless work ethic, his determination to live life on his own terms, his remarkable knack for gamesmanship and salesmanship. These were traits I admired, traits that allowed me to overlook the darker, more toxic sides of his personality. There had been moments leading up to this when I had started to peel back the layers of denial, but this letter, this threat, marked a point of no return. Dad was now Rick, and he was a threat—an extortionist, a predator. We were adults now, and the reality was stark. I had my own family to protect. It was time to face reality. No more pretending.

Laura reached for her phone. I knew she wasn't angry with me; instead, there was pity in her gaze. I didn't like it. Empathy was tough enough to accept, but pity was unbearable.

"I need to reset," I said, and went off to unpack, take a shower, and clear my head. Meanwhile, Laura dialed my mother-in-law, Irma. She was a therapist, and an inspiringly successful nonprofit founder who provided family and mental health services across Los Angeles. After moving to the States from Argentina, Irma had to go back to school and take all the licensing tests and exams over again in a different language, only to start her own nonprofit in a foreign land.

Laura's plan was to add to her mom's body of good work. She was taking it to the next level, pursuing her doctorate, an academic level above the marriage and therapy level her mom had achieved. They spoke every day, only in Spanish, and theirs was a relationship built on love and respect.

When I walked back into the room, Laura had her mom on speakerphone.

"Yes, Mom, it's extortion," Laura said. "We are being extorted."

There was a pause on the line, and I could picture my mother-in-law, the seasoned therapist, wearing her pajamas, seated on her plush, all-white, overstuffed grandma couch with a magazine and reading glasses on her lap.

"This is very serious," her mother finally replied, her tone clinical yet concerned. "Extortion is an act of desperation and manipulation."

Laura nodded, squeezing my hand.

"What do you think we should do, Mom?"

"Clearly communicate with him," she said. "If you choose to respond, tell him that his behavior is unacceptable and why. It's crucial to stand firm."

Laura turned to me, looking hopeless and empty.

"What are you going to do?" she asked.

I ran the math. After processing the scenarios, the actions I could take and outcomes they may yield, I made the straightforward decision. The best result: pay. The price to move on and play the next hand in the game was $20,000. So be it. I was running good, both in business and at home. Paying the price to continue was far better than all the alternative scenarios I found to be realistic. At best case, the family could melt down, causing distractions; worst case . . . I just couldn't bring myself to hold that image longer than an instant.

Driving to the office the next morning, I called Nigel.

"Pay him the fucking money," I said, and vowed never to speak to my father again.

———

In the office, we prepped the press release. I reviewed the language carefully—this moment was critical. Never before had a cannabis company like ours taken capital from formal investors.

We made sure to quote Fred Portnoy first, letting the money speak for itself.

"Our investment in MedMen is based on our assessment of the dynamic growth potential of the marijuana industry. It also reflects the excellent record that MedMen has established in helping more than 100 businesses navigate and succeed in the legal marijuana market."

After reviewing the final tweaks, we put the release out on the wire. I then hit the road to let the world know who we were and drum up more clients that could afford our retainer and win licenses.

———

As a team, we were growing. We needed our own office space—something that could bring us even closer together and impress new clients. Andrew and I went hunting for locations in Culver City and found an old industrial woodworking shop that some real estate folks bought, spruced up, and leased out as creative space. We rented it immediately.

In total, the place was around 3,000 square feet. We used some of the construction crew we hired to help build our dispensaries to handle the build-out for us. Andrew ordered a shipping container for his office and had it painted MedMen red. I vividly remember when they brought it in on a truck and loaded it into the open warehouse part of the office. To make it functional, Andrew had to use a laser to cut a hole in the side for a window. The entrance was just the gate to the container, so then Andrew built a ramp to walk up. To get in, you'd have to unlatch the gate, swing it open, and step into this dark, small space. At the top, he installed a vent for air through a round window, making it feel like he was floating around in a red fish tank.

———

After settling into our new office, we wanted to do something to unify the team and reflect the familial nature of our commitment to one another. Andrew designed some MedMen letterman jackets, and we ordered one for each of our 30 or so employees.

A few weeks later, the package arrived in the mail. It was a large box, and when we opened it, there they were—stacks of red jackets. Each one prominently displayed the MedMen logo.

We handed them out, and soon, everyone in the office was wearing one. It felt almost like we were members of some exclusive society. Everywhere you looked, you saw red—in meetings, at lunch, even out on the street when we went for coffee runs.

These jackets weren't just about warmth or comfort; they were a statement. Wearing them made us feel like we were part of something bigger, a movement that was pushing boundaries and making waves in culture and society. It was a small thing, but it brought us closer together, unified us under a single, bold color. The original 30 or so jackets transitioned to zip-up hoodies both for comfort but mostly cost reasons, and every MedMen employee up until the time I left was given one upon joining the mission.

The office became our new base camp—our own recruiting grounds, sales office, and propaganda center. We moved in just in time to create a lasting impression, for shortly after we finished the build-out we got a call from an editor at *Time* magazine who wanted to feature us in a story about the future of cannabis.

When they came to talk to us, I showed the reporter around the space, our crew of red-jacket believers shuttling around. At the time, I had a map of the country on a wall, highlighting our targets.

"New York is going to be a monster market," I said. "California is going to be a monster market. Florida is going to be a monster market. Those are the three big states where we wake up and point a finger at a map and say, 'What makes sense for us?'"

Outside of securing licenses, we wanted to shift perceptions and reshape culture, I explained. We wanted society to acknowledge that those who smoked weed were everyday people—normalizing cannabis use and breaking away from outdated stereotypes.

Asked to look into the future, I said, "I can see a really cool-looking MedMen commercial running on television during the Super Bowl."

OUR SECRET ARMY OF POLICY NERDS

T he fundraiser was in New York, in a cramped apartment on the Upper West Side. Stepping into the place, I felt like I was in a Woody Allen movie, the living room a mix of glasses and sweaters—a heady crowd. It was as if they had come from a symposium circa 1967; books were stacked in every direction, and the faint smell of old paper and scholarly pursuits filled the air.

"Can I have a lighter, honey?" a voice called out, adding to the bohemian atmosphere.

The discussions were intense, delving into the history of the drug war, the inequities in its enforcement, and its devastating impact on neighborhoods—specific neighborhoods in New York that these people knew like the back of their hands.

"There he is," Morgan said, pointing to the back of the room.

Rob Kampia was there, engaging with the crowd. He had an aura of determination, a man who had faced his own battles and was still fighting. Years ago, he had started the Marijuana Policy Project (MPP), growing the nonprofit into the leading advocacy group for the legalization of weed, a national policy militia that was running ballot campaigns and lobbying politicians across the country.

The conversation flowed easily with Rob, who had his own battle scars. He had been kicked out of college and spent time in jail for a small amount of weed, yet he had turned that adversity into a mission to change antiquated laws. We indeed shared a common goal.

At the end of the dinner, Kelley Crosson, his fundraising director, stood up to address the room. "This cause needs funding," she said. "Who can pledge to support our efforts? Any amount helps."

The attendees, a mix of professors and nonprofit types, began to pledge modest amounts. I quickly realized I was the only one from the business world in the room. When Kelley approached me, I asked, "How does this work?"

"Whatever you can do helps," she replied.

I thought for a moment and then said, "How about $50,000 a year? I can start with $4,000 a month."

Kelley's eyes widened. "That's incredibly generous. Thank you."

The commitment was an investment into our future. Not only would a relationship with MPP gain me insight into these emerging markets, but it could open a whole new world of opportunities I didn't yet understand. I was in a room with people who had dedicated their lives to changing drug laws. Until this point, I had only met with Stu Richlin.

We weren't a profitable business, but we were generating revenue and raising capital, believing we could become a real enterprise. Supporting organizations like the MPP was part of that vision.

Rob and I quickly became close allies, speaking every couple of weeks. He excelled at navigating the complex world of changing laws and regulations, expertly bridging the gap between the financial resources required to drive change and the officials responsible for creating, passing, and enforcing those laws. Behind the scenes, we pooled our resources and collaborated closely as Rob prepared and executed legalization campaigns at the polls. These local ballot initiatives aimed to legalize cannabis in certain states, where we and our clients could then apply for lucrative, once-in-a-lifetime licenses.

CANNAMOMS

Back in my suit, I found myself onstage at a marijuana conference in Florida, making my pitch about the importance of operations, regulation, and more. I was in my groove speaking, relishing these opportunities. Post-speech, as I made my way through the auditorium, people approached, seeking words of encouragement, advice, or to say hello.

"Hello, Adam. Very nice to meet you," one woman said, holding my hand a bit longer than normal, her eyes searching mine earnestly.

I noticed her demeanor was composed, and yet she was radiating a sense of urgency. It was palpable.

"My friends and I really need to speak with you," she continued, guiding me toward a small, makeshift seating area in the convention center's food court. The round plastic table was humble and plain, surrounded by a group of women who looked fraught with worry. She introduced herself as Jacel Delgadillo, one of the cofounders of CannaMoms, a group advocating fiercely for the legalization of medical marijuana, rooted in their gritty determination to gain access to medicine that had the potential to treat their children's severe medical conditions.

"Adam, we appreciate what you're doing—and believe you will be very successful in your business pursuits. We are here fighting for our children." Her voice cracked, saying, "They have conditions that Western medicine has no answer for."

I pulled up a chair. She introduced me to Moriah Barnhart, another mom.

"My daughter has a tumor the size of a grapefruit in her brain," Moriah said, motioning to her daughter.

"Come here, honey," she said.

Her name was Dahlia. The girl had strawberry blonde hair, bangs, light blue eyes. She had been fighting for her life since she was a toddler. She'd tried the traditional treatments, gone on chemo, only to suffer severe side effects: mouth sores, constant vomiting, atrophy of both legs, nerve damage. She was a victim of cancer and its treatment. Then she tried cannabis oil, and her symptoms improved, though getting reliable access was difficult and still illegal.

"Say hi to Adam," Moriah asked her, and she strained to give me a high five.

While Dahlia had a cancerous tumor, many medical issues the CannaMoms faced stemmed from Dravet syndrome, a rare form of epilepsy that begins in infancy or early childhood and causes frequent and prolonged seizures. The kids would also spike fevers, get sick, and struggle to develop cognitive skills and functions. Later on, it would become a challenge for these kids to walk or go to school, and the drugs designed to stop the seizures were so heavy they often made the kids sick or, depending on the case, made the seizures more intense.

"How much do you know about Charlotte's Web in Colorado?" she asked. "Did you see the *60 Minutes* episode on GW Pharmaceuticals out of England?"

Time stopped. Yes, I had seen the reports of these medical breakthroughs, but never through the eyes of a parent hunting solutions for a sick child.

"Can you help us?" they asked.

Until this moment, cannabis was all business for me. It was my path to paying rent and keeping the repo man from ever coming back.

"We've been talking to Harborside," Moriah said, referencing a dispensary in Oakland that was run by Andrew DeAngelo. He and his brother, Steve DeAngelo, were famous in the weed world. Steve had been the face of the legalization movement, fighting for medical use. Andrew ran the business, and I spent time with him on the speaking circuit. We'd appear at the same conferences and grab a bite together after our speeches.

His dispensary was experimenting with different medicines, and the CannaMoms thought they might be able to treat their kids there. According to Moriah, the moms had been in communication with Steve, who was receptive to the idea but noncommittal on timing.

"Let me see what I can do," I said.

———

By the time I returned to the office the next day, I had my plan ready. It all started with my business partner, Andrew. He was always the last one to arrive at the office, and that morning was no exception. I heard him before I saw him, his voice booming down the hallway as he yelled into his cell phone. Wearing oversized white Ray-Ban shades, a schoolboy backpack he designed in MedMen red, and clutching a vanilla soy latte with four shots, Andrew was hard to miss.

I snuck up behind him, snuck into his office before he closed the door. As he finished his call, I took off my shoes and lay down on his couch.

"What's up?" he asked in a meek surfer stoner grumble.

"I met these women in Florida, these moms, and I really want us to support them," I said, telling him the story. I knew he would balk at the logistics, and the cost.

"How much?"

"Ten grand. Can we split it?"

He hesitated.

"Can't the company pay for it?"

"No," I said.

With a sigh, Andrew nodded.

"All right."

"Thanks, man," I said and moved on to the next part of my plan.

I picked up the phone and called Andrew DeAngelo. "Hey, Andrew, it's Adam Bierman. How's it going up there?"

"Well, you know, everything is pretty damn great, Adam," he said. "My brother is just so swamped, man. I'm holding it down while he runs around doing his thing."

Andrew never complained directly about the dynamic—he was anything but a complainer. But it was clear to me that Andrew played a primary role in making their business magic and Steve got all the attention.

"We crushed all our metrics last quarter with my inventory program. You would dig it, man. I'm pursuing some deals in Mass and Illinois. We are just going to need to see if we have the bandwidth to expand outside of Cali."

"That's incredible stuff, Andrew," I said. "I totally see you and what you are doing and know how impossible it all is, hats off to you and I mean that. Listen, I met these women in Florida and they told me they had been speaking with your brother. They are called CannaMoms."

"Yes, I know who they are and I know my brother was talking with them months ago about something here in Oakland."

"Well, according to them, they haven't heard anything back in months and they will do anything to help their kids," I said. "I know how busy you are, but if I can deliver them to your door, will Harborside help?"

"I am catching up with my brother tomorrow morning in our weekly meeting and I'll bring it up," he said.

"You're the best. Thanks!"

A few days later, he called me back.

"Hey, Andrew, what's happening?"

"Adam, we're good to go. I talked to my brother and, yeah, man, this year has been crazy. We were finally able to take on investors and, fuck . . . me and my brother weren't ready for that. Dealing with these suits is so hard. I'm not built like you, man."

I asked about the CannaMoms.

"Helping those kids from Florida is something my brother really wanted to do," he said. "You stepping up here, we're so game. We are stoked; let's do it."

"Great stuff, Andrew. Let me call Moriah."

Ring, ring.

"Moriah, it's all put together."

"What's all put together?"

"You guys don't have to worry about paying for anything. We're gonna fly you guys out there, put you up in a hotel right across the street from Harborside. I'm just glad you grabbed me. We're going to pull this off."

"Adam, I just don't know how to thank you. You're literally our savior. I don't know what to say."

"Well, I just hope it makes a difference."

"I only have one issue," she said.

"What's that?"

"I am too scared to fly."

———

Moriah drove cross-country, all the way from Florida to Oakland. The hotel and dispensary were in a gritty part of Oakland, just on the brink of gentrification. Harborside had to be nearby because that's where the product was, and we were doing this as "legally" as we could. Their parents were the caregivers, and we jumped through hoops to stay within the regulations the best we could. The parents mixed the formulas and administered the medicine right there in that hotel.

They spent nearly two weeks there, making it work. And then, I flew up on the last day.

We went to lunch, and I wanted to learn about how it all went. All I remember from that lunch was ordering a salad and iced tea and being lost in my thoughts. The person next to me could have said anything, and I was just nodding, eating, barely there.

Then I looked up and saw her. The same teenage girl in a wheelchair. I had met her in Florida with the moms. Back then, she was frozen. Her meds had her so locked up she appeared catatonic. And now she was sitting across from me, cutting her food and feeding herself.

I was floored. *What the fuck is going on?* I found her mom to confirm it was the same girl. It certainly was.

The doses of cannabis oil that led to this girl's miracle were illegal and inaccessible to almost everyone else like her in the country. That miracle oil was considered illegal both in Florida (the state where these people resided) as well as at the federal level (the country where they lived). *But one can buy cigarettes at the gas station, and a 12 pack of beer at the grocery store?*

At that moment, everything shifted for me. Up until then, weed had been nothing more than a transaction, a way to earn a living. But those doses of cannabis oil at Harborside—watching them create a miracle right before my eyes—unleashed something in me. As a father, I felt unstoppable. This wasn't just business anymore.

Weed was now my mission, my calling. I felt like I had to create legal access not just for the CannaMoms and their children but for everyone. The history of the drug laws, their hypocrisy and insanity, had gone from a curious obsession to a calling to crusade for reform and justice. Cannabis was a miracle plant, and it was my destiny to bring it to the world.

DOWN AND OUT IN LAS VEGAS

I was back in Las Vegas, the afternoon sun streaming through the panoramic windows of Sky Bar, a luxurious perch on the 23rd floor of the Mandarin Oriental hotel on the Strip. The place was empty. It was an odd time for a meeting, the bar caught in a lull between the midday check-in rush and the start of the cocktail hour crowd. It felt good to be back in Vegas, especially with our success in raising the capital to secure the factory license in Reno and licenses to open dispensaries in three counties, including Las Vegas. We could sell what we produced to the whole state, not just our stores. But the whiff of our impending fortune, thanks to our victory securing these coveted licenses, was like chum in the water among our partners. A money grab was unfolding, and the more we pushed forward in Nevada, the more Kathy Gillespie wanted to seize control of our licenses, empower her loyalists, and kick me and Andrew to the curb.

She had called for an emergency meeting to hash things out. I arrived early as usual, positioning myself at one of the round tables in the bar. I don't drink alcohol, and asked the young bartender for an iced tea.

"Are you Adam Bierman?" he said, blowing my mind.

Turns out, the bartender, fresh out of college, had been interested in starting his own dispensary. He and his friends had previously attempted to apply for cannabis licenses themselves and, being well-informed, knew that I was a consultant. This was the very first time someone recognized me outside of a weed conference, that character onstage becoming the character sitting at the table.

Perhaps wanting to impress me, he then poured the largest glass of iced tea known to mankind, nearly a personal pitcher, garnished with a garden of lemon wedges.

I sipped it slowly, preparing myself for this moment. Soon enough, the long and drapey curtains that so elegantly separated the hotel's lobby from this nestled, quiet place flung open like saloon doors.

Kathy strutted in, flanked by her wingman, James Green, a former police captain from Henderson, the second largest city in Nevada. He'd been the youngest captain in that police department's history, recognized for creating one of the safest suburbs in the country. Dominick Prudenti was also there. Flanked by her loyalists, Kathy carried herself like a Roman emperor en route to a meeting of war chiefs, James and Dominic mere vassals in her shadow.

"We're going to have to change the agreement," Kathy stated bluntly as soon as they reached the table. By this point, I knew there were no niceties, no hello, just fangs.

"I don't know why you can't fucking hear me," she went on, "when I tell you that I'm going to run this day to day."

"Kathy, we all signed this agreement and MedMen is the operating partner," I said. "Why don't we discuss what's bothering you? What's on your mind?"

Her face twisted with irritation.

"I don't know why you're making such a big deal," she said, getting worked up. "This agreement will fucking change."

I lowered my tone another octave, almost like baby talk.

"But we have a signed agreement," I said.

She stood up. Then she grabbed my monster-size ice tea and hurled every ounce—all 30 of them, minus a few sips—in my face. I could feel the cold liquid on my cheeks, dripping down my neck. My shirt was drenched, ice cubes sliding down my chest.

The bartender, my friendly fanboy, sprang into action, calling security. Guards quickly moved in, locking down the bar's entrance, but it was too late, as Kathy and her minions had already scurried out.

There I stood, alone, stunned, drenched, and waiting for Kathy to strike again. This time, her attack hit my inbox, an email calling an emergency board meeting.

"Adam, we are holding an emergency board meeting," the note wrote.

"Due to your recent actions, as well as historical findings, we must meet to decide your future within MedMen of Nevada."

Kathy reveled in legal jargon, wielding it with a Don King–like flair, constantly and confidently misusing any term that sounded remotely legalistic. Her email was humorous, and sad, and an invitation to battle, only on her turf.

———

To prepare for war, I retained my own legal dream team. For the street-smart, pugnacious lawyer, I had Nigel Burns. Our relationship had stuck and grown, and he had become a dear friend and confidant. He was now my everything lawyer, acting as my own general counsel. For the seasoned and schooled corporate ace, I retained Jeffrey Berkowitz, a New York transplant who had been in Los Angeles so long he represented Frank Sinatra. And then there was the ringer, a Las Vegas corporate litigation specialist at $1,000 per hour with the silk suit to match.

We met at Kathy's lawyer's office. As I walked into the conference room, I was struck by the setup. A long, imposing table with room for all of us—Kathy's allies, my allies, the lawyers. In total, we were 13. Each seat was marked with a copy of the operating agreement for our partnership, and each had been annotated and highlighted by Kathy.

But we weren't there to be intimidated. Berkowitz and the hired litigator took their places behind us, like a mob movie scene. Always the wild card, Nigel showed up fashionably late, clutching a paper bag from Jack in the Box, having inhaled lunch in his taxi. Andrew wore shorts for the occasion, and gazed at the wall, bored out of his mind.

Asserting her dominance, Kathy called the meeting to order.

My lawyer Berkowitz piped up, disrupting her rhythm.

"You can't do that, Kathy," he said. "The operating agreement says that special meetings must be noticed and called a certain way and you did not follow that protocol."

She ignored him.

"I'm calling this meeting to order," she said.

"Can't do that, Kathy."

Her frustration mounted, and the meeting spiraled into chaos. The aftermath was a blur of shouting and accusations.

Kathy began a twisted chant.

"NO, NO, NO," she went on, standing at the head of the conference table, fully possessed. In the midst of this maelstrom, Kathy's lawyer pulled me outside the room, proposing a compromise.

"Kathy is dead set on separating from you," he said. "I'm her lawyer and have provided her my counsel, but as you know she will do things her way and this is where we find ourselves. Let's work something out so we never have to be involved in a meeting like this ever again."

I declined—always turning down the first offer; Dad's rule again—and returned to the conference room. Kathy had disappeared, but soon reappeared with a large metal dolly filled with papers. She walked around the room head down, placing one of these thick attack binders in front of each of us. I flipped open the binder and glanced through the contents. It was mostly filled with our personal tax returns—mine and Andrew's (which she had sneakily kept copies of when we printed our license applications at her shop). Her reasoning for our removal from the business? She claimed our tax returns showed we weren't individually successful enough to be trusted with running the company. It was a ridiculous argument that made no sense, but here we were, staring at the evidence of her plan.

As she made her way around the table, her cart shoved into Andrew's chair, grinding him into the table.

"Ooooww!" Andrew squeaked.

"I'm not going to speak to you like we are both idiots," Kathy's lawyer said to me on the next break. "Be reasonable—what do you want?"

So we made a deal. Kathy and her crew got the crown jewel of our assets—the license to the dispensary in Clark County (Las Vegas) and only one of eighteen total—while I and my supporters got to keep the factory license to grow our own weed in Reno, next to Google, Panasonic, and Lance Gilman's famous brothel. It was a loss for us in the short term. A Vegas dispensary would have been a cash cow for us, spitting out revenue quickly. The factory would be the longer and more valuable play, costing millions to build and develop, but establishing a product and distribution foothold on the West Coast.

If we could hold onto it.

Lance Gilman, our landlord, was still waiting for the $1 million payment that was overdue on the option we signed with him. Without the funds we'd had to postpone the deadline multiple times.

The industrial park was booming, and Lance had just scored a major win, securing Tesla's North American Gigafactory and solidifying the park's reputation as a prime destination for major tech and industrial companies. It was all great news for him, but he wasn't thrilled about Tesla's factory being so close to the location of our cannabis factory. Initially, he extended our deadline to make the final payment, on the condition we swap our land inside the park for another location across the street. We didn't care, so long as we could secure something. But we needed time, and the money.

We needed funds from a new investor or another source. I had expected to soon have $3.75 million in the bank, a war chest to secure our land in Reno and look to snatch up other licenses across the country. But the small print in our contract with Naresh was strangling us, and he and Fred Portnoy refused to release any significant funding. Our core investors were shaking us down, demanding more equity in exchange for releasing the funds. The problem was dire. If we lost the Mustang deal and thus our factory license, my play in Nevada would be over, all while my company was running out of operating funds.

We needed to come up with $1 million to save the Mustang deal, and our company. I had only a week left to find money from somewhere—anywhere—other than Nagpal.

I had no real options until, just like that, an old friend fell out of the sky.

BIG AL AND THE $1 MILLION SQUEEZE

In high school, Chris Ganan and I were both on the athlete track. I was playing second base on the baseball team. He was running point on the basketball team. We were ruthlessly competitive, both on the small side for college sports, so we trained like Russian Olympians. We spent our afternoons in his parents' garage, working the bands, straps, balls, and weights that are now common fixtures in gyms worldwide. When we were juniors in high school, we also filmed and edited each other's highlight reel videos. We then sent them to those elite East Coast universities that didn't have West Coast recruiting budgets with the hope of landing at a school where we otherwise wouldn't have been accepted. We were both hustling from childhood.

I would never tell anyone, but I was always envious of Chris. In high school, I was driving an old beat-up Camaro, worried it might break down. He was driving a Lexus, seemingly floating around without a care in the world. His uncle was a billionaire, we heard, running a commercial real estate empire. It must have been a high-pressure household because Chris was whip-smart, cocky, and could outwork anybody. By the time he graduated from Johns Hopkins, he had masterfully crafted a clear and strategic road map for his professional future.

And now here he was, stepping into my office. Dressed in a crisp white button-down, sleeves rolled up just so, Chris told his story. He had just left a fintech company where his road map fell apart after he'd raised millions for the founders, only to be squeezed out. As he recounted the betrayal, there was a fire in his eyes, a mix of anger and determination. I could relate. We were both undersized overachievers, battling to make a name for ourselves.

As we spoke, Chris was probing, asking about the legality of my business, the finances, the operations. He pulled out a laptop from his bag, flipped it open, and started taking notes. His questions were sharp, targeted. He was looking for an opening, a way to be helpful.

"I don't know anything about raising capital," I confessed. "I know that I need to access money, but I don't know how to get to it."

This was his world, not mine.

"What do you need it for?" Chris pressed on, leaning forward.

I explained our predicament with Naresh and N Squared Technologies, outlining how, after announcing our historic partnership and signing the investment documents, we were now at their mercy. By withholding the funding tranches as they were, they were putting us at risk of losing the Mustang grow deal and, ultimately, our entire business.

"You're thinking about this all wrong," he said. "The Mustang factory is a real estate investment . . ."

He'd spent most of his career in real estate and financing.

"I can help you here," Chris said confidently. "I know the right people. Let me work on this."

As Chris spoke, I realized this was more than just a business meeting. This was a reunion of two old friends, each with their own battle scars. Chris had his golden Rolodex, his knowledge of the finance world, and personal connections to capital. And I was becoming a leader on the cutting edge of the fastest growing industry in the country.

"This could be great for Ethan Penner," he went on, dropping the name of a high-profile investor, and noting that Penner had started at Drexel Burnham, the same investment house founded by junk bond king Michael Milken, an early hero of mine.

"Ethan is a mentor of mine," Chris went on, talking about a new fund he had started and a vehicle that—with a flip of the switch—could fund our Mustang project.

"I'll set the meeting up," Chris said.

———

Time was running out. With only a few days until our deadline expired, I had no choice. I had to run back to Naresh and Fred Portnoy, get down on my knees, and try to get them to agree to an updated deal that wouldn't be entirely shitty for us. Fred agreed to meet me at the Purple Parrot, the restaurant inside the Atlantis hotel in Reno, near the future site of the Mustang factory. Meanwhile, Chris was now texting me about a meeting with Penner.

"Need you, Bierman," he wrote. "Ethan is going to come in to learn about Mustang."

"K, what you need?"

"Your little ass in that conference room this afternoon to share with him what you shared with me about everything."

"I'm here all day—just give me the time."

After lunch, I heard them all arrive. I was on my yoga ball, stretching between emails, when I heard Chris in the lobby. Then my phone rang. It was the front desk secretary, announcing them.

"Please take them to the conference room. I'll be right there," I said.

Steeling myself with a hearty breath, I walked into our conference room, pumped up for the encounter with the finance mastermind Penner, and noticed—lo and behold—he was accompanied by Al Harrington, the former NBA basketball player. Al had retired from the NBA after a 16-year career and had invested in Penner's real estate fund.

"I hope it's okay that I brought Al, a friend and investor in our fund," Ethan said. "Al is my cannabis guy. He is in the business in Colorado and I want him to help me understand all this better."

"Super cool to be here—this shit's real and it's where all my passion is now that I'm done hooping," Al said, and then went on to share his company's origin story, starting with his grandmother.

"She had glaucoma," he began. "She was always reading her Bible, a deeply religious woman, you know? But the pain . . ."

He paused, collecting his thoughts.

"Then one day, I introduced her to cannabis. And you know what? It changed everything for her. The relief she got . . . miraculous. That's when I realized, cannabis isn't just a business opportunity. It's a chance to right some wrongs, to offer healing for folks while making money."

Penner nodded in agreement, his eyes flicking toward me.

"So, Adam, tell us about this Nevada project of yours."

I outlined the vision for the cultivation center, emphasizing its potential to revolutionize the industry, our neighbors Google and Panasonic,
the potential future tax benefits baked into its strategic location.

"Sounds like it could be a great addition to our fund," Ethan said.

We had no time for due diligence, no time to shuffle papers between
lawyers. The only way to secure the funding was emotional. Pure FOMO.

So I looked off to the distance, scratching my chin.

"Fuck, I wish I had met you guys a few months ago." I bluffed away
any sense of desperation, and explained we were about to sign a contract
with another party. We had a deadline. I was leaving for Reno the next
day, I mentioned, to sign the papers and close the deal.

"We can move quickly if we need to," Ethan said, his voice steady.

"Let's see what we can do," he went on, and soon was out through the
door, his NBA partner ducking under the frame.

At home that night, Mateo was ready for his bath and nightime ritual. We were sitting in his reading chair beside his crib and I was reading
aloud from one of our favorite books, *Love You Forever*, when my phone
buzzed.

It was Ethan Penner:

"Meet me at Nate & Al's, tmrw, 8 AM?"

———

The aroma of brewed coffee and pastrami hit me the moment I stepped
into Nate 'n Al's. This deli was an institution, a hive of Hollywood deals
and old-time charm. The walls seemed to whisper tales of legends who'd
dined here, and generations of studio execs and actors.

I spotted Ethan Penner in a corner booth, his gaze fixed on his phone.
He looked up as I approached, his expression unreadable. The booth was
snug, the leather creaking as I slid in opposite him. The waiter arrived,
quick and efficient. I ordered a coffee, black, no sugar, and waited for
Penner's feedback.

"We think you guys are great," he said. "We believe in the business,
and want to help."

"Appreciate that," I said. "What's on your mind?"

Penner's eyes narrowed slightly.

"What if we front you the million you need, do it quickly, and save you that trip to Reno?"

I laughed.

"That's a pretty quick turnaround," I said.

"Whoever you are dealing with, you are better with us," he said. "We can also help you develop other parts of the business."

"I am flattered," I said, and pumped up the FOMO.

"I'm flying to Reno in three hours, as I mentioned earlier. As much as I would love nothing more than to start a relationship with you, I have to respect a bird in the hand," I continued. "If we can't make this happen, we will do the next one together. If you can somehow make this happen today, then let's do it. If not, I appreciate the craziness of the timing here."

Ethan's fingers were drumming on the table.

"Let me make some calls," he said, noting that he would need to get approval from his partners for $1 million on a one-day turnaround.

"Appreciate you," I said, and raced off to the airport.

———

Reno is the biggest little city in the world, and the easiest airport to enter and exit. Within 15 minutes of departing the plane, I was at a table at the Purple Parrot, with Fred waiting in the corner. I slid into the booth, my second of the day, and waited for the hammer.

"Let's hear it," I said, bracing myself.

I listened with my mouth shut, keeping the mute button on, waiting for Fred to give me a lecture on business, the numbers, the forecast. As predicted, he did not disappoint. His monologue ran for what felt like a one-man show, extended only by the breaks when he would ask me a question—"You can't disagree with that, right?" or "Doesn't that make sense to you?"—only to have him answer the question himself.

Finally, after what felt like an eternity, came the reason we were there.

"We are prepared to invest the $1 million today, and in exchange we would need to receive a 30 percent equity stake."

"In which business?" I asked.

"In everything," he said, diving into another deep monologue, like a whale descending into the ocean. I would have to wait again for it to surface, for a whiff of oxygen, to get a few words in.

"I'll discuss it with Andrew," I said, and thanked him for making the trip across the country to meet with me and present this impossible, bullshit re-trade. Once I left the restaurant, I sprinted to the taxi stand, racing to catch an earlier flight back to Los Angeles.

Racing to the gate, I put in my earbuds and called Andrew. He picked up on the first ring, clearly anticipating my call.

"Well, we're fucked," I whispered, conscious of the bustling travelers around me.

"What happened?"

"He wants 30 percent," I replied, my voice low.

"Thirty percent of what?"

"Thirty percent of everything—MedMen, the company, everything we have in Nevada," I explained.

"He can't do that," Andrew said.

"It's currently the only deal we have," I said.

"Well then, I quit," he said. "I'd rather not work than do that deal and build all this for them. Seriously, I'll fucking quit."

I hung up and boarded the plane. I don't remember anything about the flight home. As soon as I entered the final landing stretch over LAX, soaring above Hollywood Park, Inglewood, and the 405, I switched on my phone. Within a minute, it powered up and began spitting out text messages.

One read: "Ethan gave me your number. We are excited to proceed and I've emailed you the loan documents. Please respond to my email as soon as possible."

I immediately pulled up my inbox, and there it was, right in the subject line: "Loan docs Mustang." I could hear my dad's voice in my head, the first rule of his master class on business. "Time kills deals." If there was truly an offer in my inbox that was remotely close to what had been discussed, it was imperative that I sign the documents ASAP. I couldn't afford for Ethan or anyone in his camp to "sleep on it," only to wake up the next morning and change their minds.

I checked my watch. 4:15 PM. I had 45 minutes to get to Ethan's office to sign the papers and get the blessing from our lawyer along the way, all so the money would land in our account the next day. I forwarded the doc to Jonathan Littrell, our new ace corporate attorney, and once on the jetway, I started sprinting in the terminal, out to the parking lot, and into my car.

"Jonathan, you get the doc?" I asked, nearly out of breath.

"Looks like a standard loan doc to me," he said.

"Great," I said. "Can you respond with the information they need, like, right now, please?"

I then hung up before we could find anything in the document to quibble with. Defying all laws of physics, I careened through Los Angeles's network of freeways, boulevards, and neighborhoods, to dart into Penner's office and sign the docs before they closed their doors. The next day, the $1 million was in our bank account, and I wired it to Lance Gilman and his real estate company. Mustang was ours!

THE INDIAN PLAYBOY EMERGES

I landed in Miami, where the city's usually vibrant pulse was overshadowed by the weight of the meeting ahead. Until now, Dr. Naresh Nagpal, the enigmatic doctor-turned-investor, had been only a name to me, a signature, a distant figure. Today, I was stepping onto his turf. We had secured our funding for Project Mustang from another source: Ethan Penner and his fund. Now came the aftermath. Nagpal had summoned me to his penthouse to discuss the deal and the future of our relationship.

Meanwhile, our bills were stacking up. We had clients around the country seeking our services. Our staff was toiling away to manage them. But because we were spending everything we were making, we still could not meet Naresh's investment requirements. He wanted to see cash in the bank, and we had to spend it to keep the lights on.

The elevator doors opened directly into his penthouse, revealing an expanse of opulence that was both gauche and intimidating. The place reeked an overstated affluence, from the polished marble floors to the contemporary art adorning the walls.

Nagpal's presence was as commanding as his apartment, his demeanor calm yet piercing. He gestured for me to take a seat.

"It's very nice to meet you. Thank you for coming all the way out here," he began, his voice smooth, laced with a thick Indian accent. "Fred has expressed his high regard for you, but at the end of the day, Adam, this is an investment. We must evaluate it through the lens of our returns and internal mandates. Do you understand what I am saying?"

I leaned forward.

"We just need the funds to be released under our original deal," I said. "Without the next tranche, we will fail and you will lose everything."

Nagpal walked over toward the floor-to-ceiling windows, gazing over the skyline and waves rolling onto the beach.

"We understand the risk better now," he said, "and our upside potential must be commensurate with this risk."

He was always speaking down to me, like he did everyone else.

"With all due respect, this is a re-trade," I said, "based on leverage you
think you have. Can we just be honest?"

He cut me off.

"It's not just about the money, Adam. It's about trust, about ensuring
my investment is in capable hands."

"There is nobody that will work harder to make your investment a
success than me," I said. "Have I done nothing but prove that?"

He turned back to face me, his expression unreadable. "I will consider
your request, Adam. But I make no promises."

The meeting ended with the same ambiguity it began with.

"I'll drive you back to the airport now," Naresh said and disappeared
down the elevator. "Please take the elevator and meet me out front."

I lingered to discuss a few final details with Fred, then swung my
backpack over my shoulder and emerged in the garage minutes later, where
the roar of a jet engine screamed in my ears. A red Ferrari screeched in
the parking lot, pulling up to my feet. Naresh opened the passenger door,
and I fell into the engulfing seat, more like the cockpit of a fighter plane.

Nagpal said little. I was looking for advice, and in moments like this,
I'd normally turn to Rick—the master problem-solver and manipulator.
But after his letter and threats, I couldn't make that call. Once again,
I found myself boarding another plane home, feeling utterly alone and
scrambling to find a new source of funding.

Back in Los Angeles, the office hummed along. Chris was an easy presence, setting up his office and standing desk near mine. When I returned
from Miami, he already had another investor lined up for us. The next to
appear in our conference room: Omar Mangalji.

Before we met, Chris gave me the briefing. Omar was a spoiled rich
kid, educated in Europe and a professional polo player. Majid, his dad,

owned a hotel chain in Canada and the States, and was worth billions. Omar's polo career was on the fritz, and he had come to Los Angeles with his then girlfriend Freida Pinto, the Bollywood star and *Slumdog Million-aire* actress. He was handsome, dashing with that British accent.

"So, tell me the vision," he said, and I went into our pitch, now dialed to perfection. I spoke to the future of cannabis, the cultural importance, the looming end to its prohibition, and the fortune to be made.

And as if on cue, Chris entered, talking about the business.

"We're really three businesses: a real estate company, a tech and intellectual property company, and a management company," he went on, using terms that Omar could take back to the family investment officer. A bet on us had to sound safe.

"Sounds fantastic," he said. "We would likely want to make the investment into the management company. That's what my family understands."

I took a deep breath. This was it. The ask.

"We are raising 10 million," I said, "and we plan to use the funds to buy our own assets to fuel the brand and management company."

Omar leaned back, a playful glint in his eye.

"Adam, we shall do this," he said. "This will be my magnum opus."

———

Back home, our apartment was mostly filled with typical young couple, new baby chaos. Mateo was an angel, but he struggled to sleep through the night. His cries often landed me on the couch. Laura planned to return to work after Mateo turned three months old, but our sleepless nights with Mateo continued and, soon enough, she was pregnant with Ari, our second son. We were thrilled at the news, a bigger family had always been our dream, but with the relentless demands and pressure of my work, I left Laura to feel more alone than she ever had. She had her family to help her, of course. Not mine.

"Have you thought at all about talking to your dad?" she'd say, knowing it was gnawing at me, but I was determined to keep him at bay.

I was always out the door, heading to a meeting, taking a call.

"Have you heard from your dad at all?" she'd ask again, but I had to stand firm. *No. He is a danger to us all*, I thought, and I was in too deep with MedMen and now our new investor Omar to let it fail.

With the end of the year approaching, we wanted to celebrate our monumental success with the team. And what better place to do it than Las Vegas. Thanks to all the gambling points that I racked up on the Strip, I scored us a comp deal at the Rio, giving each staff member their own room. It was a small thank-you for their hard work and faith in a vision that I understood had seemed delusional at times.

We had over 30 employees, each their own rebel. Dan Edwards left a law firm, packed up his car in San Diego, and moved to a friend's couch to be Littrell's junior. Sara Connolly was opening Dairy Queens for a franchisee in New Jersey, when she packed up her car to join Andrew trying to create first-of-their-kind systems to operate dispensary businesses. Kelsey Hernandez, our admin, was the oldest among us all, and had yet to turn 40. She was the hero of the office, driving to Vegas for the holiday party with a trunk full of Jell-o shots.

We deserved it all. Then Omar, our financier, arrived looking every bit the debonair investor in his elbow-patched sports jacket. His suave presence added an air of sophistication and promise. He made his way through the crowd, his charisma oozing, and started talking to Laura, my rock, and put his arm around her.

"You and your family will never have to worry about money again," he said.

THE HOLLYWOOD BLACK SHEEP

Back in Los Angeles, and expecting Omar's $9 million to hit our account, I started spending more time on politics. I joined the Greater Los Angeles Collective Alliance (GLACA) and began attending their meetings inside a dispensary in West Hollywood.

The dispensary was owned by Brennan Thicke, son of the actor Alan Thicke. The place felt cramped and unwelcoming. The center was dominated by those ugly and cheap-looking jewel box display cases, atop a shaggy, worn-out carpet. There was a corner dedicated to pamphlets on marijuana use, giving the place the vibe of a hospital waiting room.

Despite its lackluster ambiance, I couldn't help but see the potential. This location in such a popular area, I thought, could become the crown jewel in our retail empire, a flagship store that could set the standard for dispensaries everywhere. I knew that with Andrew's design genius and my hustle, we could transform Brennan's dumpy space and business into something extraordinary.

As the meeting went on, I was anxious to speak to Brennan to get a sense of his foot traffic and make him an offer.

"Do you know about how many patients come in here every day?" I asked casually.

Brennan shared some numbers, and I nodded along.

"Ever think of selling?" I ventured, dropping my tone and throwing the question out there to chum the waters.

To my surprise, Brennan perked up. For the right price, he said, he'd consider handing over the keys. The challenge, of course, was determining a fair market valuation for a quasi-legal business. Brennan didn't have an official license to sell cannabis in California—none of us did—but the city of West Hollywood had issued Brennan's store a city permit to operate as a medical marijuana dispensary. That was rare. West Hollywood's decision to issue four licenses in 2009 was one of the earliest examples of a city formalizing a structured licensing program. This move set West Hollywood apart, and earned it a reputation as a pioneer in cannabis regulation. Getting access to this business was an extraordinary opportunity for us.

We tossed around a few figures, settling on a price of $4 million. And with the financial backing of Omar, we could buy out Brennan, invest in rebuilding the space, and set up shop in our best location yet.

———

Back at the office, I called Omar to share the good news. His opus was underway. But the call went straight to voicemail.

I tried his personal assistant next.

"He's not in," came the brisk reply.

The following day, I made another attempt; another brush-off.

"He is skiing with his family and with limited service," she said. "I will certainly let him know to call you upon his return."

"Skiing? Where?"

Click.

I was nervous. Omar had funded the $1M as a deposit, all part of a multi-page binding term sheet for a total of $10M that his lawyers had drafted and rushed over the day after we shook hands on the deal. I went out and found the best way I could think of to spend $4 million of that investment on striking a deal with Brennan, but deep down, something felt amiss. The closing to take over the business was supposed to be in a matter of weeks.

I tried Omar and his personal assistant again. Nada. In a mix of desperation and frustration, I had no choice but to cross the line. I reached out to the only person I thought could influence Omar: his father. He had a solution. He was coming to Los Angeles, and Omar would be accompanying him.

"I will be traveling to Los Angeles as I'm inquiring about the purchase of the Beverly Hills Hotel," he wrote, like a robot programmed at Harvard Business School. "I will be taking meetings on-site during my trip and would be happy to meet you there if that's convenient."

———

I was waiting in the dining room of the hotel when Omar and his father finally made their entrance. Majid moved like royalty, the maître d' and servers all seemingly knowing his name, his smile infectious.

"Sorry to keep you waiting," his father began. He shook my hand with such grace that I nearly bent down on the carpet to kiss it. Behind him, Omar, Mr. Magnum Opus, the big swinging dick with all the answers and all the solutions, curtsying around with such ease and grace, was relegated to taking a back seat in his father's regal presence.

The meeting started with Rich Daddy expressing concerns over the situation.

"Our family is troubled by the way this matter has been communicated and handled. I regret that we have reached this point," he went on. "I apologize we find ourselves here today."

I listened, then launched into the details of our looming Thicke deal and deadline, my voice laced with excitement and our plans for our first MedMen-branded dispensary.

"So, you're planning to use part of our investment into the management company to purchase this business?" Majid asked.

"Yes, that was the plan all along," I said.

"But if our money is buying these businesses," Omar interjected, "shouldn't we own 100 percent of them outright?"

The original deal was clear to me: the Mangaljis would invest in the management company—the entity responsible for overseeing day-to-day operations. The goal was for this company to manage as many of our clients' businesses as I could bring on board, while also seeking out flagship opportunities to purchase and own outright. Owning assets was crucial to our strategy, giving us more control over our future. However, it was made explicitly clear during negotiations, and was particularly important to Omar, that their investment was strictly into the management company—they had no interest in directly owning assets. But now, as they began to understand the value of these assets and the types of opportunities they represented, they changed their stance, eager not to miss out.

The conversation spiraled from there. We argued briefly and I ultimately stormed out of the hotel, furious at the silky Mangaljis. I called Chris in a rage, venting about the injustice, how my investors (and his connections) were robbing us all blind at the last minute.

"They're trying to fuck us, Chris!" I screamed.

He laughed.

"Adam, of course they are," he said. "That's the way it works."

PRIVATE EQUITY EPIPHANIES

T he Nevada desert stretched out before us, the sun a relentless over-
seer in a cloudless sky. We were on our way to Carson City, the
capital of Nevada, to meet with a few Nevada politicians and land-
use officials. My schooling in the world of aggressive, hard money investors was well underway, graduating from Naresh to the Mangaljis. I had
conceded and made the deal with Omar on West Hollywood. He purchased the store himself and then signed a management agreement with
us to operate it under the MedMen brand. I made a decision that kept us
in the game but we needed our next solution.

Chris and I started talking to other investors, but lining up the meetings and making the presentations all took time. Meanwhile, we were
burning resources. We barreled through Nevada in our rental car, the
blare of his rap music a soundtrack to our high-speed brainstorm. The
beats were like the warm-up music before one of his basketball games, a
cue to get into the zone. We kept the windows down, the wind whipping
through the car, tangling our words.

"It's all fear; these investors are too scared," I yelled over the music,
struggling to make my voice heard.

"Nobody wants to be the first to jump into the deep end," Chris said.
"Even if there's a honey hole down there."

"We need something all these people get, and something these lawyers can at least understand," I said.

Silence fell between us, the only sound the beastly pumping of Chris's
music. We were both lost in a trance, the landscape a blur of browns and
tans.

"Why don't we just start a private equity fund?" he said, his tone dead-
pan, as if our solution had been hiding in plain sight.

The idea sounded like a joke. But it wasn't that far off. Privateer, another cannabis company based in Seattle, had recently launched a fund and was getting good write-ups in national papers like the *Wall Street Journal*. Instead of running their own stores, Privateer, funded in part by Peter Thiel and the so-called PayPal Mafia, was a holding company and invested in a portfolio of cannabis companies that were not "plant touching." In the media, they were dubbed the "Procter & Gamble of Weed." Imagine the gold rush—they were akin to the outfitters selling picks and shovels. And we were the crazed miners, seeking the gold itself.

"We do what they are doing but we go the whole way," Chris said. "We raise into a fund structure and invest directly into the licenses."

I saw his eyes light up, a spark of excitement flashing beneath his calculated demeanor.

"We get the fund to make MedMen—the management company— its flagship investment," he said, offering up some corporate logic. "Then those investors are completely aligned with us. We can own the businesses as well as the management company that operates them. It's what Omar pretended to want to do. It creates a buffer zone they can clearly understand. Investors will love this, Adam!"

I was whipped up too.

"You're a mad fucking genius!" I said, believing he had cracked the code.

THE CHICAGO CONNECTION

Back in the office, we were about to hold our weekly business development meeting. At the conference table, Kellen O'Keefe, at that time our head of business development, was buzzing. He had been cold-calling recent winners of licenses in Illinois's new medical cannabis program.

"I got a big hit yesterday," he told us.

Kellen explained that when calling PharmaCann, a newly minted cannabis license holder in Illinois, their CEO had referred him to Wicklow Capital. The company was PharmaCann's financial backer, and any potential deal had to be run through its chief investment officer, Ben Rose.

"Do you need me to get on a call to get this started?" I asked him, keeping him focused on the most direct opportunity: helping a group with no previous operational experience stand up and run their new business.

"This is the one call you can't miss," he said.

On the phone with Ben Rose for the first time, I quickly realized Wicklow wasn't just any billionaire backed investment fund—they were deeply involved in politics, actively donating to candidates and causes across the United States that aligned with their beliefs.

I saw the synergies. They wanted to end the cannabis prohibition and needed help running the operations for a company they had bought into, and we needed a giant capital partner like them that was up for creating an industry. Chris and I booked a flight to Chicago as quickly as we could to meet Wicklow's billionaire founders.

———

The Chicago skyline greeted us as we landed, and soon we were riding the posh elevator to the top floor of the Four Seasons Residence. The doors opened to reveal a lavish boardroom and the handlers of the Wicklow dynasty: Ben Rose, the sharp-minded and Harvard-educated chief investment officer, flanked by the visionary founders, Dan Tierney, who with his glasses looked like he'd been cast for *Revenge of the Nerds*, and Steve Schuler, a jolly double for John Goodman.

Chris and I made our way around the quaint room, shaking hands.

"I'm not here to mess around over small numbers," Schuler said. "I've reviewed the models you've provided and they're good enough. Let's not kid ourselves into thinking those are more than educated guesses anyway. Look, we understand startups and make no mistake—that's what you are. We would be making a bet on you. And if we're right, haggling about numbers now is just a waste of time."

I felt compelled to take action. I walked over to the whiteboard, and in the bottom right corner, I wrote the number "$25 million." My hand then started moving swiftly, the blue dry-erase marker leaving a chaotic mix of words and numbers. I was barely conscious as my intuition took over, dumping my ideas and outlining the business, the entities, and my ask: $15M for the fund, $10M for the company. A $25 million investment, in total.

"Well, holy fucking shit," Schuler blurted out, cutting off the tail end of my exercise and agreeing to fund us. I then stood back and shut up. Another lesson in sales from Dad: once a buyer says yes, don't say a word until the money hits your account.

After a flurry of documents and due diligence, the commitment came. Wicklow Capital had committed to being our anchor investor for our new fund, and Chris's brainchild sprang to life. With this stream of funding, we could propel our business into a new stratosphere. It was sufficient to cover our day-to-day costs of operating the business for what seemed like forever. There would be more than enough to bolt on new licenses for us to own and manage. With $25 million from Wicklow we were ready to take on the world, and I was geared up and tuned in to riding this momentum. Our fund documents outlined an objective to raise up to $100 million, which meant I had another $85 million to raise.

First on my list of targets to invest in our fund was Andy Rayburn, a legend in his own right. Rayburn was Ohio royalty, having transformed a simple bolt business into his own empire, and then diversifying into sports and music with the ease of a born entrepreneur. But it was his unapologetic love for weed that really set him apart in the conservative Midwest. The guy was a Deadhead, a Midwestern Cheech. I had worked with him and Rob Kampia on ballot initiatives in Ohio, huddling with him in a sleek conference room in the office of his lawyer in downtown Cleveland.

Now I was back again.

"We are just so excited, man," he said. "It's all happening. What an awesome time to be alive."

His energy was infectious.

"I'm doing this so I can be in business in Ohio," he went on. "I haven't been excited about operating a company in decades, and this will bring me out of retirement."

"But if you're ultimately in it to come out of retirement, don't you want to start now?" I asked. "This is a head start while you get ready for Ohio and your money can start working today."

Next up was Tony Visconsi, a quieter force but no less influential. His family's legacy was etched into the financial fabric of the state. When we first met, Tony told me a captivating story about his grandfather who had built the family's initial fortune. He provided the loans to create Native American bingo halls, helping transform them into the early casinos we recognize today. This investment required immense conviction and foresight, made in the face of genuine legal challenges. With his measured approach and strategic mind, Tony was a perfect ally in this complex landscape. We met in the same office conference room downtown. He brought T3, Tony Visconsi III, Tony's heir apparent, who soaked up every word, every strategy. The kid had a sharpness to him, a hunger to carve out his own legacy. They were in too.

Tony and T3 then vouched for me with their buddy Steve Samuels, a titan of Massachusetts real estate, whose family had owned and transformed the neighborhoods around Fenway Park. With his history of making the dilapidated desirable, Steve's commitment to our cannabis fund only brought more pedigree to our fundraising efforts and cause. The investment from these mega forces from the heartland, the very mom-and-pop America we aimed to reach, was another sign I was on the right path. It would be an endorsement and validation important to my highest-profile investor of all.

Chris Leavy was a Wall Street legend. He started as a fund manager at OppenheimerFunds, the mainstay of investment banks. He was so good at picking winners, he was quickly snatched up by BlackRock, one of the world's biggest and most powerful funds. Here he rose up the ranks to manage $115 billion in assets, serving as chief investment officer of Fundamental Equities. Chris was such a hard charger that he gained weight, got sick, and had to leave BlackRock for health reasons in his early forties. But he was on the health track when I met him, ready to return to the investment game and looking to personally invest in the next big thing.

I got his contact through Kellen, who had met Leavy at a cannabis conference on the outskirts of Philadelphia, where Leavy was living. We had kept in touch over the phone, and instantly I knew that his experience and rock star status among investors on Wall Street could be invaluable to us.

"How's the raise coming?" Leavy asked as I took his call while monotonously maneuvering through traffic from LAX to the office. Once the fundraising kicked off it just kept gaining momentum and I was on fire. We were on pace to raise more than $100M and close the fund. Leavy hadn't invested after our first conversation. He wanted more for his investment than others, a common expectation among this class of Masters of the Universe who are accustomed to special treatment, including their investment terms. So, when he started to ask for special treatment, I politely declined. He was flabbergasted.

"It won't make sense for me under those economics," he said. "I can help and introduce you to my network, but I would definitely need to negotiate the fees."

This time, he wanted another chance to buy in.

"I just can't find anything else in the space that competes with what you have put together," he said. "I have made some small investments that have become more of an education than anything else. The management company is the key to all this and you've pulled it off."

On the other end of the line, I closed my eyes, hoping this was not a dream. One of the most respected investors on the planet had decided that I was his best bet.

"I'm humbled, really, Chris," I said, and alongside taking in his personal investment, I crafted a plan for him to join as the general partner of the fund, giving him an additional piece of the entire company. His title: Head of Investments. He agreed, and we hung up.

"It's over! It's so fucking over!" I screamed in the car.

BREAKDOWN BRIS

When Ari was born, the moment was bittersweet. Our second son was the cutest kid, who had a wisdom about him from the very start. While we celebrated with my mother and the rest of the family, my father's absence weighed heavily on everyone. I compartmentalized it, pushing it aside as I continued to stay completely absorbed in work. On top of everything I had already been managing, the new investors and their legal teams added a whole new layer of complexity and demands for me. It wasn't just about closing deals anymore; we now had systems and processes to function as a private equity fund. Every transaction had to pass through investment committees, memos, votes, and we had to communicate all this activity succinctly through investor relations—multiplying my workload and demanding even more of my attention.

Ari's bris was nearly an hour across town in Glendale, where our rabbi lived.

"Come on, we're going to be late," Laura said, trying to get in the car, strapping Mateo into the car seat with Ari nursing on her breast at the same time.

I wasn't listening, texting with Jonathan Littrell about an obstacle in taking investor money in from Europe which, once solved, would open an even broader reach for my fundraising efforts.

"Get off your fucking phone, Adam!" Laura screamed, alerting me to the unfortunate news that, under my watch, Mateo had had a massive explosion in his diaper, the poop all up his back and ruining his outfit for the bris.

"We need to change him," she said, as I looked down at the latest message from Littrell, who needed an answer from me.

"We can be late," I said. "We have the kid. They are not going to start the bris without us," I said, my fingers pecking away.

"Today, it is your son's bris. Can you for once put the fucking phone down?"

I lost it, and unleashed my best front kick on our car's trunk door, leaving a dent and nearly splitting my suit pants.

I was losing it. I needed sleep, recovery, excercise. I had been trained to be an athlete, and there was a discipline about my routine that I could not break. Not now. With Ari crying every night and Mateo as well, nobody in the house could sleep. Laura couldn't bear the pain of sleep training. At 18 months, and after huddling with three different sleep consultants, she decided to finally commit and left Mateo crying alone in his room, hoping he'd fall asleep. After 30 minutes of tears, Mateo started projectile vomiting out of his crib. As the vomit splashed the walls and carpet, Laura burst in like a firefighter arriving to save someone from a burning building. She caressed him, bathed him, and shushed him to sleep in the rocking chair. My job was to clean up the vomit, first off the carpeted floor, then the wall, and finally from the crib before changing the sheets.

Regardless of any evening's escapades I was always up the next morning and gone for my morning run around five. By the time I was in the office, rolling my calls on the East Coast, my family was just waking up. At the officc, I felt like I had disappeared inside a video game, playing life in 15-minute power bursts, looking to pick up new weapons, gather resources, slay dragons, and claw my way to the next level.

Before coming home in the evenings, I sat in the car for 15 minutes, often a half hour, to decompress from the day.

"We miss you," she'd say.

"I only have one chance at this," I'd say. "I won't fail because of lack of focus and you know it won't be for lack of effort."

"Your kids and wife also need your attention," she'd say—a gut punch.

"You should have married a schoolteacher," I fired back.

"Please listen to me," she said. "I know what I'm talking about. Please let me find you someone to go talk to. I know it would be so good for you and help with everything."

Referred to us by one of Laura's friends, Ed Harris was a former professor and rabbi who had moved his family from Missouri to Southern

California for a warmer, easier life. Laura's friend thought he would be the perfect therapist for me, so I had my assistant add the meeting to my calendar.

Immediately, I relished these sessions. Every week, I had my sanctuary. I could turn off my phone and release everything.

"Where does your inability to connect with your life at home really start?" he'd ask.

"I can't walk in after fighting all day and be ready for Laura to throw me the kids."

"If you communicated ahead of time with her, would that one minute of effort create a day free of fighting? It sounds like she is available and wanting to be supportive of you."

"My battery is just so drained when I get home, I don't have the strength to be present."

His questions then turned to laser-guided bombs.

"Do you think those parts about your dad that are scary are also inside you?"

"I do absolutely have my dad's genetics—that's how it works. What else can I do but focus on recognizing them and try to extract the positives and kill the poisonous parts?"

He pushed me to reconcile with my father.

"Forgiveness is about you, not the person you're forgiving," he said. "Holding resentment or anger only hurts the person doing the holding. Your dad is in your brain, holding you prisoner. The only way to free yourself is to let him free—by forgiving him. He is the grandfather to Mateo and Ari, after all."

I refused to consider this.

"I don't know why I would ever be compelled to call Rick," I said. "This is who he is, and as he gets older his dark side consumes more and more of him. It's so toxic and I don't see how there's anything positive about it around my kids."

As much as I loved talking to Ed, these sessions were a time suck. Soon enough, spending 30 minutes in traffic, an hour in therapy, and driving another 30 minutes back to the office felt like an epic amount of inefficiency.

After one session, as my nerves frayed under the pressure of closing the fund, I jumped on a conference call. The night before, our head of retail had sent me updates on all projects under construction, highlighting issues we needed to make decisions on. But as I listened in, stepping out into the parking lot, I saw that my car had been blocked in by another vehicle.

"Hold on, everyone," I muttered into the phone, putting the call on mute. I returned to the building and approached the lobby attendant. She was buried in her novel.

"I'm in a bit of a hurry here," I said, trying to keep my voice calm. "Someone's blocked my car."

She glanced up, her expression blank.

"I don't know what to tell you," she said with a shrug.

"Can you please check who it is?"

She sighed, flipped through a ledger nonchalantly, then finally made a call.

Back on the conference call, I juggled apologies and struggled to focus. Just as I was back and focused, the car's owner sauntered into the lobby.

"Is that your Mercedes blocking me in?" I asked.

"You're damn right it is," she snapped back, her defiance flaring. "You folks think you can park wherever you like? Well, guess what? You're on my time now, honey. I take my lunch at noon."

She spun on her heel and left me stewing in the lobby.

"I'm sorry, guys, something has come up and I need to reschedule," I said, hanging up the call. Then I returned to the parking lot and started to kick the lady's Mercedes. I started in the back, worked my way to the front, denting the car up, lost in a fugue of anger.

By the time the police arrived, I was breathless, my dress shoes scuffed. I looked up to find Ed, who must have heard the commotion from his office, raced down to the parking lot, and explained to the officers that I was his patient.

"Go and wait in the lobby," Ed whispered in my ear, and I disappeared back into the building, only to witness Ed outside speaking to a pair of police officers on my behalf. What was he saying?

He returned and asked me to stay very calm, then explained that if I
agreed to cover all the repair costs for the dental hygienist, she wouldn't
press charges. Ed assured the officers I would pay promptly and when the
bill ran to $10,000 I was too busy to notice or care. Our initial investments
were so successful that after Chris Leavy joined, we closed and stopped
accepting new investors into our first fund, locking in the gains for our
original investors. We launched a second fund to continue to take in the
investor capital and within a blink we had raised over $150 million between
MedMen Opportunity Fund 1 and MedMen Opportunity Fund 2.

INSIDE CORPORATE WEED'S
COMMAND CENTER

ndrew and I strode through the expansive single-story building, our shoes clicking against the polished concrete floor as we envisioned the layout. The morning light streamed in through the sprawling skylights, casting sharp shadows that seemed to segment the space before us into departments.

Investing all that money into operations across the country, we had to expand our team and needed to find an office big enough to house this growing army of red-hoodie-wearing soldiers. I was eager to create an office that was functional as I, alongside my teammates, would be spending more time there than anywhere else. But I also understood our office needed to represent the mission. It needed to embody the mainstream future we were creating. Our mission statement was: "To provide an unparalleled experience that invites the world to discover the remarkable benefits of cannabis." The office needed to reflect such bold vision. I was inspired to create a space that could ignite innovation and success not just for MedMen but an entire industry. Shabby carpets and dingy cubicle spaces needed to give way to an environment we would want to brag about versus be ashamed of. If weed was going to be mainstream then the corporate headquarters of the biggest weed company in America needed to feel that way.

"So, how many employees are you planning to host here?"

I didn't know what to say.

"A hundred, maybe more," I said. "We could double overnight."

The steps of our feet echoed in the open space as we approached the center.

"Here's the heart of it all." I pointed to the middle of the floor plan, the designated spot for our glass-walled conference room. I had dreamed of this signature feature.

"Visible from every corner of the office, like a fishbowl. Every meeting, every discussion on display—transparency in action."

We took a moment to stand in the middle of the soon-to-be conference room, taking it all in. The vast, open space was silent for now, but it hummed with potential. Each space would ultimately be calculated to foster collaboration.

"Let's connect our two offices to this conference room," Andrew said. "The conference room at the center and us right here in the middle of it all."

"It's ridiculous, and I love it," I said. "Please make it happen."

————

As a result of the private equity fund's success, Chris, Andrew, and I also received hefty management and performance fees. Our first investment had by now already returned 10x to the investors. We were now playing with big numbers, and as the result of our hard work and this success, we went shopping. Andrew splurged on an $11 million mansion, a modern specimen of glass and granite complete with its own gym, steam shower, and view of the city skyline from the Birds, one of the city's most exclusive neighborhoods. Chris bought a $9 million house in Brentwood that had belonged to an entertainment executive at 20th Century Fox and was nestled in its own private forest.

I bought my family's $5 million dream house in Marina del Rey, where we could stroll around the Marina and then onto the Strand, the peaceful waterfront walkway. We had always admired this particular home. When we walked in to see it with a realtor, the interior blew us away. Big kitchen, big living room, smart dining area. Laura was so overwhelmed she walked into the bathroom on the main floor to compose herself. She didn't want the agent to see how excited she was. Out of earshot, she squeezed my hand and whispered, "This is a dream."

After closing on our own mansion, I also bought myself a gift. I had always dreamed of the biggest, comfiest Cadillac, the kind the mobster bosses in the movies used to drive. Shopping around online, I picked out the 2018 CT6, only the third year Cadillac made this flagship model, then added all the possible features including, and most important for me, whitewall tires. I watched the price in the online checkout cart cross $100,000, and purchased it. Of course I got Laura a mommy version, a white Cadillac XT-6 SUV, to match. My Caddy symbolized achieving success in a dog-eat-dog world, all while doing it my way.

SEEDS OF GROWTH

S tepping into the white plastic suit felt like gearing up for a moon landing. The synthetic fabric crinkled with every movement.

"Hang in there, boss; almost there," Damian Solomon said, as he pulled the zipper up to my chin, the sound a crisp reminder of the fortune we planned to spend growing the world's most institutional weed. Our product did not need to be the best. It was about scale and repeatability, about corporatizing a back-alley business. We understood that other "boutique growers" would always grow "better weed" than us. Our desire was efficiency and reliability.

With our private equity arm loaded, Project Mustang, our factory in Reno, was well under construction. To make the operation a success, we spent months searching for the most experienced grower we could find willing to work in cannabis. We placed him in a grow facility attached to one of our Los Angeles dispensaries, instructing him to operate a scaled-down version of Mustang to fine-tune everything for the larger project.

In the beginning, I liked that Damian did not come from the cannabis world. As a consultant in ag tech, he was using state-of-the-art technology to grow and optimize different crops. His expertise was perfect for helping us revolutionize the growing process in cannabis, creating cultivation at scale. This was a moment in history when those with experience and expertise had built businesses and fortunes around hidden grows that were able to shut down at a moment's notice. Nobody in the United States had ever truly invested in the latest technology for their marijuana farm. Why would they? Why spend millions to watch the feds come in and trash the place, seizing all the crops? I was convinced, with Damian's push, that we could be the first to grow cannabis at institutional scale, and all thanks to our license that made it legal.

"Now the gloves," he said, handing me a pair of rubber surgeon gloves, a barrier against the sticky resin I'd soon be wading through, and sealing off any entry point for stray particles.

The final touch was the hairnet and the face mask, a one-two combo to keep the cannabis safe. Any spores of mold or mildew could kill a crop. Stepping through the double doors of the facility, the cool, filtered air was a stark contrast to the heat outside. I was hit immediately by the earthy, pungent, unmistakable aroma of cannabis in full bloom. The facility stretched out like a green sea, row upon row of plants under a canopy of artificial light that hummed faintly overhead.

"These LEDs are game changers," Damian explained, gesturing toward the sleek, glowing fixtures.

As we toured the different rooms—from vegetative to flowering—the controlled environment systems hummed in the background, a symphony of technology and nature intertwined. I watched on as Damian executed the technique of checking a plant: squeezing the bud and inhaling the sweet, powerful must.

"We can tailor the spectrum to mimic the optimal conditions for growth," he went on, "far stronger than those old high-pressure sodium lamps."

His cockiness had me worried.

"Those ideas around cannabis being somehow different are ridiculous," he told me. "It's a plant that needs nutrients, water, and light. Modern agriculture has ways to deliver those elements optimally using 2017 technology. It's really that simple. Any cannabis grower not using this equipment is either stupid, lacks the funds since this is more expensive, or, yeah, just stupid."

My interactions with growers had always been marked by humility. Yes, there was pride in the quality of one's finished product, but there was always respect for other growers.

"He is a great guy, and his product, well, you have to make that decision for yourself," was the extent of any derogatory speech I was accustomed to from that world. It felt like a red flag.

But the Mustang grow was not my project. Andrew was leading the charge, and with the funds closed, I was working on the politics, spending our treasure in critical places, namely New York, where I believed we needed to have a presence in order to accomplish our mission. Through one of his banking buddies on Wall Street, Chris Ganan introduced me to Richie Yost, a Staten Island native who had somehow pulled off a miracle, snagging one of the five golden tickets—a license to grow and sell medical cannabis throughout New York State. His family reportedly had ties to organized crime, and he claimed his operation was funded by a generous loan from his mother's electrical company. The subtext wasn't lost on me; Yost was navigating treacherous waters of this emerging weed industry with what many suspected was mob money.

Despite the red flags, Yost's predicament presented an opportunity too lucrative for me to pass up. Like many cannabis startups, his venture was hemorrhaging cash, struggling under a state program that was not commercially viable. He was cut off, his investors no longer willing to carry the business, and offered to sell it to me for what he had invested so far in the venture: $26.5 million.

It was a bargain, I thought. New York issued only five initial licenses for their new program and mandated each license holder to grow their own cannabis, manufacture their own cannabis products, distribute their own cannabis to retail, and operate their own cannabis dispensaries. It was impossible to pull off, but I could see the future: a Fifth Avenue dispensary, full recreational legalization in a few years.

"It's an absolute pleasure to meet you," I said.

"We definitely got something special cookin' over here," he said. "I've been at this for years even though I'm young, and I think you'd be impressed by what I've created."

I connected with this kid from the first beat. A young hustler who no doubt had lived a level of craziness I would never uncover, but I already understood.

"Look, if you're interested in making a deal," I said, "I'll stay in New York an extra night."

He gave me the address, and we agreed to meet the following morning.

I followed the address out to Long Island and pulled up to a warehouse. I knew I was in the right place when I saw an orange Lamborghini parked outside—a clear statement, but of what, I wasn't entirely sure. Inside the huge factory, I found Richie Yost in his conference room. Around the table sat an array of executives, each more polished and seasoned than the next, their résumés filled with stints at major pharmaceutical companies and corporate giants. As they laid out their work to date and operating plans for their future inside New York's medical cannabis program, it struck me how out of their depth they were. Richie and his team were attempting to mold a cannabis company into a pharmaceutical one. The disconnect was glaring—here was a team led by a young entrepreneur trying to navigate waters better suited for Pfizer or Merck.

Despite the impressive presentation, solid competence, and previous experience, their biggest challenge was reality. New York's medical cannabis program simply wasn't commercially viable. No company could make a profit until the regulations changed.

It was so difficult for patients to receive a recommendation to purchase medical cannabis that only a tiny fraction of the adult population—less than a tenth of 1%—had access. Even if patient restrictions eased, the entire supply chain would need to be established. The program would need farmers to grow cannabis and far more than the handful of dispensaries currently allowed to sell it.

I liked Richie. I sensed a mutual understanding, a recognition of the hustle and the grit it takes to launch ambitious projects. And so, in the midst of his presentation, I boldly reached across the table, shook Richie's hand, and committed to buying his business. I needed to call in capital from my investors, I told him, and that we would have a lot of regulatory work ahead, but I was committed to making it happen.

———

Back in Los Angeles, I couldn't wait to share the news. I huddled our executive team in the conference room, including Jonathan Littrell, our legal ace.

"I got the deal done," I announced, barely containing my excitement about securing Yost's company for $26.5 million, and a chance to get our hands on a coveted New York license.

"Not gonna happen," Littrell said, throwing a bucket of ice on the transaction. "You know it's impossible to transfer licenses in New York."

He was right. I didn't care.

"We're going to have to figure out how to do it," I shot back, determined to make the deal happen, even if it meant state legislators in Albany had to rewrite the laws for us. Morgan, our government relations ace, and I had already been lobbying the governor's office and the state's new cannabis czar. We had been having clandestine meetings in the basement library of the governor's office, helping them begin to contemplate a viable commercial program. I knew they didn't want Richie to fail—if he did, the state would look foolish having the first of their pilot project bomb.

I turned to Morgan.

"Where are we in New York?" I asked, already knowing that, whatever the answer, it wasn't going to be enough.

"Slow," she said.

"We have no choice but to get this transfer approved by the end of the year," I said. "This is your number one priority until it's across the line."

And we got to work. We pumped up our lobbying efforts, shelling out retainers to bring the state's best lobbyists onto our payroll.

We also needed to find a farm to grow the weed, and a farm owner who liked the idea of growing a crop like cannabis. As it turned out, I already knew just the guy—Anthony Quintal, the owner of Brightwaters Farms in Utica, a town in the rust belt of upstate New York. A few years earlier, Anthony had hired us to provide consulting services for his application to get his own license. He lost, Richie won, and here we were.

"How are you doing, my guy?" he said, picking up the phone.

I shared our predicament, and the news about taking over Richie's business.

"You know I am down for whatever," he said, and invited me to his farm in Utica to give me a tour of the prospective site.

―――――――

Utica felt like a relic, a history lesson in blue-collar resilience and the fleeting nature of industry. To get there, I had to drive six hours from New

York, following the old rust belt route of the Erie Canal, then a triumph of transportation, floating pelt furs and other goods down from Canada. But it had all dried up, leaving this part of New York in the dumps, its bustling downtowns now case studies for urban sprawl and despair. It was all a reminder that cannabis could create new economic opportunities here and throughout the country.

In town, Anthony and I made our rounds, starting at city hall where he exchanged familiarities with the mayor. Anthony was a big guy, old world, with a soft touch. We drove on to his farm and hopped in a golf cart to tour the land, which hosted an endless plain of greenhouses, all stocked with lettuce beds. He was growing them for Costco.

"We can do whatever the fuck we want out here," he said. "We could turn this whole thing into weed, and we can expand as far as you can see."

I liked this optimism, his versatility.

"If Andrew wants it indoor to start, we can put up a building literally anywhere that direction. All that land is ours."

Back in the LA office, our team was sweating. In the event we got approved, we would only have 30 days to transfer all the plants to our new production facility. Richie was trapped in a horrible lease on Long Island for his production facility. He hadn't paid rent, and the landlord was in the process of kicking him out. Somehow, the plants would need to get to their new home, not die along the way, and get back into production. The land in Utica was raw and not set up to grow cannabis.

"We can put them in containers," Andrew said at one meeting, doodling in his notebook.

Before the trend of container homes took off, he envisioned our new cultivation center on Anthony's farm housed within a series of shipping containers.

"Brilliant," I said, thinking the idea was so nimble we might actually be able to pull it off.

Littrell received the news first via a phone call from a lawyer in the governor's office.

We would be approved. The state would need the process to be in phases. First, we would take over the operation via a management agreement with a promise to fund and run the business. Then they would approve a transfer of the license as an exception to the regulations, a one-time deal to save a company that represented 20% of their market. But the approval had one condition: moving the plants in 30 days!

Andrew got to work, organizing the purchase and transport of the containers. Then he and Damian tricked them out as mini grow houses. A van service operated by off-duty NYPD officers was commissioned to ferry the precious mother plants from Yost's facility. The operation was a ballet of precision, all against a ticking clock.

A month later, when the state inspectors arrived, everything was in place. The plants were thriving in their container sanctuary, a testament to Andrew's ingenuity and our team's unwavering dedication to creating our own reality. We had turned an impossible deadline into a showcase of MedMen's capability and resolve.

We were opening operations across the country. Capital was flowing, funding our projects in California, New York, and Nevada. As more MedMen stores opened, a brand was born.

———

Amid this madness, we received a call from a producer at *The Profit*, the popular show on CNBC hosted by Marcus Lemonis, the entrepreneur and CEO of Camping World and several other companies. We agreed to film a segment welcoming him into our popular store in West Hollywood, the same location that Omar had purchased earlier. Once our private equity fund launched, I was able to buy it back from him.

"I've never been in a pot store, ever, and I'm honestly a little nervous," he said as they filmed him making his entrance. "I don't know if I want anybody to see me going in."

I greeted him outside the front door, the microphones on. He looked in awe—of the wood paneling, the beam lighting, the endless SKUs, and brilliant packaging. Our stores had an airy, easy quality about them.

"What do you call this?" he asked me.

"I call it the future," I said, as I literally opened the doors to the store and figuratively welcomed him, his viewers on CNBC, and the world into mainstream marijuana.

"There are no bars on the windows," I said, "no guy with a gun at the front." (Although I wished there were on some days.)

The verdict?

"Definitely not what I expected," Marcus said. "I like the design, where iPads are everywhere, loaded with information, right next to gizmos you see and smell before you buy. More style, less stigma."

"I would have never imagined that the retailing of marijuana would ever be this slick, this well merchandised, and this lucrative prior to going into the store," Lemonis said.

He concluded the segment, watched by millions across the country, this way: "I would have never contemplated investing in this concept but after seeing the frozen goods, the beverages, this is a real business with a real retail footprint. You may not like it morally, but you definitely have to pay attention to it."

UNION SPIES AND LABOR POWER

I was spending so much time in Nevada that the company rented a condo for Andrew and me in Las Vegas. It was a two-bedroom at Veer Towers, overlooking the Strip, a convenient spot where we could keep a fresh change of clothes and a spare set of toiletries—everything we needed to operate. After landing at McCarran Airport, gearing up for a marathon of meetings, I stepped off the plane and made my way through the terminal, passing slot machines and gift shops selling cowboy hats. Then I was ambushed.

"Adam! Adam from MedMen, right?" the guy called out, his voice slicing through the hum of the airport.

I was standing in front of the Bud 29 Track Lounge, in the bustling heart of the terminal. I turned, my heart kicking against my chest.

"Yeah, that's me," I replied.

He extended a sweaty palm, breathing heavily from what seemed like a short sprint. His name was Frank, he said, and he was dressed in an untucked plaid shirt that screamed suburban dad more than government spy.

"I'm from the UFCW," he said. "Mutual friends told me you were landing in Vegas. I just ask for 10 minutes of your time."

The UFCW? United Food and Commercial Workers? The union? This couldn't be good.

"I'm in a rush," I said. "Can we set up a meeting later?'

Seeing my hesitation, Frank gestured toward the Budweiser bar.

"Just a quick sit-down," he said. "I swear, it's worth your time."

I followed him. We sat in the back, the noise of the airport silenced and replaced with cigarette smoke thanks to the bar's industrial-strength vents and pro-smoking policy.

"Look, the UFCW has decided that our future is in cannabis retail," he said, leaning in. "We have been the workers' partners in grocery, and now extending into cannabis. Weed is the future and grocery is dying." With that, he glanced over at a waiter.

"Budweiser, please. You want anything, Adam?"

"No thanks," I said, disgusted by him and his approach, the beer, the three minutes that had passed.

"It's going to happen," he went on, "because that's what we do and we want to be your partner. With our political muscle and your trajectory over at MedMen, this industry could be legal, national—and together, we would both be seated at the head table."

My voice felt steadier than I felt.

"Let me think about it," I said.

"Sure, take your time," he said. "But remember, the union can be a powerful ally. Or a nightmare of a headache. Depends what side you are on, I guess."

"I'll get back to you," I promised, taking his card and not trusting myself to say more.

———

The minute I rolled up to the UFCW headquarters in Koreatown, I could tell this wasn't going to be your average meet and greet. The building looked like something out of a medieval fantasy, standing stark against the backdrop of LA's industrial wasteland downtown, a stone fortress amidst a sea of concrete with the homeless tents of Skid Row nearby. I half expected a moat and a drawbridge.

I was there to meet Nam Le, the union's political director for the state, who had been trying to help focus and support the motley crew of dispensary owners in Los Angeles pushing for legalization. These owners of dispensaries all considered themselves renegades and rebels, living on the fringe of the law. They'd been resisting order and organization their entire lives. Their own attempts to organize on the most basic of issues had already backfired. Once rallied around the cause with GLACA, the trade organization I had joined, infighting ensued and that core group splintered into another, UCBA (United Cannabis Business Association). Le had organized a roundtable comprising leadership from both groups, plus lawyers, lobbyists, and of course UFCW officials. I had been invited so Le could sell me on joining and becoming the patron for his initiative.

Showing up was a purely political endeavor but I quickly became aware of the immediate business opportunity. In our race to become the industry leader in modern cannabis, we needed to grow at lightning speed. This room was filled with dispensary owners, beaten up by the grind of operating on the fringes of the law for so long, while watching their margins eaten up by knickknack expenses.

We were their solution, their savior. Our successful transaction with Brennan Thicke gave me credibility in this room. He was there, too, sitting far more relaxed with the cool $4M in his pocket after we snatched up his West Hollywood location. Others were envious. Risk off the table, legitimate cash in his bank account, and still here because of his passion for the mission. I held their keys to that same outcome, and nobody else was buying stores like me. We were creating a market. We joined the group, but as a regular member, first telling Le that we wanted to attend a few meetings before committing fully.

Quietly, I started making alliances, pushing the political agenda forward, and sussing out which of these owners and their businesses could make the best purchases to expand our footprint.

"I've got a bankroll," I'd say, "and I would love to purchase your business, now."

Tony Fong was a standout. Skinny and dressed like an accountant, Fong could blend into a boardroom or a back-alley deal without missing a beat. He was the point man for several dispensaries owned by Chinese investors. He lived in Pasadena with his family and did everything in his grows and dispensaries: trimmed the plants, kept the books, and kept cash flowing.

As we spoke in the corner, Tony described his operations around the city, and one dispensary interested me greatly: it was directly across the street from Los Angeles Airport, and a potential marketing machine, considering all the travelers passing through every day.

"Ever think of selling?" I probed, casual but calculating.

Tony hesitated.

"For the right price," he said.

We met at his location shortly after. The building had a mix of tenants, from a third-tier car rental service to a discreet dispensary marked only by blacked-out windows and the name "Venice Caregivers." The adjacent spaces, once benign storefronts, had been converted into Tony's sprawling and covert grow operation.

The building was owned by a ghost, Tony said. He knew she was an heiress to a fortune in India, and her real estate holdings were a labyrinth of holding companies. But he had never seen her.

"I am trying to arrange for a meeting with all of us," he said. "She remains unresponsive to me. I have spoken with her guy in the United States. I call him but he says we must wait."

The dispensary was on the ground floor. Walking in and then down the hallway past the elevator bank, the doors opened and a group of toddlers filed out, their tiny hands clutching lunch boxes and backpacks, chaperoned by weary-looking adults, all making their way from a Kumon learning center that was running on one of the upper floors.

It was then that I knew we had a problem. We believed that once the city passed regs, dispensaries would need to be far from "sensitive sites," and this included: schools or learning centers like Kumon, public parks, public libraries, alcohol or drug abuse recovery centers, day care centers, and permanent supportive housing.

I decided to buy it anyway. The location was worth the hassle and the risk. So close to LAX, where the world converged and diverged in equal measure, our own dispensary could be a Hollywood-style billboard for MedMen, a statement piece screaming our arrival on the global stage. Tony and I struck a deal to buy his license for $2 million, though the terms were complex, layered with contingencies based on lease negotiations with the phantom heiress and the peculiarities of the building itself. Meanwhile, I needed a way for us to get those kids out of there, in preparation for a regulated future.

We decided to go undercover. To convince Kumon and their kids out of the building, we cooked up a Hollywood-level scheme. Our real estate ninja, Chris Ganan, with his golden Rolodex, found a perfect new location for the learning center just down the street, and one far better than their current digs. It was more spacious, more accessible, and, crucially for us, far enough away for us to comply with what we anticipated the future cannabis zoning laws to be. We then got ready to rent it ourselves and pass it on to the Kumon guy.

Next up, we needed someone who could play the part convincingly. Enter Kimble Cannon, our in-house lawyer with a flair for the dramatic. We briefed Kimball on his character: an educational entrepreneur looking to make a mark. The location was so perfect for his tutoring center that he was willing to pay a fee to the Kumon owner, plus relocate him to a better location nearby. He rehearsed his backstory, his motivations, everything down to the minutiae of his fictional business plan.

The day came, and Cannon walked into the learning center, exuding the confidence of a learned man on his righteous mission. He laid out his proposal to the owner, painting a vivid picture of the bright future that awaited him in his new location down the street. The promise of a better space, coupled with a tidy sum to sweeten the deal, was compelling. After a series of discussions, marked by Cannon's unwavering charm and strategic acumen, a deal was struck and those toddlers were out of our hair. The once-shabby building was now poised to become the gateway to MedMen for travelers from across the globe, and the next in our growing portfolio.

OPENING THE ABBOT KINNEY FLAGSHIP STORE

B
ack in our new offices, we started to look at the city of Los Angeles like a board game, our own version of Marijuana Monopoly. Thanks to our private equity fund, we had the cash to purchase key locations in West Hollywood, Venice, and downtown. But as strong as those locations were, spreading our brand across the city, I was hunting for a cultural anchor. Our position in the market was always cultural, always looking to break down the stigmas that have surrounded weed. We couldn't get into a mall but we found a way to get onto Abbot Kinney.

The boulevard is like its own curated art exhibit—a seamless blend of high-end boutiques, artisan cafés, and avant-garde galleries. In 2012, *GQ* magazine even crowned it "The Coolest Block in America." From bespoke tailors and Finnish candy shops to some of the hottest restaurants in the country, Abbot Kinney isn't just a street; it's a statement, a state of mind, a place where art, fashion, and food converge in a vibrant display of Westside cool. The synergies were perfect. Picture a customer sipping single-origin coffee at a sun-drenched café before wandering into MedMen to explore our curated cannabis selections. Or imagine the buzz of local artists hosting exhibitions in our space, seamlessly blending cannabis with culture in a way that only Abbot Kinney could make possible.

But getting in—like all the cool kid places—was impossible. Leases were hard to come by, and almost impossible for us when accounting for all the restrictions and codes we would have to abide by in a regulated future.

To solve this problem, Chris Ganan went high tech. He used a blend of real estate databases, which outlined the available spaces on the street, and then cross-referenced the schools, churches, and any other sensitive-use locations that could torpedo our dispensary in a regulated future.

Looking over his shoulder, I watched his cursor flick across the screen, navigating a digital maze. Every now and then, Chris would murmur a location, only to discard it seconds later as another red zone popped up. Then, something caught his eye—a blip on the digital landscape of Los Angeles.

"Here," he said, zooming in on a stretch of Abbot Kinney that would be safe for us to open.

"See if it's for sale," I ventured, and left him to work his magic.

Chris was already on it, tapping into his network with the efficiency of a seasoned pro.

"Price tag, $18 million," he said, popping into my office.

"Can we just rent?"

"This is Abbot Kinney," he said. "No."

The thought of purchasing a building outright on Abbot Kinney was audacious, even for us. But the size of the bet never changed my decision-making process, and although it was a big chunk of our bankroll, it was going to buy real estate that would maintain or grow its value regardless of the legalization efforts of a maniac like me.

———

As the lawyers worked on the paperwork, Andrew and I made a field trip to scout out the location. We found a pair of rickety stools at La Tostaderia, a taco stand across the street. The sun was falling, casting this epic golden haze over everything, and making even the weirdest hipster art look majestic.

"Check out that group of girls over there," I said. "Where do you think they are from?"

"Uh . . . somewhere not here," he said. "Like the South or something."

As I sat there, munching on my fish tostada, every passerby seemed like a potential brand ambassador or marketing persona. First, there was a guy with a man bun and a meticulously groomed beard, straight out of a craft beer ad. Then, a group of women breezed by, their laughter cutting through the street buzz. Dressed in boho chic, they looked like the types to host yoga retreats and down green juice, but in their eyes, there was a glimmer of rebellion—like they'd be down for a toke with friends. Then, an older couple strolled by, likely longtime locals who had watched the area evolve. Arm in arm, they probably had been smoking since the '60s and would love a legal weed shop in their neighborhood. And of course the wide-eyed tourists were there too, chasing the ultimate California experience. Maybe they were on the hunt for a taste of that Sticky Icky OG.

The building itself was a beast, spanning over a hundred feet along the street. But it was chopped up, a third going to a bikini shop.

"They've got about six months left on their lease," Andrew said. "We could start with two-thirds of the space, then see if they renew."

I nearly choked on my iced tea.

"Are you out of your mind, dude? Screw the bikini store! This is Abbot Kinney, man. We need the entire space."

Andrew just sat there, silent and hiding behind his shades.

"I just don't know how much it really matters," he said. "We can just deal with it later."

"You're a genius, figure it out," I said, and was off to my next meeting about the looming election that fall.

Hillary Clinton was the clear front-runner. Not only would voters be putting a new president in Washington to fill the seat of Barack Obama, but voters in California were also signaling they were finally ready to make recreational weed legal. Early polls showed support for Proposition 64, a bill that would give everyone in the state the right to buy a joint and dispensary owners like us the legal right to sell. "This is the point of no return, if this all comes through," Morgan said, about the upcoming race.

"It's crazy that people laughed at Rob," I said of our ally at the Marijuana Policy Project. "Now all the states are gonna legalize weed on the same day!"

ANTONIO

The White House was not the only office up for grabs. At the top of the ballot in California was the race for governor, and the matchup was a tale of two cities, between the south and north of the state. Gavin Newsom, the polished mayor of San Francisco, was pitted against Antonio Villaraigosa, the scrappy former mayor of Los Angeles.

Thanks to Morgan's networking wizardry, I hosted both of these candidates and their staff in our office. We gave them all a tour, presenting our vision of a future where a joint was as legal as kombucha. We also donated heavily to each of their campaigns, maxing out the accepted limits. They toured our space, nodding approvingly at our operation. I knew our headquarters was never what any politician expected from cannabis but more what they were used to from tech in Silicon Valley. I could always see the wheels turning in their heads as they tried to make sense of our bustling bright-red command center. With politicians touring our headquarters, taking our donations, building alliances, I thought: *What's more mainstream than this?*

I was glued to the television for one of the first debates, hosted by Jorge Ramos, the popular Latino broadcaster. Early on, he lobbed a question into the fray.

"Have you ever smoked marijuana?" he asked the candidates.

Antonio's response was immediate, almost eager. His hand shot up, and with a grin that spoke volumes, he dove into his past using drugs with a candor that was both shocking and refreshing.

"Yeah, I've smoked," he admitted, his tone a mix of pride and nonchalance. "Where I'm from, it's just part of the culture. I've been around the block with this stuff."

Gavin's response, on the other hand, was more calculated—his response skimmed the surface and had the unmistakable air of a politician carefully crafting every word, projecting an image with clear ambitions for the future. Newsom sailed through the primary with ease, veneer intact.

I was disappointed. Antonio was a maverick, and we needed more leaders like him. I called him a few days after he officially dropped out of the race.

"Antonio, I know how busy you are," I said. "I wanted to check in and see how you're doing."

His laughter crackled through the line, sounding as resilient as ever.

"Adam, how many people a day do you think called me before I ended my candidacy?" he said.

The line went silent. "I don't know . . . a lot?"

"And how about now?" He chuckled.

He went on to share about his defeat and lessons learned. I was all ears. Newsom may have bested him in that race, but Antonio's spirit was as eager as ever, his energy contagious.

"You want to meet for coffee next week?" I asked, already wondering how I could convince a former mayor to join the MedMen team.

"Text me," he said. "I'll be there."

We met, hit it off, and I asked him to join our board of advisors.

He accepted, marking another milestone for us. Along with the major investors and Wall Street legends on our team, we now had the former mayor of one of the biggest cities of the country and former head of the country's association of mayors.

Antonio believed in the cause and was ready to advocate for cannabis reform at the highest levels of government. With Prop 64 on the horizon, and recreational licenses up for grabs throughout the state, we needed all the political cachet and operational firepower we could muster.

———

Racing to the UFCW headquarters before the elections one afternoon, my stomach was already staging its own rebellion. The meeting had been called by Jerred Kiloh, the then-head of the association, as a response to my indication to Nam Le that we were ready to become the benefactor of the initiative being called Measure M—the UFCW-backed Los Angeles City ballot initiative to regulate, license, and tax cannabis.

I hadn't eaten all day, a rookie mistake given the marathon of meetings on our docket. Spotting a sushi joint across from the union hall, I made an executive decision. "Morgan, I have to pull over or I won't make it through the afternoon."

We dashed across the street and I inhaled a few sushi platters like it was my last meal. By the time we arrived for the meeting, my stomach was already protesting—a guttural symphony of impending doom. I tried to stay cool, but that sushi was a ticking time bomb, threatening to go off at any moment.

"I'll meet you inside," I mumbled to Morgan, beelining for the bathroom. The explosive aftermath of my sushi binge left me weak, pale, and completely drained.

Emerging from the bathroom like a ghost of my former self, I waddled to the meeting room and joined the table, where Jerred sat resplendent in his pink mohawk.

"Adam, you look . . . rough," Jerred observed, barely concealing a smirk.

I waved him off, trying to regain my composure.

"I think that sushi spot across the street made me sick," I said.

As we dove into the heart of the discussion, my ordeal in the bathroom faded to the background, and I offered to donate $3 million to support the ballot initiative in Los Angeles that would be needed to create licensing at the city level, regardless of the state's politics. In exchange for our donation, we wanted board seats and the ability to ensure the money and the moment was not squandered inside UCBA, which had become the most prominent trade organization in the city and was working alongside the UFCW to support the ballot initiative and help pass it during the election.

In exchange for the gift and boost to UCBA's campaign war chest, I was expecting a hug, a high five, a kiss on the cheek.

Jerred was wary.

"We just want to understand what you're really in this for," he began. "We've been doing this for over a decade, and here you come with your millions, wanting to control."

I leaned back, planning my response.

"I'm not here to step on anyone's toes," I said. "I see a future where our businesses have permanence. I've got the bankroll now to make that happen, and want to support this."

I pressed on, laying out my vision for a regulated, thriving cannabis industry in Los Angeles, one where dispensary owners like Jerred and his constituents could operate without fear.

"At the end of the day, we all want the same thing," I concluded.

"And what about the little guy, Adam? How do we fit into your grand scheme?"

"Jerred, I'm building something global. I'm not interested in monopolizing LA. But without a united front, without clear rules and regulations, We're all at risk. And that's something I'm willing to spend millions to prevent."

As we parted ways, I couldn't shake this frustrated feeling. I was up against the establishment, pushing for change that would protect all of us, but the very people who stood to gain from my efforts—other "weed people"—showed me nothing but spite at every turn. I had the cash, the team, the desire to help, and yet I was somehow the enemy.

———

Back at the MedMen office, a problem was brewing on a marketing campaign I needed to solve.

"Adam, we've got a situation," Morgan said. I raised an eyebrow, still decompressing from the sushi debacle.

"What now?"

"It's Jerred. He talked to the UCBA lobbyist, who then blabbed to Herb Wesson's staff about your offer."

Herb Wesson was arguably the most powerful political force in Los Angeles. A noted advocate for social justice and affordable housing, Herb rose from blue-collar Ohio and moved west, where he quickly became a political force. He served as speaker of the California State Assembly before going on to become president of the Los Angeles City Council.

"They're all riled up about the 'three-million-dollar man' trying to buy his way in," she explained, her words hitting me like a kidney punch.

I had just offered them millions to help legalize their own businesses, and now they were trying to undermine me with the most influential political figure on the LA City Council, the one person who could actually make it happen.

We had precious licenses to win, and I couldn't have the political gate-keeper to our fortunes think we were finance punks with money. I had to fix it fast. My mind raced, calculating my next move. That's when I remembered Antonio, our political ace who was now on our payroll.

"Do you know Herb Wesson?" I asked him.

"Know him? That's my little brother, man! What's he done now?"

I briefed Antonio on the situation, my words tumbling out in a rush. "They're calling me the 'three-million-dollar man,' like I'm some villain in a comic book."

Antonio's laughter filled the phone receiver, a balm to my frayed nerves.

"Don't worry, Adam. I'll handle this."

Less than a half hour later, Antonio called back.

"You're set to meet with Herb next week," he said. "Don't fuck it up."

MEETING HERB WESSON

The office of Herb Wesson, the nerve center of Los Angeles's political system, was located in West Adams, one of the city's toughest neighborhoods. Only a short drive from our office in Culver City, gangs had been vying to control street corners there for years, the community scarred by the war on drugs. Like so many other neighborhoods across the country, West Adams was a place where weed had been both a means of survival and a ticket to incarceration and despair.

The dilapidated buildings and barbed-wire fences were stark reminders of generations of low-income residents who were trapped in the crossfire of harsh drug policies. I knew the stories all too well. Here, young men who could have been entrepreneurs were marked as criminals, their potential snuffed out by a system that favored criminal punishment for cannabis over licensing and taxation.

Despite its barbed-wired fence, Wesson's office stood as a kind of safe haven amidst this broken bottle backdrop, a testament that a hard-charging guy like him could rise up through the system. Inside, I was introduced to Andrew Westall, the right-hand man to the political boss. Like many of these younger and ambitious aides, Westall was an operator. Despite lacking the team and resources, he was accountable for getting shit done.

"This isn't just about profit," I explained as we sat and waited for his boss to appear. "It's about turning the tide, offering opportunities where there were once only dead ends."

The taxes could help support failing schools, infrastructure, or any number of programs that needed help.

"Most importantly, let's please just learn from what previous cities have already done. I can't figure out for the life of me why each new city doesn't start this exercise by analyzing every city's ordinance in the country, and pick what is working and learn about what is not."

I offered resources and information on all of them.

"This is the most important program in the country," I continued. "We have the benefit of others coming before us to learn from."

I could see a flicker of interest in Westall's eyes as I outlined how regulated dispensaries could also replace the illicit market, taking part of the drug business from the streets and bringing opportunities to neighborhoods like West Adams. Why work for a gang selling drugs when you can get a job with a company like MedMen, make a decent wage, and get health benefits too?

Soon, it was time. A secretary approached.

"The councilman will see you now," she said.

_____

Herb Wesson's lair was a space that felt plucked from a TV drama set. The office was a shrine to achievement and community, walls adorned with sports memorabilia and photos of Wesson with luminaries like President Obama and basketball star Magic Johnson.

He was a small guy, and he sat behind an enormous desk that took up most of the room. I was directed into a plush leather couch in front of the desk, and soon became the recipient of his streetwise charm and political savvy.

"What the fuck is this $3 million shit?" he asked.

I explained it all in an easy and smooth tone. The amount was only my initial commitment to funding a campaign with the union and others to pass the city's ballot initiative and secure licenses for dispensary owners. I volunteered to work with Wesson to establish a regulatory framework that could benefit the consumers, the entrepreneurs, and the communities supporting cannabis. I dove deeper, emphasizing the importance of getting LA's cannabis regulation right, considering its status as a global marijuana market.

"It's just important that we don't make the same mistakes everybody else has made," I said, offering the full support and expertise of my team to ensure LA set a gold standard in cannabis regulation. As our conversation wound down, Wesson gave me a casual assurance.

"Listen, I want to see nothing more than for weed to be legal and people in our communities to stop being locked up for selling and smoking it," he said. "I really dig what you're doing, you and I are good." Shaking my hand, a weight had been lifted off my shoulders. "Say hey to my big brother, Antonio, for me."

Our next steps were clear.

"Work with Andrew [Westall]," he said, reinforcing the sense of partnership we were forging. I now felt I was in the fold at the highest levels at city hall, and had forged a newfound alliance that could potentially reshape LA's cannabis landscape as the latest initiative was gearing up to appear on the ballots.

BEATING ADELSON

That year, cannabis initiatives weren't just stirring up California. Voters that November in California, Nevada, Arkansas, North Dakota, Montana, Massachusetts, Maine, and Florida would all be asked whether they wanted access to legal weed in their state. Nevada—our second home, and crucial to our West Coast strategy—demanded my attention, and I found myself jetting to Las Vegas often, looking to inject resources and unite allies to support the cause.

Raised on the stories of casino moguls my father told me, I'd come to learn about the titans who had sculpted the Vegas skyline. Among them, Sheldon Adelson stood out. His Venetian resort wasn't merely a hotel; it was a testament to opulence and ambition. Beyond Vegas, Adelson's empire stretched all the way to Macao, influencing far corners of the globe.

A staunch conservative, he wielded significant influence through his media holdings, including the *Las Vegas Review-Journal*. Now in his twilight years, he was pouring his vast resources into a battle deeply personal to him. His son, Mitchell, had tragically overdosed on heroin, a loss that Adelson blamed on cannabis, which he believed had acted as the gateway for his son's heroin use, abuse, and overdose.

Perceiving marijuana as the harbinger of his family's anguish, Adelson saw the pending legalization initiative as a direct threat, especially with the possibility of cannabis smoke wafting through his Venetian corridors.

As I touched down in Vegas, the weight of the impending confrontation loomed. This battle was not just about business; it was steeped in personal beliefs and tragedies, elevating the stakes immensely.

It was personal for me too. My cause was facing off against Adelson, a Vegas titan I was raised to revere. My strategy? Enlist the support of another heavyweight in Vegas, one of Adelson's competitors and my newest ally. In a city of high stakes and even more intense rivalries, this was more than a campaign—it was a clash of legacies.

———

I was an outsider in Vegas, a town defined by its tight-knit, legacy-driven community. Looking at the national stage and the importance of Nevada for the movement and for MedMen, I was pushing every button and pulling every lever to ensure a ballot win.

For extra resources, I had reached out and made a connection to Armen Yemenidjian, a new cannabis entrepreneur and Vegas power broker. His dad, Alex Yemenidjian, had been the right-hand operator to Kirk Kerkorian, the casino mogul, and one of our family's personal heroes.

Armen and I had developed the beginning of a friendship, and I wanted to support him as he led the political ground war to push the ballot initiative in Nevada. To assist, I connected Armen with Rob Kampia and his crew from Marijuana Policy Project, and implored Armen to support them. The troops at MPP were the national campaign experts, and could assist with logistics, messaging, and voter turnout. They could be his air support.

We all met in a conference room inside the MGM Grand. Rob arrived first, carefully placing his war plans in front of each seat, packets that he no doubt had printed on his home computer in DC before flying out to the desert. And soon enough, in walked Armen.

"You can see I've laid out what it will cost to ensure victory in November," Rob said, walking us through the line items of his battle plan. "I think what is going down in Nevada is too important nationally to not have every resource on it, and this is a road map I know works when followed."

"This looks great, but frankly, this is Nevada and we have our own road maps," Armen said. "You know we appreciate your efforts nationally, and will continue to support those separately."

"We can't leave anything on the table," I said. Knowing no deal would be reached during the meeting, Rob smoothly offered to follow up with

Armen, shook hands like a statesman, and headed off, likely already plotting his next campaign for legalization. Ultimately, Armen brought Rob and his team onboard in Nevada.

———

I spent election night at home. Mateo was restless as usual, and Ari was still in the bassinet on Laura's side of the bed. As the results trickled in, I retreated to our second room, which doubled as my home office. Earlier that year, I had purchased our dream home, though it wasn't ready to move into yet. Even knowing that more comfort for me and my family was on the horizon, patience was key—much like the inevitable end of marijuana prohibition. It was coming, but it would take time and persistence.

In the dim room, with the soft glow of my phone lighting the space, I lay on the air mattress, which felt like a life raft in a sea of uncertainty. Earlier, I had checked in with Rob.

"Looking good," he reassured me. He was known for picking contests.

"We win California, Nevada, Illinois, Maine, lose Florida, and Mass too close to call."

I casually checked the cannabis ballot results, confident in our strong position in California. Later, as midnight crept closer, I woke up and glanced at my phone again. The numbers for Donald Trump were climbing, an unexpected twist at the top of the ballot. Must be an error, I thought, and drifted off to sleep.

Dawn broke. I tiptoed around the house, slipping into my running clothes and readying myself for a day that was supposed to be filled with interviews and celebrations.

But it wasn't. Trump had won, and I knew nothing would be the same. The energy in the office that morning was sunken and glum, and it stayed that way throughout the day. While we had scored ballot victories in California and beyond, each of these wins that would ease the restrictions on cannabis and increase our business universe was now shadowed by the looming uncertainty surrounding the Orange Man. The Republican president had openly embraced the role of moral policeman during his campaign and now suddenly, the future of our business, our industry, and my mission had become perilously unpredictable.

The incredible triumphs of cannabis were merely a footnote in the news. The only folks who seemed to notice were MedMen's investors, all nervous that our ride was now officially over.

I fielded panicky questions from every direction.

"Adam, what do we know from Trump's camp on his real stance toward enforcement?"

"Adam, is there anything to what Kellen told me about Trump's nephew wanting to invest in us? Does that mean they are pro-cannabis?"

"If the Republicans start kicking in doors and seizing assets, what are we going to do?"

OUR CELEBRITY SUPPORTERS LINE UP

I was in the middle of a budget meeting in my office, juggling my attention between line items per department, when the notifications lit up my phone. One of them was from Laura. Intrigued, I excused myself and glanced deeper into my phone.

"You're on *The Kardashians*!"

I had never seen the show, but I knew it was big. Beyond big.

As I quickly regained focus on my meeting, Kellen O'Keefe, ever the eager messenger, rushed through the halls and peeked in my door.

"Bro, did you see this? We're on the Kardashian show!"

The best part: It wasn't the young Kardashians who were responsible. Our iconic red shopping bag, one of Andrew's greatest design triumphs, had been dropped on a gift table whose only purpose was to show off the trendiest brands and the Kardashians' personal favorites. The occasion was not for the younger daughters, however. It was for Kris Jenner, the matriarch herself, supplying us mainstream validation on a whole new level.

———

Media exposure, I learned, comes in waves. Soon after our brand's appearance on *The Kardashians*, we got hit with another surprise. I was plopping around in my office on my red bouncy ball, when Daniel Yi, our head of PR, craned his head through my door and asked to come in.

"Jimmy Kimmel reached out," he said. "They want us on the show."

Wow. The Kardashians were celebrity, sugar pop figures. But Kimmel was an influential mainstream voice in the country, watched by millions in the heartlands. Heck, my grandmother back in St. Louis watched Kimmel.

We accepted the invitation. Daniel and I brainstormed feverishly, concocting a plan for the segment. We needed a suave, good-looking, smooth-talking lead. A sexy, irresistible budtender.

Kellen O'Keefe was our obvious choice. He was perfect for the show, where he'd be fielding questions from Kimmel's sidekick and even interviewing customers live. Kellen didn't work in our stores, but who cared?

We found him lounging in his office.

"Kellen, we need to talk," I said.

"What's up, boss?"

"We've been offered a spot on the Jimmy Kimmel show," I said.

"Wow," he said. "Congrats."

"Congrats to you," I said. "You're going to be our main guy on the segment, pretending to be a budtender."

Kellen scoffed, crossing his arms defiantly. "No way. I don't work in the stores."

"But it's national television!"

"I'm management," he said.

"Kellen, this is a big opportunity for us. Put your ego aside for once, please, and do what's best for the company."

He hesitated, glancing around the room as if searching for an escape, and the best he could come up with was that he was allergic to the red cotton t-shirts our budtenders wore.

"They give me a rash," he said.

I sighed, feeling the tension mounting.

"You're either in or you're out," I said, giving him the ultimatum. Do the bit, or leave the company.

"Fine, but I'm doing this under protest," he said.

———

I never watched the show live. It was on past my bedtime. But once I got into the office, I watched the replay. The familiar set of the Kimmel show appeared on-screen, and my heart quickened with each passing second.

Then, there he was. Kellen, standing behind the counter at MedMen West Hollywood, wearing the "itchy" red budtender shirt. Despite his initial resistance, he crushed it, engaging with customers and answering questions with ease.

"We have a little something for everyone," he said. "Whether you are young or old, it doesn't matter."

I couldn't help but laugh along as I watched, a sense of pride swelling within me.

"I haven't tried anything yet," one curious customer said. "I just heard about it and thought I'd come in and check it out."

As the segment progressed, I found myself leaning closer to the screen, hanging on every word and gesture.

"Do your folks know you are in that store right now?" Kimmel asked the customer.

"No," he said, laughing.

"Would they approve?" Kimmel said.

"Sure. It's the 21st century."

———

Shortly after these media spikes, David Dancer, our new chief marketing officer, burst into my office.

"Ready to meet Gwyneth Paltrow?"

We had all seen what Paltrow had done in the consumer space, launching Goop, her own platform and line of wellness goods. Paltrow had reached out about a collaboration, curious about a market-ready product that we could share with their community.

I went to the meeting at their office in Santa Monica. The place had the ultimate startup feel, dozens of worker bees floating around the airy space with laptops.

We met in Paltrow's office. She introduced herself and shared her passion for cannabis advocacy and new consumer products.

"When are we going to see THC in tampons?" she said. "That, we could really push on Goop."

Looking around the room, watching these talented operators, I was getting goose bumps. The key to unlocking the mainstream opportunity, I always believed, was through a female audience.

In the end, MedMen provided the cannabis for the Goop annual event, and we had validated our mission further. As our teams worked together on our collaboration, I couldn't help but feel empowered with a force like Gwyneth and her worker bees buzzing on our side.

———

Each new opportunity seemed to lead to another. With Kellen O'Keefe's latest introduction, we suddenly found ourselves on the inside, smoothly navigating circles that had once felt impenetrable. Through a connection, Kellen had snagged an introduction to musical mogul Jay Brown, who was business partners with his longtime friend and luminary Jay-Z at Roc Nation.

I first met him in our office for a tight 15-minute chat. I liked him immediately. He wore his success lightly, and it quickly became apparent that Jay saw the immense potential in aligning with MedMen. He invited Laura and me to join him backstage at the Inglewood Forum, to meet a star in his stable, Shakira.

The night of the concert, Laura and I breezed through the VIP entrance. Jay was waiting for us and guided us through the maze backstage. Shakira greeted us warmly in her dressing room, offering a smile and a hug. Jay then led us to the sound board area, 50 feet from the stage, dead center. He politely asked one of the sound engineers if he could borrow an extra rolling desk chair and pulled it up to the front of the area and motioned for Laura to sit down. She had been escorted to the best seat in the house. Literally. The concert kicked off, with smoke and pulsating beats filling the air. As Shakira performed, Jay and I found a quiet spot behind the stage. We sat at a high table near the security guard station.

"I want you to know I'm here to help you," he said. "This is about supporting you. Invite me in and you'll see how much I can help."

I expressed doubts—about myself, my abilities.

"You're exactly where you need to be," Jay encouraged. "You're a genius at what you do. Don't doubt that."

In that moment, I felt a deep connection with Jay, a blend of mentorship and camaraderie. I offered him a seat on our board of advisors, and he accepted.

With Jay Brown behind us, MedMen was poised to redefine the cultural landscape. We weren't just promoting legality; we were spearheading a cultural revolution. It was clear, as we stood on the brink of change, that our mission was ushering in a new era of acceptance. And for us, the next step was to do what all mainstream companies do: go public.

PROJECT MOUNTY

Vancouver was a refreshing new destination for me—the lush, cool landscape of pine forests and mountain lakes. I headed there to meet David Subotic, an old friend who, with his wife, cofounded a frozen yogurt concept called Go Greek Yogurt, one of my and Andrew's first marketing clients.

David was a finance guy. He grew up on Bay Street, the Wall Street of Canada, and cut his teeth slinging mining company IPOs before finding his niche in casino gaming. He was a gambler at heart, and was raising money to take companies public, then working the machine to cash out on stock, earning himself a small fortune. We were meeting to talk about Captor Capital, a shell company that David and his partners controlled. As a shell company, Captor would charge a fee and take an equity stake in exchange for letting a private company merge into the already public shell. This approach allowed companies to bypass the daunting mountain of regulatory filings, checks, and scrutiny they'd face if they went through the process from scratch.

We met at Joe Fortes, a renowned fish house overlooking the harbor, the smell of the sea mingling with the scent of fresh cedar. David was already there, a grin spreading across his face as he saw me.

"Look, bullshit companies go public every day," he said, once we got into the conversation. "You actually have a real business here. Your stores do more sales per square foot than Apple!"

"We are used to dealing with people hoping a piece of dirt in some desert or forest somewhere yields gold or oil," Neil Stefanos-Taylor, one of his associates, said. "These markets up here would eat this up if you package it all the right way. I can help you put it all together."

I took a sip from my iced tea, taking it all in.

"The market is ready for a leader like MedMen," Neil went on. "You've got the brand, the business model, and the buzz."

"Public money is different," David said. "This is the access you need to really scale. You can't keep raising these small numbers and get to where you want to be."

Neil chimed in, "It's not just about going public, Adam. It's about making a market that you are the leader of. We would start by backing you now while you are private, and then start working on helping you get ready for the merger."

"I've only seen this once before," David said. "I remember when I was working on Bay Street and Steve Wynn was pumping Mirage Resorts. Every day I was in the office I would look up at the screens playing the money shows and there he was. You couldn't turn on the television without seeing his face. He was the spokesperson for a new opportunity. That's why we all ate it up; that's why he was able to do what he did. You're that, Adam, for weed."

The conversation shifted toward the nuts and bolts—valuations, potential market caps, and investor appetites. Neil laid out their proposal: "We're prepared to make a $30 million investment into you now as a private company at a valuation of $1 billion USD."

I was speechless, the figure daunting. And a valuation made by *finance people* who knew what they were talking about. It was the validation of every risk we'd taken, every late night, every setback.

"Adam, this is it—the rocket fuel MedMen needs. Let's grab this."

I only had one way to play the hand.

"Let's do it," I said, and started to work with our lawyers and investors to roll up all our assets, across all our companies, into a place that everyday investors could buy on a stock exchange.

Back in LA, the office felt foreign. I was now spending more time on the road than ever, stopping home to change clothes, kiss the kids and Laura, check on the staff, and head back out. Even when I was home, making every effort to be present for the time I was there, I was a phantom more often than not. Every morning, I would sneak out in the darkness, praying that walking on my tiptoes would save me from waking a sleeping baby and as a result the whole house. This was the discipline I felt I needed, the only way to keep my mind and body fresh for the day ahead.

"We miss you," Laura implored. "We barely see you."

"I'm in the postseason, baby," I'd say. "This is the World Series. When Albert Pujols is playing in the World Series, he is not distracted by anything and, yes, that includes his family. I just have to focus right now. Don't expect anything from me."

"What do you mean, for me or the kids?"

"You need to handle the kids and not count on me for anything," I said. "When I can participate, I obviously will because I want to. Look, I still take the kids to everything I can, do bedtime when I'm home; I'm doing the best I can. But my primary focus needs to be MedMen."

"This isn't a marriage," she said. "Your family needs you too. Your wife and kids need you."

"Yeah, but you live in this house, you drive the cars, you benefit from all this shit, and this is what it takes."

"That's just stuff, Adam."

"Yeah, and you don't love this fucking stuff and the kids don't have everything they ever wanted?"

"You don't get it."

At home, I went from absent to unavailable. At work, I felt more determined than ever to take the company public. I now stormed through our office corridors with a new plan that was as audacious as it was game-changing. Project Mounty, our covert operation to take MedMen public in Canada, was about to kick off. I handpicked a team of a dozen or so aces, each with their own unique skill set crucial for navigating the icy waters of international finance and regulation. Charts, timelines, legal documents, and financial projections were meticulously crafted under a veil of secrecy.

I was determined to prevent our attempt to go public from leaking. The world wouldn't start to learn of our plans until after I had secured a deal with the investment bankers that would ultimately take us public;

that community can't keep its mouth shut, and once word got out, it got out! As to be expected, I was fielding inbound communications from the zaniest corners of the universe. One was an email from a guy writing for the Bud Baron, an email newsletter, claiming he was excited about our impending public offering and could help boost our stock price by writing about us favorably. We then received a follow-up email reminding me that the Bud Baron was offering his services and updated the communication to include an implicit threat that if not hired, he would do the opposite and destroy our stock price. He was more than brazen when he included his price of $2.5 million. I chalked these communications up to the crazy pile and forgot about them.

OPENING IN LAS VEGAS AND RENO

Cruising back into Vegas once again, the neon skyline stretched out before me—a beacon of dreams and high-stakes gambles. It felt different this time. The grand opening of our latest MedMen store right off the Las Vegas Strip was just days away. Thanks to our lobbying efforts and the passage of those recreational marijuana laws, the state's governor, Steve Sisolak, was slated to cut the ribbon, and in our honor declare it "MedMen Day" in the state of Nevada.

As I drove down the Strip, the familiarity of the route was overshadowed by the gravity of the moment. The store, situated on a prime stretch from McCarran Airport to the heart of Vegas, was more than a retail space; it was a bold declaration to welcome every traveler from every corner of the globe to mainstream marijuana.

I dropped Laura off at Veer Towers. She came along as she often did; I tried to bring her, and the boys, to every trip I could. Understanding how absent I was at home, bringing them into the adventures, milestones, and celebrations inside my video game was my way to express my love and share with them a glimpse into what I was spending all my time on.

Pulling up to the store, the location struck me again with its potential. Yet, as I stepped inside, the expected buzz of activity from our staff was absent. The place felt dead.

"Boss, we've got a problem," said Matt Power, one of our tech leaders. "The POS system . . . it's glitching."

"What do you mean? We open in three days!"

Matt dragged me aside, his face shadowed under the neon lights.

"We failed the final inspection. The point-of-sale system—the heartbeat of our operation—isn't complying with state regulations."

"And you're telling me this now?" Our tech was supposed to be cutting-edge, seamless. Yet here we were, grappling with glitches. If we couldn't pass the inspection, our store could not open.

"It's the receipts," Matt said. "They need to detail everything from batch dates to testing results. Our system can't generate them fast enough. It's all backed up."

The grand opening had been choreographed down to the minute, and delays were not on the agenda.

"Fix it, Matt. Whatever it takes."

Back in the apartment, I paced around, trying to come up with a solution to this nightmare. I dialed Lisa Sergi, our chief legal officer, seeking any sliver of good news.

"We can't get another inspector before the opening," she informed me.

"What about Morgan's contact?" I asked.

"On vacation," she replied, her tone flat.

Desperate, I called my local power broker for another favor.

"Armen, I need a miracle," I said into the phone. I outlined our predicament, half-bluffing about the system's readiness.

His response was a brief pause, then a promise to call back.

Moments later, he did. "The inspector's boss from Carson City will fly down Saturday morning," he said. "He'll handle your inspection."

"You're a lifesaver, Armen."

The next morning, armed with coffee and donuts, I rallied the team with a new idea.

"We are going to have to fake it," I said, and outlined the plan. Instead of leaving the system to chance, we would hand-select the products for the inspector and ring these products up for him. Beforehand, we would rig the machines and hope the inspector didn't notice.

"You want me to create a receipt for five products that are ready to print, and then I hit PRINT?" Power said.

"Yes. Can you make that happen?

"Yes, of course, but—"

"Matt, please go make that happen."

———

As the sun rose over Vegas, I waited outside the store. The inspector arrived on time, lit up a cigarette, and offered me a nod. I stood there, watching the smoke spiral into the morning sky, pondering the man who held the fate of our grand opening in his hands.

"You know, I used to be an entrepreneur," he said. Intrigued yet anxious to proceed with the inspection, I indulged him, sensing this might just be part of the dance we had to perform.

"Oh, really? Doing what?" I probed.

"My brother and I owned one of the biggest condom manufacturers in the country. We got our rubber from Southeast Asia—cheapest rates you could imagine." He chuckled. "Had a bit of a labor dispute down at our factory in Alabama, but that's business, right?"

I laughed. Only in Nevada would your business inspector for a cannabis store also be a former condom tycoon.

I opened the door for him and we walked through the site together. The store was sparkling, every detail meticulously executed.

We arrived at the checkout. Showtime.

"How can I help you?" Matt asked.

We had strategically placed five items behind the checkout counter, and removed all other inventory from the store. The inspector nodded, seemingly impressed. He pointed to the only inventory anywhere inside the store, placed right above the counter.

"Great, show me. Please ring me up for all of those."

Matt processed the items, and the printer whirred to life. I held my breath, crossed my fingers and toes. The receipt slid out, and it was perfect—every item, every detail, exactly as it should be.

The inspector scrutinized the receipt, pen in hand. He circled a few items, then nodded in approval. He pulled out a folder, signed a paper, and handed it to me.

"Congratulations, and good luck this weekend," he said.

As he left, I let out a breath I hadn't realized I'd been holding. Against all odds, we made our hand once again. Before we cut the ribbon, I watched the early morning foot traffic pick up and our first customers pile into the store. As they did, I knew we were on the brink of something far bigger than I had ever imagined.

———

Soon after the Vegas store opening, I was heading back to Nevada, this time flying to Reno for the ribbon cutting of Project Mustang, our cultivation center in the industrial park. I surveyed the airplane cabin. Laura was radiant with anticipation, Mateo and Ari were immersed in their own adventure treating the seats of the private jet like a playground, with Daniel Yi and Morgan Sokol both keeping a watchful eye. Even I couldn't help but savor this moment—a testament to relentless sweat and toil, and a pivotal investment in our blitz-scaled empire.

The facility was primed. In just a few months, the inaugural harvest from MedMen would make its way to our stores in Las Vegas and other Nevada locations. And when the day finally arrived, when the federal prohibition lifted, our Mustang center could dispatch products across the West Coast within hours.

The drive from the airport in Reno to our facility took just 30 minutes. As the Escalade doors swung open, a desert windstorm greeted us with swirling sand and debris. At the facility, our MedMen team awaited, clad in red jackets and battling the relentless gusts.

"We're going to blow away," Mateo quipped, gripping my hand as we made our way to greet the crew.

In celebration, the facility was wrapped in a massive red ribbon that stretched its entire length. The local press had their cameras trained on us. I shared a few remarks, then we transitioned indoors where Damian Solomon, our lead grower, commenced the tour.

As we navigated the sea of high-tech equipment, Laura leaned in and held my hand. "*You* built all this."

Her words warmed me, but as I gazed upon the sprawling setup, doubts nagged at me. The entire operation hinged on Damian's expertise and Andrew's oversight. Was it enough to sustain our ambitious vision? And would it even work at all?

OPENING ON FIFTH AVENUE IN NEW YORK

I was back in New York, ready for another monumental event. After a grueling year of negotiations and red tape, we had finally secured the lease to 433 Fifth Avenue, a building previously owned by a Rockefeller and oozing with prestige, commanding a rent of $115,000 per month. We had then convinced the state to update the regulations so that a store could sell cannabis more "normally" out of a traditional sales floor. The regulations at the time required a buzzer door through a separate waiting room, creating a setup that felt worse to be in than an urgent care facility. That setup was not going to work long term for the marijuana program in New York but it certainly would be asinine on Fifth Ave. With Morgan's passionate and competent lobbying attack, we were able to get these updates made to the regulations allowing us to proceed with the location.

We all knew we were destined to lose money in this location. The licenses in New York were still medical, making it nearly impossible to break even. But the grandeur of Fifth Avenue was irresistible. The location could be a global beacon for the movement, and a touchpoint for the brand. And in a future where legal weed was sold in New York, I knew we wouldn't just make money, but that the revenues from this store could outperform any of the other stores in our system.

I brought Laura with me on the trip. She was due for an escape from the kids, and we were both blown away. This was Fifth Avenue, the heart of American commerce, and here I was, planting a flag for cannabis in the shadows of giants.

At the ribbon-cutting ceremony, Tish James, the aspiring attorney general, approached flanked by her entourage. The cameras surged forward. We had been an early supporter of hers, maxing out donations wherever we could. Now an ally, she gave a rousing speech bringing the crowd to cheers.

"The people of New York will benefit from this new cannabis economy," she said. "Thank you, MedMen, for showing us what the future can look like. We are on Fifth Ave, for the entire world to witness. Thank you, Adam, for your leadership and support. And let us all look toward this brighter, exciting future!"

———

Later that night, I went to meet David Subotic for dinner. He was in town to meet a few bankers—Wall Street was his world—and they had reserved a back room at a steak house in the Financial District, the kind of place where companies are bought and sold over oysters on the half shell, wet-aged porterhouse, and vintage wine.

When I arrived, the air was thick with the scent of money and meat. Servers navigated the room with military precision, balancing platters of outrageously priced crabs, their spiny shells glinting like trophies on ice.

"Adam, glad you could make it," David's voice cut through the hum. His handshake was firm, the smile all teeth.

The table was a live wire of energy, each seat occupied by someone either too important or too rich to ignore. Then, through the haze of indulgence, one of David's acquaintances emerged.

"Adam, I want you to meet Jason Adler of Gotham Green," David introduced us, his hand sweeping toward Jason like he was presenting an Egyptian pharaoh that had emerged from ancient history. Jason's eyes were sharp and calculating. Thin hair. Stocky build. A money guy.

"MedMen, right?" he asked. "I've been following you. Impressive."

As he introduced us, David explained Jason's new business.

"They are building a firm to finance cannabis companies," he said, a proposition that rang as sweet as a violin quartet in my ears. Until now, traditional lenders or investment funds had been so gun-shy investing into companies like ours that any new option, especially one with friendly connections, was a major piece of good news.

"We want to institutionalize cannabis," Jason said, a line that sounded so familiar because I had been using it for years.

Jason was based in New York, but he was moving to Los Angeles.

"Thinking of Santa Monica," he said. "Better for the kids."

"That's a great area," I said. "If you need help getting settled, my wife, Laura, can help you and your family. We know the schools. Makes the transition smoother if you know someone."

"Appreciated." Jason smiled, his phone buzzing in his hand—a silent summons he couldn't ignore. "I have to take this, but let's keep this conversation going. There's potential here."

With a final nod, Jason Adler was gone, slipping away as smoothly as he arrived.

"That guy could change our game," David murmured of Adler, though how could I know in that moment that he could end it all too?

———

Flying home, the drone of the engines muffled our tense conversation. I had left Laura behind to attend that dinner, and after years of waiting around for me, juggling the kids and sacrificing her own career, she was despondent. Her voice cut through the air, sharp and accusatory. Then she started crying.

"What do you really want?" she said.

"What do *you* want?" I shot back, as if providing for the family was not enough.

"For what? When will it end? What about us? What about the kids?"

"I have one shot at this," I said, "and won't let up, period!"

"But what about us?" she persisted, her eyes searching mine for answers I wasn't sure I had.

"I totally get it, but it won't change," I said. "I have to be honest right now. MedMen is more important because without MedMen we don't have any of what our life is today. I won't live with regrets."

"But what about now?" she pressed. "What about the present? What about our family?"

I struggled to find the right words, to bridge the gap between us that seemed to widen with each passing moment.

"Laura, I want respect for what I'm doing," I said finally. "I can't fight the outside world and come home to fight too."

Silence fell between us.

I wanted to console her. But I couldn't.

"We're not in the same place we were on that Super Bowl date night," I said, my voice firm. "We can't pretend like nothing's changed. This is our life for now, and I'm fully committed to MedMen and my mission."

BOOK 3

BOOK 3

GOING PUBLIC

Back at the Four Seasons, in the suite where I started this story, I bolted upright. On the nightstand of the hotel room, my phone erupted with notifications, piercing the early morning silence. Amidst the digital frenzy, one message stood out:

"What the fuck? What are we going to do about this?"

Chris Ganan's words screamed at me from the glowing screen. The ensuing flood of messages echoed the same tone of urgency, threatening to distract and overwhelm me on this critical day. In only a few hours, we would be going public. I had to focus.

With a grim determination, I silenced my phone and pushed it aside. I had a routine to uphold, a ritual of preparation, my way to summon my game face.

I was already in motion before dawn, lacing up my running shoes and gulping down water in hurried swallows. The morning darkness enveloped me and soon I pounded the pavement of the paths in Central Park, the rhythmic thud of my footsteps echoing in the stillness of the early hour. Through my headphones, my go-to ballad was turned up and Eminem was pumping through my ears once again. Behind me, Roy followed me through the park on a bike.

Roy was part of my executive protection team. In preparation to go public, security was a global concern and project. We had to think about keeping our employees, stores, factories, offices, and intellectual property safe. Based on the analysis prepared by the experts, with tales of kidnapping and corporate espionage among other threats, our board voted to require me to have full-time security. This meant armed guards with or around me and my family 24/7. For me it was just a component of the video game. For Laura and the kids, it was intrusive, disruptive, and downright confusing. Pre-school drop offs were definitely awkward, as they pulled up to the school with our armed guards as drivers.

Once broke and bluffing my way into deals at the Trump International Hotel & Tower only a few years ago, I now picked up the pace as Roy chased behind, having manifested my fantastical idea that weed, along with me, would be reckoned with and ultimately respected.

As the first light painted the sky in hues of pink and gold, I was sweat-drenched and pumped up from the run. The polished golden staircase of the hotel greeted me like an old friend. I held onto it like a piece of gym equipment, stretching and flexing my muscles, the cleaning crew casting curious glances my way, and others saluting me like I was the hotel owner. I had been spending so much time in New York between our lobbying and fundraising, the hotel had become a familiar place to lay my head.

"Morning, Mr. Bierman."

"Hi, Mr. Bierman."

"Good day, Mr. Bierman."

Breakfast was a solitary affair, the weight of responsibility heavy on my shoulders, until Daniel Yi met me in the dining room. We sifted through the deluge of messages and emails, preparing for our big media day.

It was then, amidst the clatter of cutlery and the muted chatter of the dining room, that I started reading the texts and emails from our staff and the gravity of the situation fully dawned on me.

That morning, a blogger in Canada named the Wolf of Weed Street had pushed a newsletter and post slamming our company and attacking me. The Wolf's persona was an homage to Jordan Belfort—the infamous stockbroker portrayed by Leonardo DiCaprio in *The Wolf of Wall Street*, who was associated with unethical financial practices.

He claimed that I had pilfered company funds. We had just raised over $100 million in the largest road show in the history of American weed, and it was definitely all safe in our company account.

The ridiculousness didn't matter.

I looked at Daniel. "What the hell is going on? This lying scum cannot possibly be fucking with our opening day?!"

"I called legal already," he said. "And this guy's post may not even be where it ends. There's a handful of these newsletter guys in Canada trying to shake down companies."

"What can we do about this?"

"Nothing today, I think," he said. "The damage has been done." The Wolf had sunk his fangs in my leg, tearing it clear off, and had informed his subscribers to short our stock, sending it tumbling before the first bell, landing a direct hit and destroying any potential opening momentum we could have hoped for.

Breakfast had yet to arrive. I felt helpless, beaten before the game started. The vicious attack on our credibility, orchestrated by an unseen adversary, threatened to derail everything we had worked for. But what choice did we have? I pushed aside the doubts and distractions, focusing instead on the task at hand.

"First stop, trading floor of the New York Stock Exchange," Daniel, the day's timekeeper and cheerleader, said as we got into the Escalade and hid behind the tinted windows. Our first press appearance was on the trading floor, and I knew that once the market heard our story, our share price (and future) would rise.

To focus, I slipped on my headphones. I cued up Joey Alexander, the young jazz prodigy. The sharp, emotional notes were a light soundtrack to the maelstrom in my mind, the scenarios, questions, answers, and objectives for the day. It was my pregame ritual, feeling like Albert Pujols riding the bus to the stadium for a game in the World Series. Instead of a ball game, I was driving to deliver the most dynamic messaging I could muster around MedMen, marijuana, and my mission on this planet.

———

Beyond the tinted windows of the car, I could see commuters with their coffee cups scurrying on the way to work, piling into subway terminals, crossing the street in throngs. Planted in the back seat of the Escalade, I wasn't scurrying anymore. I had ascended, bringing the weed world with me.

At the Stock Exchange downtown, I felt like I was moving in slow motion, passing through security, the X-ray machines, the metal detector. Once through, I reached into a bowl to retrieve my phone and wallet and followed Daniel through a maze of hallways that felt more like the underbelly of a worn-out sports stadium. And then, through a final hallway, we stepped into the open lair of the exchange floor.

Looking up, the place was awash with the glow of countless screens flickering with pre-market data. Traders, huddled in clusters or pacing with purpose, murmured their strategies into headsets, their voices a low, urgent drone against the backdrop of ringing phones and clattering keyboards. The iconic bell podium loomed over the trading floor, a silent sentinel awaiting the moment to unleash the day's chaos.

We walked onto the trading floor, where the television networks rent out booths to broadcast their shows live. I got in a director's chair, the usual layer of powder and makeup applied.

"Boss, we might have to wait a bit," Yi said, whispering in my ear.

"What's up?" I asked.

"This news out of Italy is bigger than we thought."

Turns out, in addition to getting blindsided by rogue newsletter writers in Canada, the economy in Italy had collapsed the day before. In Europe, the markets went spiraling out of control, and the shitstorm was making the rounds, now landing on American shores. How would the new instability in Italy affect Wall Street? The Dow was down 500 points after the opening bell and sliding.

A new line of talking heads were on their way in, and an international economist was now next to me.

"What do you do?" he said.

"Cannabis," I said, sitting there and fuming. Finally, a production assistant came over with another water bottle to hold us over. Daniel was pacing. Every minute that passed, we knew our chance to tell the world our story on this crucial day was evaporating. Finally, I saw Daniel exchange terse words with a younger producer. He came my way, his face red, his backpack over his shoulder.

"Let's go," he said, explaining that I had been bumped. "Fucking Italy. I think I can get us in later in the afternoon."

I followed him down the stairs.

"We have our next hit at CNBC," he added, as we jumped back in the car. The CNBC studios were located across the river from Lower Manhattan at the network's headquarters in Paramus, New Jersey. We were cruising up the West Side Highway and soon pulled on the George Washington Bridge to cross over into the state. Next to me, Daniel was working the phones, trying to line up more gigs.

"Fuck me," he said.

"What?"

"They canceled the segment," he said. "We just have to keep our heads down and stay focused."

Our driver turned around to face me.

"Where to now, boss?"

"Ask Daniel."

I looked out the window, clenching my jaw and knowing a vein must be popping out of my forehead somewhere. For nearly the last decade, I had been trying to mainstream cannabis, and these bookings on these shows were the proof that I did it. No weed person had ever been on these shows before. We were the first. I was the first. Today was the ultimate culmination, the coming-out party.

"Back to the Stock Exchange," Daniel said, after lining up an afternoon hit with another network.

On my phone, I was watching messages in my inbox pile up. Investors were calling and leaving messages, all in a panic. How could I respond? I had no plan, no way to control the fallout from the Wolf and Italy's economic disaster. I just let them all go to voicemail.

"This is just fucking perfect!" I fumed.

"Breathe, boss," Daniel said.

"Of course this is how it has to play out."

"We can control what we can control," he said. "I'm already working on rescheduling and lining up new stuff; the whole team is on it."

We pulled up at the Stock Exchange again and followed the same routine as before, working our way to the media platform.

I had another layer of makeup applied.

"Boss, be patient."

"What is it now? We literally made history today. Does anybody at all give a flying fuck?!"

I noticed another CEO type appear on the stairs and take a seat in the director's chair next to me.

"This is going to be a while," Daniel said.

I looked around the floor. The traders bustled about, their voices echoing through the cavernous halls of the exchange. Papers fluttered to the ground, discarded and forgotten. Lights flickered, then dimmed, as the day's proceedings drew to a close.

"Don't we have any other options?" I asked Daniel.

He looked around the press section. He noticed one camera crew still had their lights on. It was Cheddar TV, then an upstart. I saw him locate the producer, put a hand on his shoulder, and point my way.

Waving his hands, Daniel motioned me over.

"Last interview of the day; we got five minutes," he told me.

So I sat in the Cheddar TV director's chair. The host of the show was scanning the web on a laptop, doing some last-minute research. Finally, a chance for us to celebrate this moment.

"And we're rolling," the producer said.

I twisted around, getting comfortable, clearing my throat, ready to share how proud we were, and how important it was that investors could now support corporate cannabis, buy MMEN stock, and be a part of this brighter future.

"So, it is opening day and it looks like your stock is down 18 percent," she said. "Do you have a response to this initial feedback from the market?"

Back at the Four Seasons that night, I didn't bother greeting my mom, Laura, or the family. I went into my room, closed the door, and ran the shower. I must have been in there for half an hour. I looked down at the floor of the bathroom, and every drip of water looked like blood. A chum line had started to form. I was bleeding everywhere. First wounded by the Wolf of Weed Street, then the tizzy of the day, the Italian market collapse. My Michael Milken moment: a bomb.

On opening day, stocks are supposed to go up. What else could I say, other than, *Sorry, it has nothing to do with our actual business and I'm sure it will all work out over time?* Along with our investors, I got nailed too. My entire net worth was wrapped up in my stock. In one day, on paper, I lost $60 million.

We had dinner plans with the family, a table reserved at Blue Ribbon Sushi, one of those places that was just high end enough to celebrate and casual enough to take the kids. The family was already there, the plates nearly licked clean by the time I arrived. I could not sit down. I could not eat. My face pale and energy spent, I hugged everyone and slipped out. On the sidewalk, with cabs honking around me, I dialed Ed Harris, my rabbi turned therapist. By now, Ed was on board at MedMen full-time to support our team through the wild experience we were living. From team-building retreats and workshops to one-on-one sessions with employees, he provided a level of care that I knew firsthand could make a difference. I wanted the whole company to have access to what I had found invaluable. "I am having a fucking nervous meltdown," I screamed through the receiver, looking like a lunatic on the street.

"Thanks for calling. Now, if you can, take a breath," Harris said, his voice carrying a zen-like calm.

"Now take your time and tell me what's going on."

He had managed to quell my fury and capture my focus. Next thing I knew, I was sitting on the curb outside a sushi restaurant in New York City, pouring out the day's events to Ed.

I wanted answers, a plan.

"Adam, I can't give you advice on the business stuff, but on a personal level, I just ask you to reflect," Ed said.

I closed my eyes, sitting on this busy, filthy New York City street curb. Why couldn't it feel like a success? Was I broken? Maybe I just wasn't capable of the success that people like Chris Ganan and Armen Yemenidjian wore so effortlessly.

"Look at what you have accomplished," he went on. "You still have your family, and they are inside waiting for you."

I could hear the words, but I wasn't listening. I needed a plan to share with our investors, and to get our stock price up again.

MEETING BIG BOY

The next morning, I was back in Los Angeles, the sun piercing through the windshield, heading into the office. As I sifted through my messages, one name stood out like a dagger: Ben Rose, our chairman of the board. He'd called several times. With a deep breath, I dialed his number, bracing myself for the conversation that was about to unfold.

"Where the fuck have you been?" he asked.

I could feel the venom mounting, the bite of each word.

"First, when I call you, you call me back," he said. "Second, what the fuck is going on with the stock price?"

I didn't have any good answers, and the aggressive tone surprised me.

"What the fuck, Ben?" I shot back. "I've had a million things on my plate. You know that."

But Ben's tirade continued, the accusations flying like ninja stars.

"Look, we need to talk," he said. "We need to talk about your compensation package, your super voting rights."

"Unacceptable, Ben. Absolutely fucking unacceptable," I said, seething. "I created these structures with you, with your approval, and this is your reaction to our first real adversity?"

My words tumbled out in a rush of anger and indignation.

"You're supposed to have my back, man. We're supposed to be in this together."

———

I was too angry to speak once I arrived at our building. I kept my head down, beelined to my office, and shut the door. As I approached my desk, I noticed a colorful array of cards scattered across its surface. Congratulatory messages from my team, each one a reminder of the support around me.

One card in particular caught my eye, adorned with a heartfelt message from Matt Power, our head of technology.

"There are very few people who truly make a dent in the universe," it read. "You are one of them."

I was too much in damage control mode to care. As the morning wore on and the office began to fill with the buzz of activity, I found myself preparing for our company-wide, all-hands meeting.

We piled into the open bullpen area of the office, the staff a unified sea of MedMen red, donning their hoodies and letterman jackets. Nearly 100 employees crowded in, standing against the walls. We also streamed the speech into every MedMen store, grow, and office across the country. We had just made history and the "we" was now over 1,000 dedicated, mission-based evangelists. I wanted to share the moment with every single one of them if I could. In the room, I stood at the front, summoning a dwindling supply of inspiration.

I had to fire them up, even though I felt completely beaten down—emotionally and physically spent from the relentless fight, the late-night flight, and overall awful start to the public listing.

"At the end of the day, people are going to talk shit," I said. "But we're the biggest, baddest motherfucking marijuana company on planet Earth. We are on a mission and we will not be denied."

The room erupted into applause. I raced back to my office to hide, then heard the knock at my door. It was Ed Harris.

"How are you?" he inquired, his soothing voice carrying a note of genuine care, and referring to my near meltdown the night before.

"Fine," I said, deflecting him. He knew better. My time to be open enough to assess how I was personally "doing" was relegated to our sessions, 50 minutes per week, no more. He knew better than to fuck with my workday by bringing any feelings into this.

"Adam, I wanted to talk to you about something," he went on. "Do you think all the vulgarity is necessary? Do you need to say 'motherfucking'? Can you say 'biggest, baddest'? I mean, there were 1,000 people listening to that speech. It's just something I want you to think about."

Determined to protect our stock price from the baseless and harmful attacks from the Wolf of Weed Street, I tapped Daniel Yi to run point, and we mapped out a plan to combat the relentless assault on our business. A treasure chest had been cracked open by the Wolf and the financial bloggers and pirate newsletters in Canada were all scrapping to extract their spoils before it was all gone.

Through another cannabis company that dealt with a similar problem, we hired a private investigations company that specialized in stock market manipulation and asked them to identify the perpetrators. Meanwhile, I delved into the final reports, dissecting every detail in search of a solution.

We were stuck. Despite identifying the likely culprits through IP addresses, what could we do about it? Pursuing criminal charges seemed futile, especially when the real criminality was happening across the border in Canada. The Ontario Securities Commission had jurisdiction there, and there was little hope of justice being served. I didn't know what to do.

For advice, I called a Bay Street veteran in Toronto familiar with the fuckery of the Canadian public markets. I dialed his number with a sense of trepidation, knowing that this conversation could lead to all kinds of traps. I laid out the situation, detailing the relentless attacks on our company's stock price and reputation. His response was disheartening.

"It's a game," he told me. "And you are either in or you're out."

I listened in silence as he revealed the ugly truth behind the facade of legitimacy that had cloaked the stock market in Canada.

"Everyone has to eat," he said. "The marketers, the investors, the hedge funds. And you should know everyone plays this game. All the American companies that are going public now after you are playing. You should not spend energy on this, or it could take you down in ways I promise you can't even imagine."

But amidst the despair, I was optimistic. If this was the game we had to play, then we would play it—but on our own terms.

"Can you help introduce me to someone who could help, if I decided to play the game?"

"Sure," he said. "His name is Big Boy. I'll send a group message introducing you now."

My secretaries planned the meeting in secret. On my calendar, I was headed to Las Vegas, though when our jet took off, we flew north, touching down on a private airstrip in Vancouver.

I found Big Boy waiting for me in the outdoor seating area. It was late morning, and he was sipping on a beer. He looked every bit the model—tall, lean, with perfectly styled hair, moussed and blow-dried into place like he'd just stepped off a runway. Flashy rings adorned his fingers, and a thick gold chain gleamed around his neck, catching the light. But behind that polished, pretty-boy exterior was a sharp and calculating financial mind, as ruthless as they come.

"My friends and I control investor lists across the country," he said. "I will find out what parts of your business are most exciting and pump those in our emails."

"Well, that would be great," I said. "We are absolutely crushing our core business; our performance is off the charts. Compare our business to these Canadian weed companies and it's a joke. But that's not what anybody in your investor world is talking about."

He chuckled and took a swig from his pint.

"How much would it cost for you to help us?" I asked.

"$2 million," he said.

I wondered about the action. Was it a lot for a newsletter or two, or a pittance? For every 10% rise in our stock, our company value increased over $100 million.

"How do I pay you?" I asked.

"I send you an invoice," he said. "It will say 'Marketing Services.' That's how I do it with everyone."

He didn't miss a beat or lose eye contact. As much as I respected his steadfastness, I needed to get out of there as quickly as we could get cleared to exit. I could never do business with a guy like this on behalf of

MedMen. My habit was always to act as if someone was watching me, but for sure this motherfucker had many people watching him.

So I began my exit by asking him to send me a formal proposal, outlining the deliverables. I could have our lawyers draw up a contract, I said, to make it official.

He declined.

"Just an invoice and your promise?" I asked, looking around behind him, wondering who was recording this conversation.

"My word is everything," he said.

I got up and apologized.

"I'm sorry to have wasted your time," I said, citing the need for contracts and deliverables. "I wish you nothing but the best, but now that I understand your business, I won't be able to proceed."

We needed another way. Back in the office, Daniel Yi had another plan. Why not hire a financial newsletter writer in the States. There were many who offered similar services, namely producing "advertorials" for totally legit pay-to-play marketing opportunities.

We initially reached out to Alan Brochstein, widely regarded as the first financial cannabis newsletter guru in the United States. In addition to being a cannabis financial analyst, he earned his living by providing public relations services, digital marketing, content publishing, and social media advertising for companies like ours. His response, however, was less than enthusiastic.

Daniel then found an advertorial writer from Texas—someone who was the perfect counterbalance to Big Boy's aggressive approach and Brochstein's oddly tepid response. This writer was a marketing whiz, skilled at pushing boundaries while staying within the lines. Everything was done through contracts and completely aboveboard. It was exactly what we needed—a calculated way to fire back and regain control.

Our plan to play it safe backfired. I found myself summoned to our general counsel's office shortly after our new friend in Texas published a glowing "sponsored" piece about MedMen. Daniel and I were happy with the ad highlighting our core business, our unbelievable retail-level performance, the value of the brand, and the industry's bright future.

A letter from the Securities and Exchange Commission arrived, making it clear that our activities had raised some red flags with the SEC enforcement division in Washington. They weren't happy. We were warned about violating stock promotion laws and were ordered to issue our own press release, acknowledging our marketing tactics and pledging not to repeat them. It was little more than a slap on the wrist from lower-level personnel, but enough to make me rethink our next steps and wonder just who in Washington, DC, I was pissing off. After taking office, Donald Trump had appointed Bill Barr, a conservative lawyer and former prosecutor, to run the Department of Justice. Barr was no fan of weed reform, just another overweight bureaucrat with no vision and without a progressive bone in his body. At one Senate committee meeting on marijuana reform, he got the opportunity to make himself crystal clear on the issue: "Personally, I would still favor one uniform federal rule against marijuana."

After so many wins, it now felt like we were marching into a losing battle, with each step sinking us deeper. The stock price kept falling, and no matter what I did, it seemed beyond my control—even though, back in our stores, MedMen was thriving. Business was booming, and we were on our greatest tear yet.

THE DONUT-MUNCHING, WHISKEY-GUZZLING MR. MOOCH

I was traveling nonstop, the days blurring. I remember once waking up in New York to have breakfast with a group of investors, then flying to Toronto for lunch with bankers, and then dashing back home to Los Angeles for dinner with a target for a dispensary acquisition. After the dinner meeting, I picked Laura up from the house and we went out for ice cream. My days were extended, squeezing the time zones and using them to achieve a level of hyper-productivity. Now, I was fully living inside my own video game, huddling with security experts, operations teams, marketing groups, acquisition firms, lawyers, accountants, all in a single day. Often, an impromptu media interview popped up, or a new investment opportunity, or a deal meeting. I was addicted to squeezing every last morsel of potential from each 24-hour period. I had a growing army of believers, not to mention our growing legion of MedMen employees to protect, along with weed advocates the world over. I was monomaniacal, ruthless in the quest to make as many decisions per day as possible.

I spent most of the month on the road, texting nonstop, fielding conference calls from the car, and putting out brush fires from the 66 active licenses we were managing.

"The earnings call is fucked," Ben Rose blurted out one day.

"Fucked? Why the hell is it fucked, Ben?" I asked.

"Have you seen this initial script?" he pushed.

"Not yet. If someone sent it to me, I haven't seen it."

Ben went on to bash James Parker, our CFO, and I quickly extracted the two issues we were facing. The first was that our auditor was required to validate or sign off on different aspects of our financial reports, and Parker was light-years behind on getting this done. The second was we needed a compelling, well-organized, and optimistic script for me to read to the investors and for the financial world to lap up. On both accounts, Ben made it clear we were headed to Disasterland.

As CFO, James was responsible for our numbers. He purported to have a background in both operations and finance, and he looked the part. In my view, he seemed out of his league, and despite our best efforts to hire another CFO through a headhunter, or poach one from another company, no experienced CFO would take our calls. The cannabis industry was still off limits to the most seasoned professionals.

James was bold. Shortly after we moved into our headquarters, he installed a bar in his office, bringing in a rolling cart of high-end whiskeys and tequilas. It was hard to make a big deal of it then, though, when our office was filled with rebel stoners. So we let it go. But I felt that his work product was not what we hoped for, and now the first test of his CFO abilities at a public company—the earnings call—was approaching. It was crunch time. When we pushed him on his reports, he blamed the cannabis industry.

"I'm working on it. You have to understand this just has never been done before," he'd say.

I wasn't buying it.

"A budget for an operating business has never been created before?" I probed.

"Not in this business, within these structures, regs, and taxes."

"Bullshit. I'm sorry," I said. "We need to see the finished product by the end of the month."

Ben was freaking out, and effectively took over the earnings call prep. My job was to work on the script to ensure it matched our enthusiasm, captured our growth, and excited investors.

We worked on several versions. We then sent the script to the lawyers for them to sign off on. The night before the call, we made our finishing touches.

"It's great," Rose said, an example of our team coming together.

An hour before the call, I strode into our Fifth Avenue dispensary, walked up the stairs in the back, and into the conference room on the second floor. And there was James Parker, our flailing CFO, king of the castle, feet propped up on the desk, sipping his coffee like he had all the time in the world. We both happened to be in New York at the time of the call and agreed to take it from the dispensary conference room.

When I arrived, I saw he had brought his assistant to New York as well. She was buzzing around the room and serving him a platter of white-frosted donuts with rainbow sprinkles.

"You ready for this?" I asked.

"Easy stuff," he said. "No problem."

The whole scene was so grotesque, everything wrong with corporate America wrapped up in one decadent, donut-filled package. I was embarrassed that this was my company. Despite all my zealous efforts, it felt out of control. I was losing my grip.

The recording lasted 40 minutes, and now it was showtime—a live Q&A with the investors. No safety net, just raw, unscripted interaction.

"Okay, Adam, We're live for the Q&A," Zeeshan Hyder's voice crackled through. I nodded to myself, took a deep breath.

"Thank you for joining today's call. We're now open for questions," I announced, my heart pounding.

The first question came from a well-known analyst, and it was sharp and probing.

"Adam, can you elaborate on your strategy for the next quarter given the current market dynamics?"

I leaned into the speaker on the conference table.

"We are blitz scaling," I said. "It's growth at all costs, because we believe this is a race. The zoning restrictions around cannabis retail are such that the first to plant their flag around the country in the most strategic locations will have a moat around their businesses for time immemorial."

The questions kept coming, each a curveball that I managed to hit.

"Adam, there's concern about the sustainability of your growth rates. How do you respond to that?"

I chuckled lightly before replying, trying to inject a bit of warmth into the exchange. "We are creating an industry, asset class, and company all at the same time. It's been a rocket ship almost since the start. That's how we will realize our mission to mainstream marijuana."

Finally, as the last questions trickled in, I concluded, "Thank you all for your insightful questions and for your continued support for our vision. We're excited about what the future holds and look forward to updating you next quarter."

Hanging up the call, the adrenaline slowly ebbed from my veins. We had navigated the treacherous waters of our first live Q&A without capsizing. I turned to high-five James, who said little, and noticed a strange if not ominous look in his eyes.

"THIS STOCK IS TOO HOT TO OWN"

The sun was setting over the rooftop of our home in Marina del Rey, transforming it into a makeshift dance floor. Ben Rose was in Los Angeles to work with us for the week, and he'd brought his son with him on this trip. My son Ari was dancing to Michael Jackson, and Ben's kid joined in, their little feet grooving to the rhythm of "Billie Jean." The laughter and music swirled around us—a rare slice of normalcy and joy amidst the relentless pace of our lives.

Ben and I watched on with pride and amusement.

"They've got moves, huh?" Ben chuckled.

"Ari can't stop blasting Michael all over the house," I said.

Ben nodded, sipping his Perrier. I had come to like Ben and identify with him. Like me, he was an athlete in high school and he went on to play football at Harvard. He was spending about a week with us every month in Los Angeles, working out of our office.

"Everything good with Wicklow?" I asked.

Ben set his water down, his demeanor shifting slightly.

"Actually, that's one thing I wanted to talk to you about. I have an idea."

The music rolled into another jam, but the mood between us had changed. I gestured for him to continue, intrigued.

"MedMen and PharmaCann," Ben mused. "What if we combined them?"

"Merger?" I asked

"I think we should refer to the combination as an acquisition, not a merger," he said.

"Interesting. How would you do that?" I asked him.

"MedMen buys PharmaCann, and you become CEO of the whole thing. Everyone wins; you lock in national dominance, gain access to

PharmaCann's cash reserves and assets in markets you aren't in yet. It's kinda perfect if you think about it."

I could only imagine the conversation that his bosses and our investors Tierney and Schuler had with him before he came over. Ben was acting as a messenger, pitching me on what they must have wanted all along.

"It doubles your footprint," he went on. "It cuts down operational costs and adds cash to your balance sheet."

The big winner was Wicklow, who had stakes in both companies.

"I'm always down to chase big shit," I said, and I meant it.

———

The acquisition talks continued at the highest levels between both companies. A few weeks later, Schuler, John McCarthy, the corporate lawyer at Wicklow, and the leadership teams from Wicklow and PharmaCann flew to Los Angeles to work out the final kinks in the deal. MedMen would purchase PharmaCann in stock, and we'd start a transition to organize the systems, the inventory, the assets, and the culture. Ben's project had turned out to be an idea so brilliant, we only wished we'd thought of it sooner.

"Adam, you're the guy at the top of this thing," Ben told me, buttering me up. "You just need to keep going, faster. This is absolute rocket fuel for your machine."

But I knew the hard part was coming. Percentages. Equity. Control. Schu took over, outlining the distribution of shares. I felt my stomach tighten. The numbers weren't adding up the way I'd hoped. When Schu was done presenting his overly researched, analyzed, and articulated economics of the deal, it was hard to imagine how many fucked-up things were happening here. Schu and Tierney were the largest owners in both companies. They were holding the strings. I was the marionette.

"Schu, I appreciate all that underwriting and analysis, but this doesn't add up," I said. "We are a public company and PharmaCann is not. We are a national brand and PharmaCann is not. Let's make a deal, but let's not bullshit."

Schu's eyes narrowed slightly.

"Adam, we're not here to hand out favors. We want a deal that benefits everyone, but let's be clear—PharmaCann brings significant assets to the table."

The room grew hotter, the tension thicker.

"Significant? Significant in Tier 2 and Tier 3 markets, yes. A great fit for MedMen's platform, yes. I'm in full agreement there."

Ben saw the storm brewing and stepped in.

"Gentlemen, we're on the same team here."

I was about to retort when Ben laid his hand on my arm, a silent plea. "Let's find a middle ground," Ben said. "We all want this combination. Let's focus on how we can make it work."

The discussion went on, each of us bending, albeit grudgingly. Numbers were crunched, scenarios debated. We left the room that day with a handshake agreement. A few weeks later, it was converted to executable documents—the first of their kind—with legal teams from Canada, California, Illinois, and DC buttoning up the documentation around the largest acquisition in American weed history at the time.

I walked into our conference room. The papers had been brought in, and laid around the table were signature pages the legal team had meticulously lined up. I started making the rounds with the pen in my hand, and after a swift walk all the way around the long conference room table, I had scribbled my mark on each of them. The size of the acquisition, once it was announced, was $628 million. I had started the Treehouse for $13,000.

We announced the acquisition the next day—MedMen was buying PharmaCann. By the time I woke up, my phone was ablaze with notifications. The press release had hit the wires, and it was as if we'd injected adrenaline straight into the veins of the market. Our stock, which had been languishing around $4 a share, was now climbing. The core business itself was booming. Our stores were turning on. Sitting in my office, I scrolled through the flood of congratulations, queries, and a few envious jabs from competitors.

Finally! I leaned back, letting the gravity of what we'd accomplished wash over me. We weren't just a company; we were a market force, leaders of a new industry. We had gone public, created a new asset class, and had now pulled off the kind of M&A deal you would find in a traditional industry. Soon after, Daniel Yi burst through the door.

"Jim Cramer wants you on *Mad Money* to talk about the acquisition!"

Soon after, I was on a plane to New York to film the segment. Stepping into Cramer's studio at CNBC's headquarters in Paramus, New Jersey, felt like revenge. I knew I would be back after the shitstorm of my own opening day and that I would bring my A-game. I wasn't worried about the performance. I just needed the chance.

In the studio, I watched on as he read from the teleprompter, lavishing praise on our ambition and unbelievable performance.

"MedMen sales per square foot exceed those of the Apple Store," Cramer said. "They want to be known as the Apple of Weed, but they might be selling themselves short."

He then went on to talk about our stock price.

"MedMen stock has soared since they went public last year," Cramer said, and mentioning the announced PharmaCann deal, he pushed a button on his control panel, the lights in the studio flickering.

"I think this stock is too hot to own," he pronounced, and we got into it.

"We're trying to build an asset class that's investable," I said. "From retail investors that wanted to own shares, to the institutional investors that are now investing tens of millions, if not more."

"You feel confident the trajectory is still very strong?" Cramer asked.

"Retail is defensible," I said, explaining that the number of licenses were limited, and the demand only growing.

"Will you start reporting same store sales, so we know how each store is doing?" Cramer asked.

"We will, absolutely," I said. "We have our first earnings call coming up. Maybe you'll call in."

"I most certainly will," he said.

Back home, I felt a true sense of achievement. Now trading at almost $7 a share, we had nearly tripled the stock price from its low point earlier that same year. On paper, my stake in the company was now valued at nearly $600 million.

Privately, I was encouraged to take money off the table and sell a portion of my stock. In the office, Laura and I had financial advisors come in and present us with a plan to sell a percentage of stock and diversify our portfolios. I rushed them all out. We were the industry leader. I wasn't going to entertain the notion of not being all in. And I would never sell a stock I knew was just going to keep going up. How stupid would that be? Besides, I was on a mission. I had a society to make safer, healthier, and happier. I didn't need any more. We owned our own home, owned our own cars, and had our kids' education paid for. We didn't worry about eviction or the repo man anymore. I had already made it.

The acquisition was truly transformational. As part of the deal, we would be bolting on assets in six markets for us—Massachusetts, Maryland, Ohio, Pennsylvania, Michigan, and Virginia—bringing the Med-Men red shopping bag to a dozen total states. To access this new footprint, we had to start immediately planning for MedMen to absorb up to 500 new employees in an integration that would need to unify operating procedures, systems, and, perhaps most important, culture.

Incredibly, the teams at both companies were getting along, inspired by this addition of a whole new battalion to our army of mission-based warriors. I was receiving enthusiastic feedback from our investors and employees.

And then I got a text from Littrell.

"You'll never guess."

"Prohibition is over," I responded.

"Nope. Even better. The announcement of MedMen buying PharmaCann was such a big deal that the Department of Justice has ordered a review of the transaction because they think—get this—that merging the two companies could violate federal antitrust laws."

"Does that mean we can't do the merger?"

"No, it means they are reviewing."

"How long will it take?"

"They have six months to file a formal review."

"That's a long time. Can we do anything?"

"Only wait," he said, and went shopping for a white-shoe firm in Washington, DC, that could push them to drop the review.

I chuckled at the ludicrousness of it all. Our business was federally illegal. If the DOJ had an issue, they could always prosecute us for the manufacturing and distribution of a Schedule I narcotic. Now they wanted to "review" our deal like we were Amazon or Apple. And the antitrust stuff was to protect consumers against monopolies. It was bogus, unfair, and targeted. What in the fuck was going on here? Who had decided to stop me? The advertorial scolding was out of place but now it was a part of this pattern. I just don't know how to fight against a ghost.

We put out a press release, announcing the DOJ review, and the stock price dropped, tumbled, and crashed. Back in Washington, I imagined Bill Barr at his desk, an impish grin on his face, somehow personally putting the kibosh on our plans.

I wanted to call my dad for advice, or just to have him listen. His Full Tilt Poker journey had been wiped out by the feds on Black Friday. Now, I was about to go through the same fight. Often, driving to meetings or waiting on a runway somewhere to take off, I would think of calling him. But still, I couldn't.

"Have you communicated with your dad at all?" Laura would ask at home, and I just couldn't pay attention. Not now. The video game was in overdrive and I was en route to the Marijuana Business Daily conference in Las Vegas, the annual gathering of the entire cannabis industry. As a leader in the space, I could not afford any distractions.

THE RUSSIAN BEAR AND
THE MEETING OF THE FIVE FAMILIES

Before heading to Vegas for the conference, Morgan and I flew to New York to meet with the governor's staff, and to lobby the state to allow the current license holders a chance to open more dispensaries. At the time, we were limited to only five stores per license and given that the program in New York was still so extremely limited, each store was struggling. The justification for more stores was straightforward. The state was forcing us to be vertically integrated, growing way more weed than we could possibly sell. More stores would mean more outlets for the product we were being forced to grow, and more stores would mean more access for the patients the program was created to serve. We ended the trip, making our final plea to Axel Bernabe, who by now had become an ally, connected by the common objective of making the New York State cannabis program viable. We left our meeting with the state's cannabis czar and flew back West. On the way back, I received a call from Rob Chalmers, a banker in Toronto, who by now had become an important part of our Canadian ecosystem and a personal friend.

"So, I hear Uncle Boris is pissed at you," he said.

"Boris? Who the hell is Uncle Boris?"

"You don't know who Boris is?" he asked, and told me that Boris Jordan was among the most powerful players in the global cannabis trade. He was born in New York, worked for Russian power brokers in Moscow, and was running cannabis and other businesses in the States.

"You need to read a book called *Red Notice*," Chalmers told me. "Listen to me. Don't blow it off. Figure out how to make it right."

I wasn't a fan of homework or anyone telling me what to do, but Rob's tone suggested this wasn't advice; it was a directive.

"All right, I'll read the book. What's his issue with me?"

"Did you show up in his neighborhood and not introduce yourself first?" he said.

Before getting on the jet, I downloaded a copy of the book and started to learn about how deep Boris Jordan and his connections truly were.

His résumé read like a financial thriller. After the fall of the Soviet Union, Boris was an advisor to Vladimir Olegovich Potanin, the former prime minister of Russia. Boris was also a close ally of Vladimir Putin and Roman Abramovich, the infamous oligarch, whom it was confirmed had been quietly investing substantial amounts into Curaleaf, Boris's cannabis operation.

Finishing the book, a new weight settled on my shoulders. We weren't only fighting the old American laws and venture funds and dispensary owners. I was making a high-stakes play on a global chessboard. And with Russia's elite controlling many of the pieces, I had just moved my pawn into the path of a queen.

———

In Las Vegas for the cannabis conference, Boris had summoned me and the heads of the major cannabis companies to a private meeting. When MedMen went public, we blasted open a path through which a wave of companies followed. Boris was at the helm of one such company, Curaleaf. In a span of months, from MedMen being the first to go public, there were now a dozen of us, all running our public companies in Canada and battling for market share in the States.

The location for the meeting was a high-roller suite at the Encore. Accompanied by Roy, my bodyguard, I felt like I was walking into a *Godfather* scene, a meeting of the five families, only instead of older Italian wiseguys, the table was filled with stoner executives. And, of course, Uncle Boris.

"I've heard much about you," he said, welcoming me at the door. He smiled, but there was not much warmth in it.

"You are ambitious," he went on, and invited me to take a seat around the table with the others. I knew them, or at least I knew of them.

Next to me: Ben Kovler, sitting with a phone pressed to his ear, his family legacy in liquor with Jim Beam paving his way into cannabis.

Next to him: Hadley Ford, the CEO of iAnthus, adjusted his glasses nervously. His company was on the rise, having recently taken an infusion of cash from Gotham Green—the company run by Jason Adler, David Subotic's acquaintance. With the funding, they were growing quickly.

Next to Hadley: Jason Vedadi, another rebel turned mogul. After navigating illicit grows in New Mexico, he launched and was running Harvest Health & Recreation, another publicly traded juggernaut.

Soon, Boris joined us.

"Look, guys. On changing the laws, regulations, making this work—we can't fuck it up. We can't get in our own way," he said and scanned the room, his gaze lingering on me.

"Adam, we had New York. What are you doing fucking around in New York?"

I bristled at the accusation, my defenses rising.

"Fucking around? I'm the only person doing anything in New York," I said, and then went on to relay what most of us already knew, complaining about the overregulation. But unbeknownst to me, Boris was even further behind the scenes than I was and pushing his own lobbying efforts. We both came up short in our initiatives that go-around, but instead of blaming the legislators in New York for his setback, now Boris was pointing his finger at me.

"We've got to work together," Boris said.

I apologized for not understanding his efforts and committed to communicating and working together next time.

"I couldn't agree with you more," I said. "Then why is nobody acting like it?! Guys, we're covering 99 percent of this country with our footprints," I continued. "Every time I see a pitch deck from any of you slamming MedMen, you realize that hurts the whole industry? We should not be slamming each other; we should be propping each other up. I can tell you right now I've never talked shit about anyone in this room. When asked by an investor what I think, I always say that there is room for all of us to win, as different as we may be."

Hadley Ford interjected.

"Adam, we need to compare to show why we're better investments," he said. "That's just how it works in the big leagues."

Jason Vedadi chimed in, his voice smooth, a mediator's tone. "I'm not going to take sides here with you two, but Adam's right about one thing— we shouldn't be knocking each other down. It's bad for all of us."

Then the oddest thing happened when the geeky banker decided to stare down the rogue industrialist. Hadley, a former Goldman Sachs and Bank of America investment banker and the epitome of the quiet, nerdy type, shocked everyone when he stared directly at Vedadi and declared, "If it means coming for you, Jason, then I'll come for you."

Jason snapped back, "If you shoot, don't miss."

I left early, leaving the others to bicker and rant. I had seen these squabbles before in the trade groups and unions. Cannabis was an industry made of rebels and misfits, not logicians or cooperators. As the others ranted and bickered, Boris and I left that first encounter understanding one another. I thanked Boris for hosting and with a handshake cemented a commitment to stay out of his way, which blossomed into a mutually respectful relationship that I always valued.

PROJECT SPOTLIGHT

Every month, I felt the singe of our burn. We were constantly raising money, which fell squarely on my shoulders. With a growing staff across the country—post PharmaCann we would be over 1,500 people and blitz scaling at every turn. We had these trips down pat, flying into Toronto and sometimes to Vancouver to meet with Canadian bankers and hedge funds. Unlike their counterparts in the States, the Canadian hedge funds were investing in weed, and investment banks were banking weed clients.

One fund manager I clicked with immediately was Moez Kassam. Unlike the other stuffy and older finance guys in Canada, Moez was about my age. He had long hair, a can-do attitude, and was hungry to take big swings. He'd been a scrappy young kid, and despite being socially awkward and somewhat of an outcast, his financial acumen and savant-like performance created massive returns in the public markets earning him a stellar reputation. By the time I met him, he was managing Anson Funds, one of the most revered hedge funds in Canada, and he was actively investing in cannabis.

I felt a youthful connection with him. We were both playing high-stakes games in a world dominated by people much older than us. And I think he was used to being pitched to by boring, old Canadian businesspeople.

From the start, it wasn't the usual, "Talk to my analyst and we'll see if it's worth it."

No, with Moez, it was more direct. "I want to invest in you. Let's do it."

Anson's investments started incrementally, over about the course of six months, and our teams built a solid relationship. They were investing in almost every round we put together and doing well in their returns.

On one of my trips to Canada, I mentioned we were gearing up for another raise. The amount: $20 million. Moez, in his usual decisive manner, said, "Let's just do it together. I'll handle the whole thing."

Our teams then went to work, spending about a month on the deal. It was nuanced and detailed, involving specific share types, rights, and possible bonuses or sweeteners for every dollar they invested. Both teams worked through these complexities, and we were both very excited about the deal. It was something we planned to finalize imminently.

Then I got a call from Jason Adler from Gotham Green. He'd moved his family to Santa Monica, just as he promised when we met in New York, and his kids were now going to the same school as my kids. Rachel, his wife, had become friendly with Laura, sharing birthday brunches and day trips together.

Jason and I had become friendly, running into each other at school events or on the weekend. He'd pitched me on working with Gotham Green, but every time it came up we asked for more details and he was never ready.

"Dinner tonight?" he texted, out of the blue.

We met at Charcoal, my go-to bistro, down the street from our house.

"I've been chasing you around now for years," he said, settling into the reason we were here. "I've been working on an analysis of MedMen. I call it Project Spotlight."

"Project Spotlight?" I raised an eyebrow, intrigued.

"Yeah." Jason nodded. "All I want to do is be your investor. I don't want to see you running around raising money like you're doing in Canada, spending your energy chasing these deals, when you should be 100 percent focused on building MedMen and building an industry."

I sighed, the weight of constant fundraising always on my shoulders. "I appreciate that, Jason. But how much money are we talking about here?"

"How much money do you need so that you don't have to be raising money and you can be focused on building the business?" Jason asked, his eyes locking onto mine.

I hesitated, thinking about the numbers. "I don't know, Jason. I mean, over the next couple years, I'm raising . . . We're now about to close on another $20 million with Anson. We have a lot of work to do."

Jason leaned back in his chair, a serious expression on his face.

"Well, Adam, for $250 million, do you think that you wouldn't have to think about raising money again anytime soon?"

"$250 million?" I repeated, the number almost too large to comprehend. "No, Jason, I don't. I don't think for $250 million I'd have to worry about it anytime soon."

Jason leaned forward, a determined look in his eyes. "Okay, Adam, well, then let's stop playing games. Why don't you stop messing around in Canada. Let me figure out how to get you $250 million so you can do what you were put on this earth to do."

I was taken aback by his passion and commitment.

"Fuck. I'm flattered."

"Well, I'm serious now. I'm not fucking around, so think about it."

I sat there, the enormity of the offer sinking in. "This . . . this is what I want to do," Jason continued, his voice firm. "Let's make it happen."

"Okay, Jason," I finally said, a sense of relief and excitement washing over me. "I really appreciate your support."

Leaving the restaurant, I was stunned. Jason Adler was not a fly-by-night loan shark. I was starting to understand his game. He was trying to use his financial genius, which had earned him a fortune on Wall Street, to become weed's *greatest* loan shark. He'd been a Wall Street hedge fund manager for years, shared a business attorney with David Subotic, one of our own investors and among my fiercest allies. And he had moved to Los Angeles to launch and operate his weed fund. His offer was real.

I called Andrew to share the news.

"Are you fucking kidding me, man?" he exclaimed. "I would get that deal done right now."

"Yeah, but are we letting a fox in the henhouse?" I said, playing the scenarios, wondering what could go wrong.

"Yeah, but it's like so much money," he said, and besides, we already had so many foxes in our henhouse.

I called David Subotic, relaying Adler's offer.

"Adam, you got to be real careful," David said.

"Yeah, I know about the fox and the henhouse," I said, "but if it really were the kind of fox that was bringing that much money, it would truly be game over for us."

"Be careful, that's all I can say."

The next day, I huddled our finance team in the office. I told them about the potential deal with Gotham Green—the deal of all deals—a $250 million infusion of cash to set up MedMen for life.

Zeeshan Hyder, our razor-sharp head of finance, and who internally had become one of my strongest allies, had doubts.

"What about Moez?" Zeeshan asked, referring to the paperwork that he and the others had spent the last month drawing up.

"No question, we go with the Jason deal," I said, echoing Jason himself. "After this, we won't have to ever raise again."

"Are you sure, Adam?" Zeeshan said. "I mean, these guys at Anson are good and we'll get a deal done with them."

"We're talking about a whole other league here," I said.

"I just want to be careful when it comes to Gotham and Jason and those guys," he said.

"Look, we know who we are dealing with," I went on, "and let's figure out how to get it done. Can you do your part communicating with the team at Anson Funds and let those guys know, and I'll text Moez personally?"

I made the intro for Zeeshan to speak with Alex Wang, Jason Adler's righthand guy at Gotham Green, to start the paperwork with the lawyers. Then, in a state of euphoria, I texted Moez.

"Moez, I really appreciate all the work that you and your team have put in so far. I gotta put a pause on it. Something has come up. Let's connect soon and I will fill you in."

A few weeks later, they came—Jason Adler, Alex Wang, their lawyers, and his team at Gotham were in the MedMen conference room, with reams of papers to sign. Our lawyers had gone over them, too, along with our board, approving the terms. The deal was irresistible and real: $250 million, in five tranches, based on a host of conditions. The massive deal was mostly all in debt, meaning we would not have to give up equity once we paid it back. We were set to continue growing, buying licenses, and blitz scaling our way to become the single biggest weed company on the planet. The only catch? Just like the Nagpal and Omar deals years ago, there was a list of conditions we had to maintain in order to not find ourselves in default. Trigger default, Gotham owns MedMen. But that wasn't a concern. Despite the empty probe at the Department of Justice—which would only prolong our PharmaCann acquisition—we were churning revenue. When I was on *Mad Money*, and Cramer asked me what I was most excited about, I told him: our path to $1B in annual revenues. There was nothing in the PharmaCann deal that was illegal, and no grounds for it being blocked. On the other side of the PharmaCann acquisition, we'd emerge as the national leader in cannabis. We'd become American Airlines. Jason Adler, I thought, would not be a problem.

THE SUPER BOWL AD OF DOOM

Backstage appearances had started to feel normal. Jay Brown of Roc Nation invited Laura and me to another concert, this time giving us access to his business partner and best friend, Jay-Z, during a performance at the Rose Bowl for his "On the Run Tour 2" with his wife, Beyoncé. We arrived in style, chauffeured like royalty, surrounded by the electric atmosphere of the night. Lines of cars stretched for miles around Pasadena, everyone eager to witness the spectacle about to unfold.

We cruised through the VIP entrance and were whisked away to the dressing room. Instead of Shakira and her entourage, this time it was Jay-Z and Beyoncé. Beyoncé's father was there. Kobe Bryant popped in, dressed to the nines in a sporty blazer. Chris Martin, the musician, was lounging around as if he were in a friend's living room. I found myself in the corner talking to Jesse Williams, the actor who made his career on the show *Grey's Anatomy*, and among the faces of the Black Lives Matter movement.

On a morning run the following week, it hit me. I shot Williams a text, asking him to come into the office to hear a pitch for a monster ad campaign we had brewing whose centerpiece was the first-ever cannabis Super Bowl commercial. I had been quoted in *Time* magazine back in 2015, over three years earlier, wanting to one day be so mainstream we would launch a Super Bowl ad campaign. Maybe he could be the voice?

He rolled into our conference room.

"I have an idea," I said, and shared the vision for the campaign. We wanted a political piece, a statement that could usher in a new era for cannabis. I was inspired by the iconic 1984 Apple commercial. That commercial wasn't selling computers; it was referencing a permanent cultural shift into the future alongside technology. I kept having this recurring thought that airing a statement like this on television reaching as many demos as possible at the same time would be a watershed moment for the industry. The statement: responsible cannabis use was The New Normal. The Super Bowl was that platform, and I asked Jesse to be part of it.

"Let's do it," he agreed.

A few days later, one of my creative team members burst into my office with an update.

"Adam, you won't believe this," he said. "We've placed a creative brief around town, and guess who wants in? Spike Jonze!"

Spike believed in legalization. He wanted to place his mark on history. The following week, the legendary director was in our office, pitching us his idea for a short film.

"I see the story unfolding in a museum, chronicling the pain and cruelty of cannabis prohibition as the start," he suggested. MedMen would be alluded to but never at the center.

We all liked his historic take. This wasn't just an ad; it was a statement that cannabis had become mainstream and was here to stay. Along with the ad, Andrew and his team started mocking up billboard ads and other campaign elements. We needed CBS to approve Spike's storyboard so we could get started. The process was fairly frictionless; a vice president from CBS Sports came to the office, reviewed the storyboards with us, then made us wait a week or so before receiving an email from the network's legal team telling us we needed to remove all the weed leaves. We did, and we were in!

I spent a few days on the set. From the corner of the room, I looked on as Spike worked his magic. Every detail was meticulously crafted, every shot a work of art. One day, as I pulled into the studio parking lot, I stepped out from the car and nearly bumped into Brad Pitt.

"Hey, how's it going? Are you looking for someone?" I asked, trying to play it cool.

"Nah, just trying to track down my buddy Spike," he replied.

"Ah, he's over there, shooting a commercial for my company," I said.

"What's the company?" Brad asked.

"MedMen," I replied. "We run dispensaries . . ."

"Ah, I love MedMen," he said. "We buy all our weed there."

We marched into the studio together, and I watched Brad sneak around the crew to surprise Spike with a bear hug. It was surreal, standing there amidst the glitz of the entertainment industry, knowing that our mission and my determination had all brought us here.

After the shooting wrapped, a fight broke out in post production. Andrew and Spike, the two creatives, started warring over a logo placement. Andrew wanted it in the video. Spike wanted an editorial piece, letting the story do its job without selling anything. I saw both sides, but Andrew was insistent.

"I'm out, bro," Jonze told me, threatening to leave.

After a night of playing mediator between two creative geniuses, who in moments like this can act more like adolescents, we found a way back on track. I had personal conversations with each, and we brought everyone in alignment on a conference call. The final cut was locked and I was excited to have made history—at least that's what I thought would happen.

The final step was to send the ad to CBS for approval. I could almost hear the TVs at Super Bowl parties across the world halting conversations, drawing all attention to our spot. I envisioned people from all corners of the globe watching the ad online the next day, with MedMen, a cannabis company, sparking discussions across various geographies and audiences.

The final work was strong. As I sat at my desk, bouncing on my yoga ball, I watched the ad on repeat. We had done it; this was to weed what the Apple commercial was to technology. The idea of life imitating art, using this commercial to convince society that weed *was* mainstream, had manifested itself as a masterpiece, and the Super Bowl would be the ultimate megaphone. Then I got a call from Littrell, our lawyer.

"We got rejected," he said.

"Rejected from what?"

"The Super Bowl."

"Who told you?"

"The network. I am so sorry," he said, and explained they gave him some lame, fake reason that they would not be in a position to accept our advertising in connection with this year's Super Bowl.

ENTER PHIL STUTZ

I was feeling frustrated and boxed in. Once again, the fine print on these deals felt like a noose around our throat, and our stock continued to dwindle as antitrust regulators at the Department of Justice twiddled their thumbs on our PharmaCann deal. Meanwhile, far from assuming the role of the shining knight in the industry, I was lampooned as a villain, a soulless corporate suit. It got so bad that *South Park*, the popular animated show, mocked us all.

In one episode, a pair of MedMen execs show up to a weed farm called Integrity Farms, looking to persuade a farmer.

"So, you guys want to pool our money together and we go fuck this town up so nobody can grow their own weed again?" the farmer asks. "I'm totally in."

Within the industry, we were persona non grata to many. The more I touted corporate cannabis, the more others turned against us.

I started playing poker again, a relief. Once I sat down at the table, at least the uncertainties were certain. At least in poker, a full house beats a straight every time.

I stayed in contact with Spike Jonze, sharing battle tales.

"Why don't you see Stutz," he said, referring to Phil Stutz, the noted psychologist, author, and coach.

"He's not taking new clients, but I can get you in," Jonze said.

And now here I was, opening the door to Stutz's apartment. His condo felt like stepping into the past, a world where time moved a little slower. The furniture was old-fashioned, if not dated, and the rug worn and welcoming.

Phil sat in the corner, behind a desk cluttered by stacks of papers and Post-it notes, his hands trembling slightly—a result of his Parkinson's—as he scribbled and doodled.

He introduced himself with a warning.

"I'm not a shrink, not anymore," he said. "I refuse to renew my license."

I settled into the couch, feeling a mixture of anticipation and excitement. I was an unconventional business guy and had an unorthodox story. I didn't want cookie-cutter advice.

"So, what's been on your mind lately?" he asked.

I hesitated for a moment, unsure of where to begin. The weight of the company I had built was bearing down on me. I had investors, regulators, employees, customers, growers, marketing folks, business ops, finance, my kids, wife, my dad . . .

"I . . . I don't know where to start," I admitted. "My life is a war. Every day I wake up, put on my armor, and depart for that day's battle. Every night I come home covered in blood, wash it off my body, and go to sleep. Physically next to Laura, but all alone."

Phil nodded knowingly, his expression sympathetic.

"It's not easy," he said softly and then smiled. His tone changed. "Sometimes when we feel like we're losing control, it's actually an invitation to let go—to surrender to the flow of life, rather than trying to force things to always go our way."

His words resonated with me. I had spent so long fighting against the current to fulfill my mission, both personally and professionally. And yet, the farther along we got, the more attacks we had to defend from those looking to sap our mojo and steal our market share.

"I know it's scary," Phil continued, his voice filled with empathy. "But sometimes, the greatest breakthroughs come when we surrender to the unknown, when we embrace uncertainty."

I sat in silence for a moment, letting his words sink in. Despite the tremors in his hands, there was a steadiness in Phil's presence—a sense of calm and assurance that filled me with a newfound sense of hope.

I came back every week. He'd start the sessions the same, as if he were the coach of my team or a loving, selfless father.

"Give me the updates," Phil said, his voice a raspy whisper.

I revealed all, and he took notes.

"It doesn't matter if you are right or wrong," he told me once, and shared a system to alleviate inaction. He drew a series of circles on a Post-it note, and labeled the first circle "Intuition."

"It starts with intuition, because if you're not going to make a decision on intuition, then you are never actually making a decision."

Then he drew the next circles and labeled them "Decision," "Action," and "Final Consequence," and pointed down with his pen.

"Your intuition leads to a decision, and we want as little time between decision and action as possible," he went on. "Once you've made that decision, I need you to take action, because we need that consequence which will better inform our next decision."

The consequence was the goal, he said. Not the perfect decision. Chasing the illusion of perfection will only lead to the inability to act, he said. Action is the only way forward, and action is the only way to force learning. It was all a cycle, and one that resonated so quickly and deeply for me. This is how the game of poker is played—you are making decisions with incomplete information, then receiving an immediate consequence. With the information gained in that hand, you are dealt your next and intuitively decide yet again whether you're in or out.

"The consequence of your action will always inform your next decision," he said. "You are capable of living that consciously."

Success was not a goal, he said. It was an attitude. "The mountaintop is rented space," Stutz told me. "Enjoy it while you're there, and then get ready to climb the fuck back up."

Soon, our conversations spiraled back to my father. The absence of communication had been weighing on me, and he'd yet to meet Ari, who was now crawling. With some encouragement from Stutz, I reached out to Rick, in the safest way possible: typing up a distant letter, sending an email, and following up with a meeting on my calendar.

We met in my office. My turf. I told him it was unfair to let the distance between us bother me anymore, that we needed to move on. He said he wanted to have a relationship with the kids. He never apologized for threatening us. I never apologized for blackballing him. And soon it was time for my next meeting, he was gone from my office, and we were all back in his world.

JAY-Z IS IN THE OFFICE

The day was a mess. I had a morning full of calls with lawyers in Washington about the PharmaCann deal, and an afternoon spent with accountants and finance folks to prep for our earnings call. And then, looking down at my calendar, I noticed a familiar name: Jay-Z.

We had finally landed a business sit-down with Jay-Z on the books. My first idea was to bring Jay-Z in as our chief brand officer (a title I made up that was my best attempt to encompass what he could mean to MedMen), get him on the payroll, then create his own line of products. Jay-Z was always around peripherally, giving feedback to Jay Brown. But this was him coming in officially to be pitched to join his name with ours and take on the mainstreaming of marijuana together.

As chief brand officer, I envisioned Jay-Z crafting the feel and flow of our stores, the layouts, the product selection, placing his Midas touch on the platform we had created. I knew he could make it better. We only had a few days to prepare for the meeting, and part of the plan was for Andrew to deliver a mock-up of a Jay-Z branded product line.

We'd only have one chance. And I needed the presentation to be irresistible. I knew enough by now to leave Andrew alone. He wouldn't show me his creations until he was ready, and when he did, they were another masterstroke. Sleek and sophisticated, he chose to use midnight black, almost like onyx, a classic and sexy color. The vape pens, pre-roll joints, and loose flower packaging all looked like something you'd find in a high-end spirits shop.

He arrived alone and sat down in our conference room. Andrew unveiled the line by removing a white linen sheet from a metal tray.

"I love it; shit's clean," he said.

We all nodded, and I turned the conversation toward offering him the position of chief brand officer.

He laughed.

"What you need to understand is I'm outta my fucking mind," he said. "When I made my deal with Puma, I told them now let's buy a fuckin' jet and paint it black. We need the superstars to want to be associated with the shit and nobody wanted to be associated with Puma. They listened and it worked. It's the only way that I work."

"Well, great, 'cause I'm outta my fucking mind as well," I said. "How do you think we got here?"

"Put it together with my people," he said. We shook hands, he thanked Andrew, and he was out the door.

———

The early morning light was flooding through the windows of the empty Roc Nation offices as the city below hustled about getting ready for work. With the staff yet to arrive, the energy was still. The space was sleek, posh, with wood paneling and modern art everywhere. The walls were a testament to Jay and Jay's specific appreciation for black artists. Even amid the empty leather chairs in the conference room, the air hummed with a quiet and powerful energy, a palpable aura of success.

"Once Jay gets behind a brand, it becomes a success," Desiree Perez, the CEO of Roc Nation, said, sitting at the head of the conference table. She was gushing about their recent deals. She dropped the names of Armand de Brignac, the champagne brand that Jay-Z bought a stake in and rebranded as Ace of Spades, along with D'USSÉ, a cognac brand he had recently launched. Cannabis was a similar play in Desiree's opinion.

"We're talking to a few farms," she said.

Huh? She was talking to a few farms? I had met with Jay and he told me to make the deal with his people, not go on an audition with Desiree, who knew nothing about the cannabis business.

"That's all great, but alcohol is different from cannabis," I said, and went into our pitch, our backstory, and solution.

"With us you have the farms, distribution, and retail," I said. "It's immediate and national, from coast to coast. You need to be licensed in each state you intend to do business. So even a deal for you guys with one farm in Florida means you can only play in Florida. We can bring you to 12 states on day one."

"All right, I get you," Desiree said, blowing me off. "Let me talk to some of our people. We'll get back to you."

After the meeting, I was furious. *Talk to her people?* Jay-Z already wanted in. Jay Brown wanted in. I called Jay Brown in a huff.

"'Talk to some of your people'? Like, what the fuck, Jay?" I asked.

"She's got to work her process," he said. "She'll get through it."

It was a week or so later when my assistant received an email from Desiree's assistant inviting me to have dinner in Los Angeles and discuss the project.

———

I arrived early for dinner, per tradition. The spot she chose was the Waldorf Astoria, newly opened. Fighting my yawns after having gotten up so early, I rolled into the dining room and coincidentally spotted David Subotic, my old friend and trusted advisor. He was having dinner with his wife, Tanja. Together, this couple had supported me throughout my career. I gave them both hugs as they half stood up from their chairs.

"Please tell Laura I say hi and miss her," Tanja said.

"Let's please get together soon, maybe dinner," David said.

I then excused myself to get to the table. Soon and from a distance, in walked Perez, and although the invitation was for a dinner for two, she had duped me and she was walking toward me with her arm wrapped around Jay-Z. They skipped into the dining room, laughing like kids.

"Thanks for meeting with Desiree in New York," Jay said, sitting down.

"I fuckin hate LA," she said. "I won't come here for nothing or nobody. Just ask Jay. He can't get me out here."

Only recently, Jay and Beyoncé had purchased a $100 million mega mansion in Beverly Hills, signaling their intention to live in LA most of the year. The mansion was near Jay Brown and the Roc Nation office. But Desiree's New York street sensibilities were a stark contrast to the bright fakeness of Hollywood's glitz and bullshit.

Jay-Z opened the conversation by sharing about TIDAL, his subscription-based streaming service that was staring into an abyss of accusations. It was his way of acknowledging the negative media garbage being tossed my way and finding a common footing to say to me, *I go through the same shit every day.*

"So let's talk about MedMen and me," he said

This was my cue to turn the mute button off and make the most of the airspace.

"It all starts with your product line," I said. I went back into the idea of his national product line distributed in our 12 states. I did my best to convince them of how hard it would be to go make a bunch of one-off deals versus making one universal deal with me.

"And I would love you to come in and imagine what's next for retail." I was so excited about the potential of getting Jay-Z involved in our customers' experience. Jay-Z had his finger on the pulse of popular culture and was in a class all his own. Andrew had done an amazing job creating the concept of mainstream marijuana retail, but I was convinced Jay-Z could steer it to an even more appealing and inclusive future. I wanted him to clearly understand I wanted nothing more than to let him run wild.

"I dig this shit and we know Jay [Brown] is all about it," he said.

He instructed Desiree to work with his lawyers to bring him a deal he "could sign" as MedMen's latest executive: chief brand officer.

After dinner, I picked up the tab and bid goodbye to David and Tanja, who grabbed my hand, pulled me close, and whispered in my ear, "Did you just have dinner with Jay-Z?"

Driving home in the dark, I sensed a light shining ahead. Finally, with Jay-Z onboard, attention would come easier, more opportunities would come our way, and the stock price would rise. I was thrilled to share the Jay-Z news around the office. But once again, something was curiously amiss. James Parker, our CFO, was missing.

Strange. At first, we had no idea what happened. Suspicious, I had my security follow him to a cabin, where he wouldn't leave for hours. What was he up to? As an officer of our company, we needed his signatures on financial reports, but he went dark. We wrote emails. We called. Nothing. Then his lawyer sent us a letter making the bogus claim that Parker had been "constructively discharged," whatever that meant, and would only return to the office and sign off on critical docs if we paid him. The price? $10 million.

I refused to pay, claiming extortion. Then James sued us, cooking up bogus claims, trying to fight his way into a settlement. We fought back with cross-claims for breach of contract and breach of loyalty, ultimately prevailing on both counts. The court found no evidence of constructive discharge.

As I read the lawsuit on the night before it was going to be filed, it wasn't the crybaby nonsense he was suing us for that bothered me. He knew the legal causes of action were all bullshit. "Constructive discharge" for a CFO earning six figures with his own plush office and bar cart? Nobody was feeling bad for Lazy James. The bigger issue was the story laid out in the suit's inner pages, designed to publicly destroy me. He made completely fabricated and ludicrous claims that I was running a toxic workplace at MedMen, that I was anti-gay, anti-female, and, in his final fabrication, claiming I was racist and had called Herb Wesson, my friend and our ally in city hall, a "midget Negro."

Feeling a need to escape, I went home early, only to find the house unusually quiet, the family out. I always gravitated toward Ari's room upstairs, tucked in a corner—it offered a safe, protected kind of feeling for me. Seeking solitude in a place generally untouched by the chaos of my life, I shut the door, sank to the floor, and pulled out my phone. I knew I had to start making phone calls. It was critical that our supporters heard directly from me, before this hit the internet.

First, I called Herb Wesson. Our friendship and working relationship had only grown.

"Herb, what's up?" I started.

"What's happening, man? How are you doing? How's life, big dog?"

Herb's voice was warm, a balm in these harsh moments. His casual tone was a reminder of normalcy, something I craved desperately.

"Well, it's not good, Herb," and I dropped the bomb on him.

"I've got this CFO who's been trying to blackmail me for months. Told him to go fuck himself. Now, he's filed a lawsuit trying to check every box. And one of the accusations he threw out there is that I run around calling you a 'midget Negro.'"

There was a heavy pause.

"Motherfucker, I am a midget Negro," he said. "That's good shit. Adam, I know you wouldn't say that. Come on, man. I got your back. You're my dog."

Herb laughed it all off, his humor defusing the tension.

"I know, Herb. Obviously I didn't say that, but I had to call. You had to hear it from me first."

"That's why you're my man. Thanks for telling me. We're good, man. We're good, little brother."

With Herb's assurance, a slight weight lifted off my shoulders, but there was more cleanup. Next, I called Jesse Williams, another friendly ally and the face of the Black Lives Matter movement, who had recently partnered with us to address injustices in cannabis policy.

"Jesse, how are you?"

"Hey, Adam. How are you doing, man? Everything all right?"

"Not really. Here's what happened with my CFO . . ."

I explained the nightmare lawsuit in full.

"Fuck him, man. Fuck all these people," Jesse interjected. "Are we on a farm in 1936 somewhere in Mississippi? Who the fuck talks like that?"

"Thanks, Jesse. I appreciate you, man. Really do. I had to have you hear it from me."

With each call, the absurdity of the situation grew, and so did the solidarity from those who truly knew me. As I ended my calls, reassured yet weary, I dialed Jay Brown at Roc Nation. He was our connection to massive growth, through our looming partnership with Jay-Z, then slated to have his own cannabis line and become our chief brand officer.

The Jay-Z deal was off.

"He can't talk about it right now with all this fucking noise around you," Jay Brown told me.

At home, Laura was furious. It was one of those rare nights when I was home for dinner, tucked the kids in, and we were lying in bed, trying to watch a show on television. But she couldn't watch, nor hide her anger.

"How are you not more mad?" she said, diving into a monologue about the danger of putting others first, and wondering why the other executives at the company and in the industry were not supporting me in a more vocal way.

"I just don't get how nobody is saying anything to have your back," she continued. "How can all these people sit there and not say anything? You're telling me Morgan or Andrew can't just figure out how to take a stand for you? Just tell the truth? It's fucking ridiculous to me you want to pretend these people are our friends."

I sat there, staring into space.

"Jay Brown can't just call a reporter and tell them the truth? You're a racist? You? It's just fucked. If any of these people were your friends, they would stick up for you and say something in response to all this. It makes me sick, literally sick."

BILL BARR'S DOJ COMES TO THE OFFICE

Our lawyers had been watching the calendar. After sending us a letter about their antitrust investigation, the Department of Justice had six months to take action, or else their window to hold up the deal would expire. I could only imagine it. Bill Fucking Barr, with his fat face and cascading series of chins, plopped on his throne in Washington, munching on a Big Mac and complaining to his pencil pushing minions at the DOJ about how stinky weed is, and how he hates stoners, and that by the power of God himself and the ghosts of Reagan and Bush, he will do everything in his power to prevent these United States from a cannabis takeover. And on the very last day of the six-month period, our make-or-break day, I got a call from Jonathan Littrell, our lawyer.

"They filed," he said. "For an extension. Six more months. But it gets worse. They are coming to the office to make copies of the hard drives and do their data extracts."

Consumed with the daily brushfires inside the office and other burdens of running a public company, I had forgotten all about Bill Barr and his henchmen's intrusion, until I rolled into the office on the day of their visit.

"Today is the day," one of my assistants said. "I'll need you to hand over your cell phone. It could be almost all day."

"You have got to be fucking kidding," I said, rolling on by.

But she grabbed my arm. Reluctantly, I surrendered my phone, which felt like relinquishing a piece of myself, but I knew there was no avoiding it. The DOJ had descended upon us and had now set up shop in our office like an occupying force. They had emerged in unison, setting up their data extraction units, and were working methodically.

As I glanced over at them, I couldn't help but notice the stark contrast between their demeanor and the vibrant energy of our workspace. Clad in dark suits and white shirts, the feds exuded an air of authority that seemed out of whack with our pirate crew, scurrying around in red hoodies and jackets and stinking of weed. It was a striking clash between the monochrome agents of law enforcement and the perma-stoned, Technicolor world of MedMen.

The arrival of federal agents reminded me of my father's lowest points. He'd warned me about attracting the attention of the feds my entire life. Incredibly, and only later would we learn, an illegal effort at the highest levels of Trump's Department of Justice had indeed been started to stymie the growth of the cannabis industry. Prosecutors in the antitrust division had been tasked with launching phony investigations into cannabis mergers to stop the industry's growth. I was target *numero uno* for Barr and his crusade and it had been Barr behind the scenes all along taking shots at ending me and my big red machine.

I wasn't worried, though. If prosecutors wanted to comb through my phone and scrutinize every detail of my life, they were welcome. I had seen federal agents in windbreakers when I was a kid. We had been overly cautious. I had nothing to hide. But their timing was punishing. With every delay of the merger, our stock continued to slip. Our burn rate was tremendous, and by this point, Zeeshan, our newly appointed ambitious CFO with a gift for both finance and people, was in my office regularly. He'd risen to his role with an unshakable command of our accounts, and he was more than anxious about our cash reserves running dangerously low. He warned that a default on the Gotham loan was nearing—a potentially catastrophic event for MedMen. We would have more than enough money once we could access the cash in the PharmaCann bank accounts, but that couldn't happen until our deal closed. And if closing took much longer, the problem could be fatal for us.

Then came the sledgehammer—John McCarthy started calling. John's official title was general counsel for Wicklow Partners, and it was to that post which he was loyal. After Wicklow's investment into PharmaCann, he started working with their executive team as a legal voice of reason and a sounding board for business decisions. After we went public, he started showing up at our board meetings as the guest of Ben Rose, our chairman at MedMen and his colleague at Wicklow. Before I could blink, he was now in the most conflicted position of all: a legal consigliere to us, our key investor, and our investor's other cannabis investment that was now our acquisition target. The conflicts, nonsense, and noise didn't matter to me. I just needed PharmaCann to close. Now, all of a sudden, he was standing in the way.

"We need to break the deal," he told me one day, with all the grace of a military field general. "There is too much pressure from the PharmaCann investors and Schu is going to have a literal heart attack over the stress."

"We are almost finished," I pleaded, "and there is absolutely nothing for them to discover. We have an agreement and we have done nothing but honor it, you can't just break it."

"We will sue you in Delaware, and we will win," he said, now threatening me.

The walls were caving in. The more I fought with lawyers, the finance folks were soon after me, too, as our reserves were depleting. We negotiated a release of the PharmaCann deal in exchange for receiving compensatory licenses in Illinois and Virginia. A staff that was meant to integrate all of PharmaCann was bloated for the purpose of standalone MedMen, our bank accounts, which were planning to receive PharmaCann's cash reserves, were depleted and we were locked in a death stare with the covenants in the Gotham Green loan, now the most ominous aspect of our financial predicament.

To cut costs, I put the first version of a restructuring plan in place, looking to reduce our spending across the country. But you can only cut so deep; we needed cash to make it through.

"How much do you need?" Ben Rose asked one day, on the phone.

"I think $20 million gets us through structuring," I said.

"Can you raise it?"

"We can try, and if we can't, John and Dan [his bosses at Wicklow Capital] better be able to write a check."

"You know I have your back, and we won't let Jason get out of line," Ben said. "But I need you to do everything you can to raise it somewhere else first."

"Let me try and reason with Jason first," I said. "We were friends. Or at least that's what I thought."

I drove out to Santa Monica. Along the way, I thought of all the touchpoints adding up as if part of a master plan. The first meeting in New York, getting friendly with our family in Los Angeles, now him baring his fangs, pushing us to fail and drooling at the prospect. Jason was in his office talking to his finance guy, Alex Wang, when I arrived.

"Give us a moment," he said to Alex, and we were alone.

"I need more time," I said. "We all got so royally fucked on the PharmaCann deal but we are still crushing it. I actually think it could be a blessing to stay more focused on the markets we are already in. Dan even wants me to sell off non-core markets like Arizona, which I'll totally do in order to get our feet underneath us."

"You know I can't give you more time," he said, a coldness in his voice.

"Why not?"

"Those are not the terms we agreed to," he said.

"But, Jason, you said you wanted to be partners," I said, lowering my voice and staring right through him. "You said you wanted me to go and run the business, never have to raise again."

"Okay, I hear you. Let me talk to a few people," he said, but in a way that I knew he never would.

———

Laura and I were watching Mateo play soccer. The kids were out on the field, trying not to trip over the ball. I sat by Laura, holding her hand, soaking up this precious moment witnessing my son so blissfully, carelessly playing. Then my phone buzzed in my pocket.

"Can we talk?" Jay Brown texted, summoning me to speak with him in person at the Roc Nation offices east of La Brea. The place was all sleek lines and designer cushions, like a chic hotel.

I sat across from him, excited to be in his office. I knew it was ominous the moment we locked eyes. I let him update me on the tick tock of his life while I waited for the hammer.

"What's going on, Jay?" I asked.

He leaned back in his chair.

"Alex Wang stopped by," he said, referring to Jason Adler's right-hand man. My heart skipped a beat. What was Jason Adler, one of my biggest investors and former friend, doing going behind my back with one of my board members?

"What did they want?" I said, my eyes narrowing with suspicion.

"What do you think?" he said. "They want you out as CEO."

I was stunned.

"He showed me a binder," Brown continued. "It was filled with candidates for your job."

I took a breath, steadying my nerves.

"Appreciate the heads-up," I said.

I knew there was more. That binder of candidates must have been accompanied by a sales pitch about throwing me out, not to mention an incentive for Jay to take part in the coup. But I did not pry. I appreciated Jay too much to dig. He gave me the intel I needed.

Later that day, I called Jason Adler to set the record straight. He didn't pick up. The next day, I called again. No answer. Finally, I tried one more time. Crickets.

FAMILY NIGHT AT THE CARDINALS GAME

We stepped into the entrance of Busch Stadium in St. Louis, my familial hometown. The night air had all the energy of the playoffs, the stands pulsating with 45,000 fervent Cardinals fans. The smell of popcorn mingled with aromas of tangy mustard, the burnt char of hot dogs, and sweet cotton candy. I felt like a kid again, going back to Jack Murphy Stadium, where my dad would take me as a kid to watch the Padres play and of course never missing a Cardinals game when they were in town. He would buy us the cheapest tickets up in the nosebleeds, and we would arrive right as the gates opened and head straight down to the infield to watch batting practice from the front row. I would lean over and snag balls for a solid hour before the rest of the crowd even started to enter the stadium. If we were lucky, nobody would ever show up for the seats we started in, or we would shuffle around, row to row, snatching up the best views until they were gone. Here we were now, sitting in those premium seats because they were ours, at this epic playoff game in St. Louis—not San Diego.

We were all here, three generations—Dad, Mom, the kids, Laura. We had all traveled here to celebrate my grandmother Harriet's 90th birthday and here she was with us at the game, drinking a beer and watching batting practice.

Walking the stadium corridors with my dad and his grandkids, I could sense how proud he was. Seeing him in that moment was everything for me—a culmination of a lifetime of devotion to his beloved team, and with his family.

"This could be Wainwright's last start as a Cardinal," my uncle Jon said, reminding me.

"I'm just so stoked to all be here together," I said.

Through the tunnels to the infield, I caught glimpses of the field

below, the pastoral green of the outfield bathed in the soft glow of stadium lights. I paused, my gaze drawn to the diamond below, where players moved with a grace and precision that bordered on artistry. The crack
of the bat echoed through the air, a familiar sound that stirred something
elemental within me.

Amidst the sea of jerseys and caps, we found our seats above the box
on the first base side, a prime vantage point to witness the action on the
field below. And as the first notes of the national anthem filled the air, I
also felt a swell of pride in my chest. Nine innings to play. Finally, I could
enjoy this. I deserved it.

And then my phone started to buzz. I glanced at the screen, my brow
furrowing in confusion as I struggled to reconcile the weight of the incoming call with the euphoria of this treasured moment.

———

The phone call from Jason Adler hit me like a foul ball in the forehead.
Seeing his name on the screen, I excused myself from our seats and disappeared back into the maw of the stadium, near the concessions.

"I know I haven't been available but I owed you a call back," Jason
said.

"Well, thanks for calling me back. How can we work through this?"

"There is nothing I can do if you break any of the covenants," he said.
"And to be clear, we're not going to approve you raising any debt."

"So you're just going to run out the clock and let us die out here?"

"You signed the documents," he went on, "and this is what the documents say. There's nothing I can do."

"There has to be another way," I said.

The timing of the call was strange. I had been hounding Adler for
weeks to meet in person, and he had been ignoring me. Now, once I was
out of town, he emerged, but only at a safe distance, on the phone.

"Can't you give us more time?"

"I'm sorry," he said. "You're going to have to raise equity or things are
going to change."

"You know I can't raise equity with our stock price."

"I'm sorry," he said.

"Well, that's not fucking good enough," I said, feeling the walls closing in. It was a make-or-break moment, and Jason Adler and Gotham Green held all the cards. I called Chris Ganan, my mind reeling.

"Chris, we gotta raise some fucking equity, whatever it takes," I shouted, relaying the content of the Adler call. "Bring me into the meetings as soon as they're real."

I then called Zeeshan, who had a pulse on our bank account.

"Z, how long do we actually have until these fucks can take any action?"

"Probably seven weeks if things don't change," he said.

I was now pacing in the hallways of the stadium, shouting into my phone, oblivious to the game and roar of the crowd. I looked up for a second. My dad was facing me. He'd gotten up from his seat to find me, wondering what was wrong. I was pacing, on the phone, and now he was pacing, too, shadowing me like that concerned friend, trying to learn what tragedy had caused me to miss the game and our family moment.

I needed to find cash quick, or even sell the company before Adler took it over and ran it into the ground.

I dialed our chairman, Ben Rose, back in Chicago.

"I need Wicklow to step the fuck up," I told him. "I just got off the phone with Jason [Adler] and he told me they're coming to take the fucking business, man."

"How much do you need?"

"It's the same number I gave you when we started restructuring—$20 million. But it's time for Dan [Tierney] to write a check."

"Okay. I'm gonna call now," he said.

My mind swirled. Who else to call? As I waited for a response from Ben Rose, it hit me. Ben Kovler, one of our competitors and the scion of the Jim Beam whiskey family, was also nearby in Chicago. After launching his own company, Kovler was proving himself a master at managing investors and his stock price. He followed us by taking his own company public. His operation was smaller than ours, the business less exciting, but he was a bona fide master of the universe and had proven to be above the swamp of shit my business was wading through. He had no Jason Adlers at his doorstep. In fact, he had Leon Cooperman, a legend in the investment world often compared to Warren Buffett, attend his first earnings call. It must have been staged, because Leon made a statement about his personal support for the company and specifically Ben, who he had known since birth. That's the level Kovler was playing at. Maybe I could join him?

The flight from St. Louis to Chicago was only a puddle jump. I called him. I hadn't seen him since Uncle Boris's summit in Las Vegas.

"Bierdog!" he said. "What's up, my man?"

"Hey, any chance you are in Chicago?"

"Yeah."

"What are you doing tomorrow? Can we have lunch?"

"Sure," he said.

"Great," I said, hung up, and called my assistant.

"I need to stop in Chicago tomorrow for a couple hours on my way home," I said.

When I got off the phone, the game was over and the family had migrated to Imo's Pizza, across from the stadium. I had missed it, though I had managed to score a late inning meeting with Ben Kovler, one of the few cannabis kings who had the power to purchase our company by signing a napkin, bring MedMen into the Beam family fold, and save us all from imminent doom.

———

The streets of Chicago were silent behind the windows of our Escalade as we snaked through the maze of skyscrapers downtown. The iconic skyline loomed overhead, a testament to the city's resilience and ambition. I dropped Laura, my parents, and the kids off at the Navy Pier to spend a few hours there as tourists, licking ice cream cones and strolling along. I then headed over to the restaurant. I was in my pregame mode. No margin for error. I had to protect our company.

As we approached Palmer's, the old-school steak house exuded an air of timeless elegance. Its brick facade and classic signage stood out against the modern glass structures that surrounded it. Inside, the restaurant was a haven of warmth and luxury. Red leather booths lined the walls, while white tablecloths lent an air of refinement. The murmur of conversation filled the air, punctuated by the clinking of glasses and the occasional burst of laughter—yup, this was a place where deals were closed.

Ben Kovler sat waiting at a corner table.

"What's up, Bierdog!" he said, rising and giving me a hug. "Glad you could make it."

I sank into the plush leather of the booth, the soft lighting casting a warm glow over the table.

The waiter appeared, a veteran in a crisp white shirt and black apron. Ben ordered the garbage salad, a house special of filet, veggies, and cold meats all mixed together. I did the same, sans meat.

"Good to see you, man," he said. "What brings you to town?"

I braced myself for what was to come, knowing that this lunch could determine everything I'd worked so hard to build.

"If I can't pull something off, Adler's going to take the company," I said, diving headfirst into our internal sagas.

"I'll do whatever it takes to save the business," I said, and proposed an idea. "What do you think about merging?"

Kovler fiddled with his napkin, sitting back.

"It's a bit messy," he said.

"Combine our footprints and we are clearly the leader," I said.

"It's a lot of debt," he said. "This feels like something we should revisit in like a year."

"A year?!" I exclaimed, my frustration flashing hot. Didn't he get it? We needed the $20 million now.

He looked away. The garbage salads had yet to arrive, and the chance of merging or selling to Ben Kovler was gone. As we waited awkwardly for our salads to come, I started scanning my phone for another way out.

LAURA GOES UNDERCOVER

With the PharmaCann acquisition terminated, our bank accounts depleted, and Adler holding a gun to our head, we needed to cut as deep and fast as possible, restructuring the company faster than I had planned. One afternoon, I was in my office going over forecasts when Zeeshan stepped in with a concerned look on his face. Without uttering a word, his expression told me everything I needed to know. Adler's deadline was looming, and I felt like I was on the *Titanic*, with the water filling up in a room and two people trapped looking at each other before that last breath as the water reached the roof, closing off the last centimeter of air supply.

We were on the verge of losing everything we'd worked so hard to build to Jason Adler and Gotham Green. A domino effect of events had transpired that set us up to come crashing down. I had built us billions in value and they loaned us less than $60 million and were trying to take everything. This was like Bluestar Airlines from the movie *Wall Street*. I knew I had to take action and I couldn't be shy until I had found a resolution. Heading home one day, desperate for an angle, I shot Jason a text. Not having spoken since the Cardinals game, I figured there was nothing to lose in attempting some face-to-face communication. I was not expecting a response.

"Are you in Santa Monica?" I texted.

"Yes," he texted right back. It was the first response from him in forever; but for whatever reason, he gave me a window.

"See you at your office in 15 minutes," I texted back, and had Roy swing the car around to head straight for Adler's office.

Sitting across from him, I remembered the day David Subotic introduced us at the steak house in New York, sealing the handshake that would eventually lead us here.

"You came to me, saying you wanted to be a partner," I said. "This doesn't feel like a partnership."

Adler leaned back and shrugged.

"The numbers weren't what we thought they were. You knew what you were getting into when you signed that contract."

It was clear now—this was a trap. Jason had no intention of working with us, only of starving us of the funds we needed, backing us into a corner until he could seize control of the company. My last-ditch effort at diplomacy had failed, and I was left scrambling to find the $20 million before we defaulted.

Later that night, as I was brushing my teeth, I saw Laura appear behind me in the mirror.

"What's wrong?" she asked.

I told her about my encounter with Adler, about how he was deliberately withholding funds to force us into default. Predatory lending at its finest.

"Why don't I talk to his wife?" she suggested. "He definitely listens to her. He wouldn't want her knowing he's pulling this shady shit. Reputation matters to them."

I wasn't there when they spoke. I can't vouch for what happened, but I do know what Laura told me shortly after. She had asked Rachel out to coffee at Superba, the hipster café and restaurant in Venice.

Rachel was already there, waiting for a table.

"Hey, I'm not going to be able to stay for coffee," Laura said, marching in, "but I just wanted to let you know your husband is doing some shady shit. I'm sure he's probably not telling you, but if he keeps this up, he could end up in jail," she went on.

"I know you're sitting here, trying to connect and make relationships with all the parents [in the school], but this is not how you do it, and I don't want any part of it." And with that Rachel's face turned pale and Laura turned back toward the car and drove away.

STROKE OF FATE

Back in the office, I was preparing for a meeting on tax strategy. Chris Ganan barged in.

"So, last night I was at a party up in the Hollywood Hills," he started, spinning a tale about how a friend introduced him to an Egyptian businessman she was dating. "The guy owned those Roadside Grills on the West Coast," he explained. "Sold big, and now he's dabbling around and wants to throw some money into ..."

I perked up.

"You guessed it. Cannabis."

The prospect of a late-inning investor, manna from heaven, lifted my spirits. I felt light, hungry again.

"I'm trying to get him to come in at the end of the day today," Chris said. "If he can, are you here?"

"If he can, I'll be anywhere you need me to be."

Later that day, Chris and I exchanged a determined nod as we headed to the conference room. Pushing open the door, we saw Sabi sitting at the head of the table.

"Mr. Sabi, it's a pleasure to meet you," I said, extending my hand. He stood up to shake it, his smile gracious.

"The pleasure is mine," he responded, his voice rich with the musical cadence of his Egyptian accent.

With our company on the hook, I took a seat and listened. Daddy Rick always said, "You're selling them on what they want to buy. Shut the fuck up and let them tell you."

Sabi opened up.

"My partners and I have a lot of operational expertise, and we want to invest into cannabis. I spoke with Chris briefly about purchasing dispensaries and he asked me to come in to meet with you."

"Makes sense," I responded, eager but measured. "How many dispensaries were you thinking of purchasing, and where? What was your plan before you spoke with Chris?"

Sabi nodded along.

"We have about $25 million to invest," he said. "Our idea was to purchase two or three dispensaries inside a single region. Chris said something about Arizona."

"I'm certain operationally you can find efficiencies and probably evolve even where we are operating today," I said. "I think it's all about timing and cost. The cost to become educated, make mistakes, formulate a plan. You're a real businessman—you get it. Nothing is magic. Why not partner with us and place that investment into a company that has 30 open stores already across the country," I went on

I could structure a deal for him to invest in MedMen, I explained, which would give him ownership in the entire business and all its assets.

"Let me talk to my partners," he said, sharing that the main investor was living in Saudi Arabia.

"Please just follow up with Chris when you're ready for next steps," I said. "Like so many of these deals, the timing is admittedly crazy and perfect. I hope we can make it happen."

Chris got the confirmation the next day. Ayman Sabi and his group's $25 million was exactly what I needed to get us through this restructuring, fully recover from the PharmaCann opportunity escaping us, and put us back in line to receive the balance of Gotham's investment.

"We look forward to working with you and your partners," I said, seizing his hand and shaking it, assuming the close.

———

Later that day, Ganan, Zeeshan, and I met in my office. I gave Chris a golf clap and told Zeeshan to make sure the $25 million could budget out to last through restructuring whatever it took. We would endure it. For now, we had staved off Adler.

I was itching to tell Adler immediately, but this news was too good for just a text or call. Plus, shaking a hand to signing a series of long-form investment docs is a multi-week process. A few weeks later, the docs were in final form, and I was headed to Las Vegas to the annual Marijuana Biz Daily conference for the second year in a row as the CEO of MedMen, the public company. In advance, I had Zeeshan set up a face-to-face meeting with Adler and his cronies. I was ready to flip the script on them, live.

Hidden within the grandeur of Mandalay Bay, the bar at the Four Seasons was the spot to talk real deals, a luxury zone away from the grit of the casino floor. The place was lit with sunlight, gleaming wood, and the glint of martini glasses. Amidst the throngs of tailored suits and whispered conversations, we waited for Jason Adler and his crew to enter and break the tension.

As the minutes passed, my senses heightened. Every clink of ice against glass sounded louder, every hushed exchange a screaming match.

The night before, we had struck first by announcing Sabi's investment, an equity deal that Jason could not block. We had all the paperwork signed, and wanted to broadcast to all our colleagues in the cannabis industry at the conference that MedMen would survive the PharmaCann fallout and come out the other side stronger than ever. The Parker noise and caricature he painted of me could finally be left behind, and we could move on to focusing completely on our mission.

"You think they'll show?" Zeeshan asked.

In the distance, I could hear a cacophony of sounds—the jingle of slot machines, the distant rumble of traffic—all a backdrop to this silent vigil, a reminder of the chaos that swirled outside.

"I don't think they're coming," he said.

As we rose from our chairs and made our way toward the exit, the bar remained unchanged. The absence of Adler and his people hung heavy in the air. It was a silent testament to the gravity of our confrontation, a reminder that the battle was far from over and a declaration of full-on war between MedMen and Gotham Green.

THE ASPEN MASSACRE

As our plane descended through the veil of darkness, the twinkling lights of Aspen came into view, casting a warm glow against the snowy landscape below. The mountains looked majestic in the moonlit sky, their peaks dusted with fresh snow shimmering like diamonds under the stars.

Stepping out onto the frosty tarmac, the biting cold of the winter night wrapped around Mateo, Ari, Laura, and me. The air was crisp and clear, filled with the smell of pine and wood smoke drifting from distant chimneys. Aspen looked like a fairy-tale village to me, its streets alive with late-night revelers and holiday shoppers.

We were here for a much-needed holiday vacation for the family, and despite the enchanting scene before me, the tug of tiny hands and loads of hugs, something didn't feel right. Sabi had signed the docs on behalf of his investment company. The paperwork was in the clear. But the money was supposed to hit our account that day. And it did not.

The next morning, the frigid mountain air nipped at my cheeks as I proudly watched my kids falling on their faces, simply trying to shuffle over to the bunny hill. I laughed and finally felt light. I needed this holiday. I needed this clean oxygen.

Just as I was about to join them, my phone rang. I glanced at the caller ID and saw that it was Chris Ganan, my heart sinking at the sight. I stepped aside to take the call, my stomach churning.

"Well, we've got a problem," Chris said. "The Saudi Arabian partner, the primary funder for the investment, he's had a stroke and apparently he's in critical care."

"He signed the docs, right?" I asked.

"Yeah."

"And they sent the wire?"

"Well, that's the problem. The guy had the stroke the day before he was supposed to wire the money . . ."

"Have you spoken to your guy, the Roadside Grill guy, in Brentwood?"

"That's who told me."

"What can we do to get this money in?"

"The Saudi partner is the lead; it's not happening without him."

I closed my eyes. The lifeline we needed to keep the company afloat was now uncertain, and literally in the critical care unit.

"Let me know when you hear something," I said to Chris, and marched aimlessly in the snow. I had to do something. *What the fuck?!*

I scrolled to Ben Rose's name on my phone and hit the CALL button.

My fingers were freezing as I pulled off my ski gloves to use the touch screen. "The primary investor in this deal had a stroke, Ben," I said. "This is just so out of control."

"Is this a joke? What's up?"

"The day this guy was supposed to wire the money, he had the stroke, and is now in a critical care unit."

I listened and watched as Mateo was holding the rope tow up the bunny slope.

"I got no other options," I went on. "It's time for Wicklow to step up so we can finally move forward. Obviously, I pursued all other alternatives but I'm going to need the money from Wicklow."

At the base of the hill, Laura was zipping up Ari's coat, the final touch of a bundle that included ski pants and long underwear. Now he had to pee again, forcing her to walk him back to the lodge.

"You know I've always believed in you," Ben went on. "But Dan has made it clear he's not putting any money in. He sees it as a tax write-off for Wicklow."

"Excuse me? I don't understand. Ben, you told me to find it elsewhere, but as a stopgap, Wicklow would be there."

"But I'm not the one calling the shots here," he said. "Dan doesn't have any more appetite to inject capital."

I felt short of breath, like I was suffocating.

"This is a fucking joke. I'll call Dan myself," I said.

"He's at his home in Europe," Ben said. "It's the middle of the night over there. Wait until the morning."

I hung up the phone and called him at his "castle" in Europe. But there was no answer, just the cold emptiness of voicemail.

"Come on, Tierney, pick up," I muttered under my breath. *Come on.* I hung up and dialed again, the cycle repeating itself like a relentless drumbeat.

"Dammit!" I cursed, my frustration boiling over as I slammed my fist against the table. "Answer the goddamn phone, Tierney!"

Desperate, I redoubled my efforts, dialing again and again with a manic determination. Finally, I received a text.

"I'll call you in five minutes," Tierney wrote.

———

When he called, his voice was laced with angry annoyance.

"Why are you waking my family?"

"Hey, man, here's the deal," I said. "There's over a thousand fucking people whose families rely on us to deliver them paychecks to live! This isn't a game. It's Christmas. I can't have a thousand families not get their paychecks and lose our company, Dan. What do you want?"

But Tierney's response was dismissive, his words a cold slap in the face.

"I told you this would happen," he said. "You know what happens when you fly too close to the sun."

"So you're going to let this all go?"

"I guess so," he said, and hung up the phone.

I was gripping my phone tighter now, about to crush the case. I dialed Ben again.

"What the fuck are we going to do about this?" I pressed. "You're really going to let this happen? Fuck your boss. You gave me your word. What is that worth to you?"

Ben was over-the-top explicit with me earlier when the PharmaCann deal broke that if I was unsuccessful in raising this equity, Wicklow would invest the money we needed to get us through restructuring.

"Let me see what I can do," he said.

He hung up and I wandered again aimlessly in the snow, oblivious to the world around me. The phone rang, breaking through my thoughts. Ben again.

"Okay, I had a long talk with Dan," he said. "He'll put up half of what you need, so $10 million, if you can find the other half. That's his current offer."

I put down the phone and looked up at the mountain. The sun was in a different place; the day was nearly over. I didn't know where my kids were. Over by the lodge, a fire was roaring in the outdoor chimney. Wineglasses were out. But my day of hustling had just begun. I had secured $10 million from Dan Tierney, but now I needed to find the rest. Where?

I scanned my mind for leads, searching the contacts we'd pursued over the years. The first was a fund in Vancouver that had been ready to invest tens of millions in an equity raise we were working out of Canada over a year before. We had blown them off—surely they remembered—but business is business.

I called Zeeshan. He was the lead in that relationship.

"I got the $10 million locked down with Tierney. We need another $10 million. Can you reach out to your guy from Vancouver?"

"Long shot, but I'll try," he replied.

I wandered off to the slopes, trying to find the kids and feeling weary and exhausted.

Back at the condo, I collapsed, putting my phone on my chest and waiting for news from Zeeshan.

The buzz of the phone finally woke me up.

"Good news, boss," he said. "They are in."

"Were they pissed?"

"Yep, but I told him, look, it's not personal. You are getting a better deal now and we are just looking to move forward."

"Great," I said. "Can you get the lawyers going and send around an email, cc'ing Ben Rose?"

"Will do," he said. I don't remember the rest. I must have blacked out from nerves, exhaustion, and the satisfaction that we had pulled off another miracle.

————

The next morning, the sun was out and the world felt glorious. Laura and the kids were off to a local playground, which had turned into a snow-covered fantasyland where Mateo and Ari were climbing, sliding, jumping, and bouncing everywhere.

I called Ben Rose.

"We did it," I said. "We got the rest of the money."

He seemed shocked, his tone odd.

"Congratulations," he said.

"The term sheet is getting signed today," I said.

"I got to see it signed and in," he said, and the conversation ended.

I spent the morning with the family down at the playground, only stopping for the kids to drink hot chocolate we bought from a fairy-tale candy store. I sat on a bench across the street from the store, staring into my phone, living inside my video game and glancing up occasionally at my family. "Anything yet?" I asked Zeeshan, checking to see if the new investors had signed the term sheet. "Nothing," he said. "It's early."

A few hours later, back to Zeeshan.

"Anything?"

"Nothing."

"Want to text your guy?"

"Already did."

"Keep me posted."

The sun was setting. The business day was over in Vancouver. I was on the line with Zeeshan one more time.

"What the fuck?"

"I don't know. I've called the guy a dozen times."

I didn't know what to say anymore.

When Zeeshan called again, I was sleeping.

"I just heard," he said.

"Well?"

"He sent me a text message."

"What does it say?"

"It says, 'Tell Adam that payback is a bitch. Merry Christmas.'"

———

As the snowflakes blanketed Aspen on the morning of Christmas Eve, we all found ourselves back at the playground. As the kids played in the snow, I racked my brain to think of the one person who could commit to a $10 million check on Christmas Eve. Who did I know, I asked myself, that was not celebrating the holiday and loved an amazing deal?

The answer: Moez Kassam, of Anson Funds. He's Muslim, so he was not celebrating Christmas. His wife, Jewish. Perfect. It was Anson Funds that was set to lead that equity investment from Canada before I let Jason Adler swoop in and swap Moez for Gotham Green.

I called him.

"Moez, long time," I began, my voice laden with sincerity and urgency. "First off, let me say that I fucked up getting in bed with Adler. You were always great to me."

"Yeah, you all fucked us there, but I appreciate you saying so."

"Won't happen again," I said, and went into our tangled tale of Gotham Green, and how our investor who had the stroke was on life support, and how we were on the verge of losing the company to Jason Adler.

"I'm in a fucked spot. Wicklow said they'll put up half the money, but I need the other half."

"How much do you need?" he said.

"$10 million," I said. "It's a sweetheart deal. You see where the stock is—like, it's ridiculous. If you want to be our capital provider again, I'd love to learn my lesson."

"Okay, Adam, well, first of all, I'm still pissed about how you dealt with this in the past, but I appreciate you saying that. You want to move forward. Let's make money," he declared.

With newfound resolve, I set to work, rallying the troops again and orchestrating the intricate dance of negotiations. Emails and term sheets flew, and voices echoed through the cramped confines of the Aspen condo as the final pieces of the puzzle fell into place.

Moez's term sheet got signed on Christmas Eve, and our lawyers sent it to Dan Tierney and Ben Rose. Crisis averted. Time to hang with the kids. I got ready to leave the condo, but Ben Rose was calling again.

"Ben, what's up?"

"Yeah, I don't know, man. I feel horrible, but Dan wants a personal guarantee on this money."

"What? What does that even mean?"

"That means that he puts the money up and if in a year he's not able to get it all back, you guys have to make up the difference," Ben said.

"Ben, that's not the deal, man."

"It's out of left field. I might resign over this," he said. I could hear the frustration in Ben's voice, but was he faking it? Was this all an act, given that I knew they were in cahoots to oust me anyway?

"That's ridiculous," I said. "I'm not getting anything out of it personally. You guys are putting this money up so that the company can survive. I'm not putting it in my fucking bank account."

"I know," he said. "But you need to sign a personal guarantee. You can split it with Chris and Andrew."

"I'll get back to you," I said, hung up, and did nothing. Laura and the boys were splashing around outside in the Jacuzzi as the snow gently fell. I sat and tried to breathe and dialed Chris, asking him to patch in Andrew for an emergency call.

"Well, the good news is that over the last two days we have gotten the money to keep Adler off our back," I told them both. "The bad news is that Dan Tierney is putting up half of it and now he wants a personal guarantee. That means, if we don't pay the money back, we're liable for it on our own."

"What the fuck?" Andrew said. "I'm not signing a personal guarantee."

"This is just him being overprotective," Chris said. "They're not going to fuck us. It's either this or we lose the company."

"This is the only deal available," I said.

"Adam will figure something else out," Andrew said.

"Guys, it'll be fine," Chris said. "I talk to John [McCarthy] all the time. He's my friend. Let's just sign it and fucking move on."

Reluctantly, I agreed. And finally, Andrew did too.

I called Ben back.

"Okay, Ben, we'll sign your personal guarantee," I conceded and hung up the phone. Then I started packing and joined the family as we filed out the door of the condo, ending our family vacation.

Goodbye, Aspen.

MY DAD'S EMERGENCY MEETING

My phone buzzed insistently, interrupting the steady stream of emails and notifications demanding my attention. Glancing down at the screen, I was greeted by an urgent message from my father:

"We need to talk," he wrote, like he was my business partner.

"Coffee later this week?" I responded.

"Now," he wrote.

With a deep breath, I told my assistant to cancel my next series of meetings and I made my way over to meet Dad at the Culver Hotel, an old-world place nestled among the studios.

As I stepped through the ornate entrance of the lobby bar, the mood was elevated, historic. The dimly lit interior exuded a sense of quiet grandeur, with plush velvet curtains framing the windows and pristine white tablecloths adorning each table. I could almost hear the conversations of Charlie Chaplin's and Grace Kelly's ghosts in the corner.

My father was already seated at a corner table, his commanding presence staking claim to the power seat in the room, just as he had taught me to do so many years ago. He was wearing a golf shirt like always, and it was clear that this was no ordinary catch-up.

"Look, I saw your announcement," he said. "I saw your stuff, but with the $20 million, you're not going to make it six months."

I sighed, looking down into my phone. I was running a public company. I had started it all from scratch. I didn't need a lecture.

"Dad, I appreciate your concern, but I've got a plan in place. We're restructuring—"

"You need to fucking go farther," he interrupted, his voice stern. "You can't do this, Adam. You need to bring somebody else in."

He went on, talking about bringing in that "blue-blazered

motherfucker," an older, experienced CEO that had run medium-sized companies before, a steady hand that would ease the worries of our investors and stabilize our stock. Our business was edgy, but it needed an experienced leader to run it all, he felt, someone who had decades of experience managing a nationwide operation.

"The business is too nuanced," I said, leaning back in my chair. "If I can't do it, I don't know who can."

"No, you don't get it, Adam. You fucking can't do this," he insisted. "You need to bring someone else in."

His words stung, hitting a nerve deep within me.

"You've done a great job. Being a leader, being a visionary. Hats off. But you can't do this going forward."

I clenched my jaw, struggling to maintain my composure.

"I appreciate it, Dad. Thank you so much for caring. But there's nobody that could understand what we're doing other than us."

THE LAST GURGLES

In the stark, glass-walled conference room in the office, sunlight spilled across the polished table, setting a somber stage. The room hummed with the low buzz of the air-conditioning. I stood at the head, my gaze sweeping across the faces of MedMen's department heads—finance, operations, marketing, each one braced for the blow.

"Thank you all for coming on short notice," I started, betraying none of the turmoil churning inside.

"We're at a critical juncture," I continued. "The reality is we evolve or die. We were growing at all costs and now need to hunker down and operate like maniacs for a while. We will cut and sell off and do whatever we need to in order for this money to get us through profitability. This money needs to take us through being self-sustaining; it's as simple as that."

I let the words hang in the air, watching as they settled over the room, drawing nods, resigned sighs.

"I'm asking for a 30 percent cut from each of your budgets," I stated. "This includes staffing."

Murmurs broke out.

"I know what I'm asking," I said, my tone softening. "But we don't just need to survive; we need to come out leaner, stronger."

Esther Song, our chief marketing officer, shifted in her seat, her face a mix of concern and resolve.

"Adam, about the cuts—"

"Yes, they include more layoffs," I cut in, anticipating her question. "The business has no choice; this is just reality. Or else there is no business."

———

The layoffs were scheduled for a Friday. Coordinating the day with human resources, my security team had advised me to stay away from the office.

They didn't want me there in case things turned ugly with the departing employees. And so, instead of heading into the chaos, I found myself alone, grappling with the weight of my decisions.

As I looked at my reflection in the mirror, a sense of emptiness washed over me. Once a bloody corpse with a missing leg and arm, I felt that I was only left with heart and head, vital organs to barely survive. I looked into the future, playing out the hand, and knew that my chances of surviving as the leader of a flourishing MedMen were grim.

"This thing's going to outlive me," I said to myself. The company, the industry—they would continue on their path. And then, with a sense of clarity that cut through the uncertainty, I made a decision. I couldn't continue to lead from the front. It was time to step back, to work from behind the scenes and let someone else take the reins. But before I faded into the sunset, I had to leave the company on stable footing. Jay Brown had told me once that my goal should be to end up like him and Jay-Z, on the board of the company they started, shielded from the day-to-day noise, left to be inspired, create, and do what they do best. That's now what I wanted for myself.

"I have to get us through the restructuring," I murmured, the words heavy on my tongue. "I'll get us through. It'll take the rest of me."

I reached for the phone, dialing Ben Rose, our chairman—playing his angles across MedMen, PharmaCann, Wicklow, and Gotham Green. He was now also holding a multi-million-dollar personal guarantee over my head, tightening his grip on the entire operation. "Hey, Ben," I said, my voice steady despite the turmoil raging inside me. "I've been thinking . . . On the other side of the restructuring, I think I need to replace myself as the CEO."

There was a pause on the other end of the line.

"I'm shocked," he said, and I could almost see the smile washing over him. But his support was unwavering, his words—if I could believe them—a balm to my troubled mind.

"I'm supportive of you being the CEO forever," he said. "I am also supportive of you transitioning to the board tomorrow. I want to support you."

It was a weight lifted off my shoulders.

"I want to let you know in case I get hit by a bus today that Ryan Lissack is the best choice to replace me," I said.

Ryan had come to us from Disney and was a second-generation Med-Men employee. He joined after we were public and after the stigma had started to shift. At the time, he was serving as chief technology officer, running all of our digital infrastructure. I believed the future was about technological efficiencies. "I'm going to put a plan together," I told Ben.

As I hung up the phone, I knew that the next several months would be tricky. But they always were. With Ben's support and guided by the intuition that I was making the best move for the company, I felt a sense of peace settle over me. I admired Ryan, and it was time to let someone else take the lead and guide us all into our next chapter. And for the first time in a long while, I felt hopeful for our future.

HOW TO PLAY POCKET KINGS

had been playing well all year and looking forward to this game. I filled my backpack with cash from my poker bankroll and picked up my dad for a father-son weekend. I had been invited by Jean-Robert Bellande, a legendary poker player and host, to play in his impossible-to-get-into, no-limit cash game at the Encore. What made the game so legendary were the pop stars, athletes, and bored rich assholes that Jean-Robert got to show up. He curated the game so there was just enough elite talent there to make you feel like you were playing in the Major Leagues, just with some players on the field better suited for wiffle ball.

For Dad and me, this game was our own World Series, the culmination of decades of preparation. Our relationship had been a twisted roller coaster, demented and sociopathic, toxic yet undeniably founded in love. In this moment it felt like we were back on track, chasing a dream paved by the legends of Vegas—Lansky, Siegel. The closer we got to Vegas, the more we shed the weight of the past. We felt like more than just father and son; we were partners in crime again, ready to take on the town, and with me having fought my way to earning a seat at the big game.

And as Vegas appeared on the horizon, a beacon of dreams and desperation, I knew this trip would be the ultimate test. Not of skills at the poker table, but of the fragile bond that was slowly mending between me and my dad. He had pushed his addiction on me, and I was able to harness it into a superpower in the world of business.

———

The casino inside the Encore was loud and bright, like walking onto a stage set for a drama in which we were both stars and spectators. The game was held in a back room, and the journey to this secluded enclave was a sensory overload—a cacophony of lights, sounds, and the seductive clinking of chips. But as we moved through the sliding doors into the private gambling salon, the world outside faded to a distant hum, replaced by an atmosphere charged with anticipation and the sharp, electric, and ruthless scent of its hustlers.

The room itself was a study in sham opulence, bathed in soft, golden light that reflected off polished surfaces. Televisions mounted on the walls played silently, their flickering images casting a surreal glow over the scene. The sound of cards being shuffled was a rhythmic heartbeat, syncing with my own pulse, which had picked up pace as the reality of the situation settled in.

The poker table, an altar at the center of the room, was surrounded by players deep in concentration. It was clear that this was no ordinary game. I bought into the game for $250,000, with a second bullet (buy-in) in my backpack.

As the doors slid shut behind us, I glanced back at Dad. His expression was unreadable, a mask honed from years of his own shitstorms, but I thought I caught a flicker of excitement in his eyes. It was a rare glimpse into the soul of this lifetime gambler who had been my inspiration.

"We're in it now," I muttered, half to Dad, half to myself.

The game began, and with each hand dealt, I felt a growing sense of clarity. This was where I was meant to be, not just to play, but to prove something—to myself, to Dad, to the ghosts of gamblers past that haunted the neon-lit corridors of Vegas. In the back room of the Encore, I found a piece of myself I hadn't known was lost.

———

For the first hour, I didn't find myself in any big hands, I was down a few thousand bucks, and everybody was ready for the game to heat up.

We agreed to raise the stakes, adding a round of straddles, which essentially doubles the size of the blinds. We were playing with blinds of $200 and $400, and the straddle was added for $800. The cards were dealt, and I looked down.

Two red kings. It was a hand that could make or break the session, a moment of déjà vu from that game a decade ago that jump-started my career. Now, I was ready to play it differently.

I could hear the old pool contractor from the Bike, and those lines he passed to me so long ago: "If you play pocket kings that way, you have no business being in this game."

I was different now. I had no doubts. With a raise and re-raise before my turn to act, I raised the pot to an even $30,000.

The room was quiet, tense.

"Hey, pops, how are you doing back there?" Andrew Robl, another poker legend, said, looking back at my dad, who kept quiet.

With one player calling, the dealer discarded the top card and flipped the next three. Nothing much there. Untextured or disconnected, as they say. Best of all for me, no ace.

"Check," my opponent said, as he was first to act.

"$55,000," I countered.

"Call," my opponent reluctantly sent his chips towards the middle of the felt.

A seemingly harmless four of diamonds was placed down by the dealer as the turn card and my opponent checked yet again. I had about the same amount of chips in front of me as the size of the pot.

"All in," I said, pushing my chips in.

He folded, and I raked in the pot.

———

For dinner, Dad and I walked over to Carbone and its retro-glam feel and reputation for serving Las Vegas's best Italian plates (which Dad of course loves). The restaurant was on fire, every table packed and over an hour wait. We found ourselves sitting at the bar for dinner, hungry after hours of playing, and studying the menus.

"I know what you're thinking," I said, breaking the silence as I glanced over the wine list. "The Amarone, right?" It was my dad's favorite—a bold Italian red, intense and heavy, thick like prune juice.

"Yeah, let's see what they've got," he said.

The bartender laid out our options: the Low Roller Amarone, which cost over a hundred dollars, and the High Roller bottle, for $500.

Without missing a beat, Dad pointed to the cheapest.

"This one's fine. Thank you."

"Hold on," I said. "When have you ever tried the other one? You always say you can tell the difference. Why settle now?"

"Adam, I can buy that bottle for $200 back home. We don't need to spend $500 on it here."

But something in me snapped—a mix of pride and defiance.

"I am in the middle of playing $200/$400 this weekend, and you're worried about $500?" I insisted. "Can we just please enjoy tonight with none of the bullshit?"

"Okay. I'll try."

As the High Roller Amarone was poured, its rich aroma filling the space between us, the wine felt like a symbol, uniting us. He was now drinking his favorite wine with his son, a winner against all odds, all in defiance of the system.

"Now this is pretty good," he said of the Amarone, pouring another glass—a sign from him, in his own twisted way, that he was proud of me.

SNEAK ATTACK IN THE BOARDROOM

As I arrived at the office early on Monday morning, my trusty purple lunch box in tow, I passed by the conference room and saw Ben Rose and John McCarthy, the attorney from Wicklow, lingering there with their laptops open. This was a bizarre sight indeed, given that Rose and McCarthy were based halfway across the country in Chicago and must have flown in on the sly to be here.

"What's up, guys?" I greeted them, cautiously joining them at the table, my mind racing to make sense of the situation.

They looked at each other, and Ben mustered up the courage to speak. His words hit me like a right cross to the chin.

"Adam, you've lost all credibility, not only with investors on the street but inside of the company itself," he said.

The speech felt overly rehearsed.

"You've lost complete control," he went on. "Today's your last day. Get the fuck out," he said.

John leaned in with a more sympathetic tone, attempting to soften the blow of Ben's harsh words.

"Ben, I think you need to leave the room," he said, assuming the good cop role in the routine.

"Adam, he shouldn't have been so personal," John said. "You've done so much for all of us, and nobody's questioning your commitment. You built this fucking industry. But he is right, so let's work on a transition. I know that you already have an idea, and this has got to be your last week."

"I have to go work," I said, and shuffled down the hall and disappeared into my office.

I closed the door, trying to gather my thoughts. I emptied the contents of my lunchbox and placed the cold items in my mini-fridge. The

Post-it Laura snuck in saying "We love you, have the best day!" hit me like the perfect liver punch, squeezing every cell in my body. My mind now raced between reality, Laura and the kids, and my video game waiting for me in the conference room. All the thoughts were flying, with no room to breathe. I turned and put on my best stoic warrior face to find Dan Edwards, one of our attorneys, standing in my office.

"Adam, I don't know what's happening, but these guys are running around in the legal office saying you're leaving?"

I glanced across the office and saw Esther seated in her office with McCarthy and Ben Rose. It was clear they were up to no good, conspiring to sabotage my position.

Before I could even process the betrayal, Chris Ganan burst into my office, his face twisted with concern.

"Adam, this shit is fucked up. We gotta deal with this," he exclaimed, his frustration palpable.

As I continued with my meetings, a sense of unease lingered. I couldn't focus. Eventually, Chris returned.

"They apologize," he said, bearing the message like a Swiss ambassador. "They shouldn't have ambushed you. They want to have lunch."

———

We ordered from Sweetgreen, the salad and sandwich shop, and sat in the conference room. The salads were laid out in front of us, the tension thick. John started, his tone contrite and determined.

"Adam, sorry, you know, but we're going to have to get this done."

"Okay, guys, I'll think about what you're saying," I replied evenly, though every fiber of my being was screaming in protest. Did they even have the authority to oust me?

"You told us that you're leaving anyway," Ben said. "I'm telling you now, we can't raise money with you as CEO. We can't do anything unless you're gone. So work with John and let's get it done, man."

He was twisting my words and using them against me.

"I'll think about it," I said, and made an excuse to leave.

Instead of heading back to my office, I told my assistant to clear my afternoon. I didn't know where to go, just that I had to disappear.

"Where to?" Roy asked.

"I don't know, just drive around," I said.

We drove aimlessly for a while, made a turn back, and somehow landed around Culver City Park.

"Let's stop here," I said, and I walked down the path and out onto the grass. I found an empty patch, lay down, and stared up into the clouds, waiting for them to all crash down on me. It had been 10 years since I met the blue-haired lady and opened the Treehouse with nothing to lose. I had been fighting and winning and losing and building for a long time. Each victory had placed me in the next arena, only to face more sophisticated and ruthless opponents. I had stayed alive and somehow kept dancing between the raindrops. Ben and John showing up to ambush me felt like the end. Maybe I could beat them back one last time, but my mind was tired of dancing.

———

Back in my CT6, I called Phil Stutz. He agreed to see me.

"Give me the updates," he said when I arrived at his office.

I told him about the sneak attack from the Wicklow folks.

"It's like I come home every day soaked in blood and I'm just exhausted from the fighting," I said.

"Why don't you just leave?" he asked.

"I don't think it's about leaving to fix this," I said.

I tried to defend sticking it out, adding this battle to my ever-growing list, contemplating prevailing one final time.

"Adam, I have been on this earth a long time, and these people are not going to ever stop or pay you a penny."

I was listening, cringing, not wanting to believe him.

"How much would you pay to never have to talk to these people again, to never have to go work in that environment again?" he asked, his words hitting home with brutal clarity.

"It's a real fucking question," he went on. "Answer the question!"

"Probably everything I have, except what I need to eat and clothe and shelter my family."

"Okay, well, then there you have it," he said. "Don't look at this like, *how much are you willing to fight to stay.* Look at this like, *how much are you willing to pay to leave.* How much are you willing to pay them to fucking disconnect forever?"

FAREWELL SPEECH

ater that week, I found myself at the front of that big bullpen area at headquarters, the same perch where I had broadcast so many proclamations, spewing our mission and victories out into the world. I signed a settlement agreement that allowed me to keep my stock, stay on as a board member, and coach Ryan Lissack in his CEO role. It was time for a transition, and now here I was addressing the company as CEO for the last time. Laura was in the back, others were tuning in via livestream. My voice was trembling, holding back an emotional bottleneck that had been building so deep in my system that it felt like burning magma as it bubbled to the surface. I couldn't get the first sentence out. The words got stuck in my throat like shards of glass. Tears flowed.

"Ten years ago, Andrew and I embarked on a journey, not knowing where it would lead us," I said, the memories flooding like a torrential downpour, each one a testament to the trials we had faced together.

"But what a ride it has been," I continued, my voice thick with emotion. "Access to legal cannabis makes the world a safer, healthier, happier place and each person here has made their mark in that pursuit. When we started, weed was being sold behind blacked-out windows and buzzer doors. Now we sell weed in Beverly Hills and on Fifth Avenue."

My eyes shimmered with unshed tears as I reflected on the evolution of MedMen, the weed empire we had battled to build.

"As I stand here today, my role in this incredible journey evolves," I said. "Nobody is bigger than MedMen and certainly nobody is bigger than this industry, and it's time for me to step aside and make room for what's next."

I spoke of the qualities the company needed in its next leader, my words a reminder of the challenges and opportunities that lay ahead.

"Above all else," I said, my voice cracking, "we need someone who is passionately committed to the legalization movement, who believes in the power of this plant and its ability to change lives."

And then I spoke of Ryan Lissack, a flicker of hope amidst the darkness of farewell.

"Ryan is our leader for what's next," I said, my voice filled with pride. "He has the potential to become one of the great CEOs of our generation, and it's an honor to pass the torch to him."

With a final, heartfelt expression of gratitude, I thanked everyone in the room and others watching from our stores around the country, my words echoing in the silent room like a benediction. I then bowed my head and stepped away, mopping at the tears streaming down my cheeks, feeling like a man who had just given the eulogy at his own funeral.

———

The morning after my announcement, I woke up next to Laura, feeling light and free. I put on an old T-shirt and sweatpants. As I descended the staircase into the playroom, the sound of my children's laughter filled the air. It was just the four of us and I had nowhere else to be.

"Daddy, watch me jump!" Ari said.

"No, watch me," Mateo countered.

And I watched. And we played together. In that moment, everything felt right. I had done it. It was over. I had won.

Jason Adler and his predatory goons were at bay. I had crafted a restructuring plan that would make MedMen sustainable. We had the most enviable footprint across the country and were soon to be profitable. I had passed the reins to Ryan, who I truly believed in. And best of all, after negotiating my terms with MedMen, I could still stick around and enjoy it all, assist from behind the scenes, and play the role of wise elder.

Financially, we were set. Our marriage now had a chance to receive my energy. I felt proud and changed. I had built the most recognized cannabis company in the world. We helped convince American investors for the first time to look at cannabis as an industry and one that now employs more people than coal. We convinced high-functioning executives to join and work in our industry. We helped convince lawmakers, investment bankers, and stockbrokers to treat cannabis companies like any other. We forged the first national partnership with the unions, providing store-level employees union wages. We helped convince working moms and soccer dads to feel comfortable enough to access legal cannabis for the first time. Even my mother-in-law was carrying a vape pen in her purse. I had gone from living with my girlfriend on a mattress in my parents' living room to the tip of the spear in a movement putting a "dent" in the universe. Even though the value of my stock had been reduced by 90%, I had earned enough to retire for life, all at the age of 37.

————

As I stepped into the office the next Monday morning, I was in the best mood, having had breakfast with the kids and taken them to school, and looking forward to embracing my new role as board member and mentor to Ryan. But as I approached my office, it all felt like the first scene of a nightmare. Ben Rose was in there, his earbuds in. My office, once my sanctuary and mission control, was now occupied by my backstabbing chairman.

"What are you doing here?" Ben barked, his tone laced with disdain as he brushed past me, his earbuds firmly in place.

I was confused. I was on the board of directors, assigned to help Ryan from behind-the-scenes, while helping the next generation of red-jacketed warriors navigate the future.

"What the fuck are you doing here?" he asked again, dragging me into my old office, and lacing into me, each word another lash of the whip.

"I can't have you here," he said. "You're a fucking poison. You're a cancer. Get the fuck out."

————

Back at home, I collapsed on the couch and stared at the ceiling.

Soon, I reached for my phone to check my emails, but the familiar ding of incoming messages failed to sound. My inbox remained stubbornly empty.

Frowning, I attempted to refresh the page on my phone, but nothing was working. My email wasn't loading.

I reached for my laptop, hoping to gain access through another device. But as I logged in, I hit the same issue.

I called my guy in the office from tech support who always helped out when my email was glitching or computer had a problem.

"Hey, bro, my email is not working," I told him.

"I am so sorry," he said. "They told me to shut everything down."

"Who told you?"

"That guy Ben walked in here and told me to shut all of your access down."

"Fuck, what does that even mean?"

"Like your key card and your email, I had to shut it all down."

Despite the agreements I signed, securing my position on the board, Ben wasted no time in locking me out, determined to erase any trace of my presence. I had built a monster in MedMen, and it had just eaten me alive, swallowing me whole.

LAST CALL TO SAVE MEDMEN

The weeks slipped by, first in a funk, a bubble of anger, then a blur. Each day felt indistinguishable from the others. Wrapped in a Medmen red bathrobe, I didn't know who I was. I needed to learn how to be a father and husband, and in the void, ready to cross that gap, I filled the emptiness with poker. The games were long, the focus absolute, and the competition engaging.

It was during one of these aimless days that the phone rang. I stared at the caller ID, a sense of ambivalence in my stomach.

"Adam, are you free?" asked Brian Kabot, the chief investment officer for Stable Road Capital, a family office and significant MedMen investor. They had loaned us millions over the years and were our third biggest lender. Their office was on Abbot Kinney, across the street from the MedMen store.

"You know there's a board meeting coming up," he said. "You need to be there. Adler is making his final move to steal MedMen."

His voice trailed off, but the implication hung in the air, heavy and suffocating. The legacy I had poured my heart and soul into reduced to a bargain-bin acquisition by those I once called allies.

"This deal will kill us," he said. "Can you have lunch?"

————

The midday sun bathed Abbot Kinney in a glow that felt oddly out of sync with the darkness churning inside me. Brian was waiting for me at Greenleaf, a local salad spot near the MedMen store.

"Adler reached out to me, wanted me on board with their plan," Brian said. "We can't touch it, but they're bringing their offer to the board to vote on it. And, Adam, it's a shit offer."

Sipping my coffee, I felt the weight of months spent in isolation away from the battlefield where my empire was being threatened.

"Okay," I muttered.

But Brian was relentless. "So, what are you going to do about it?"

I looked up.

"Man, I'm not in charge anymore. What can I possibly do?"

"This deal is fucking atrocious, Adam," he said. "Ben Rose and Adler are into something sneaky together. You need to counter it, match it, or better it. You're still on the board. You can't let them get away with this."

After lunch, I slumped into the driver's seat of my Cadillac. This beast of a machine, a trophy from the days when MedMen's equity fund was juiced, now felt like a relic of a past life. Lighting up a joint, I let the smoke fill the car, enveloping me in a haze that seemed to blur the edges of reality. Abbot Kinney Boulevard faded into the background as I smoked and became lost in thought about Brian's words, the looming board meeting, and the vultures circling.

"I guess this had to happen for the movie," I chuckled to myself, the smoke curling around me like a cocoon. The price of the Adler offer—$20 million—was so low, maybe I could match it and take the business back.

I called David Subotic, my longtime friend and investor.

"Can you meet later?"

"Sure," he said.

I then called Jay Brown, who always gave the best advice.

"You have time to give me some advice today in person?"

"Can we do it later, at the house?" he wrote back.

"Great," I said, and finally called Scooter Braun, another music mogul who invested in us, asking for a sit-down.

"Later, sure," he said.

The joint that I was smoking was now gone, and I had three meetings with some of the most influential figures in Los Angeles that night.

———

The mission began at Jay Brown's house. He could help raise the capital in a phone call. Once a cornerstone of support, Brown now seemed distant, his patience for my plight worn thin.

"Adam, I'm out," he said.

The disappointment was bitter, but there was no time to dwell on it. Next was Scooter's house, deep into Brentwood. His security waved me through, the mansion quiet. Scooter was awake, ready to listen, to offer counsel, as I laid bare the betrayal by Wicklow and Adler, his attempts to take over the company and my tiny crack in a window of opportunity to play the hero and come back as its savior. I understood how pathetic and unrealistic I sounded. The words still came out.

"I haven't sold a single share," I confessed, laying out the ludicrousness of the deal on the table, the fortune that I had lost, and feeling the weight of my entire journey pressing down on me.

"I just went through this with Justin [Bieber], and he is going to start fresh and come out the other side more than fine," Braun said, giving me a strange dose of comfort.

"Sometimes we just have to start over," he said, and offered to support and help fund my next venture, whatever that was.

The night's final stop was David's condo in Century City. Ever the big brother figure, David didn't sugarcoat his words.

"If Adler and Wicklow are really teamed up, you're over," he said bluntly.

———

The clatter of chips was back in the air at the Bike, my escape hatch. But today was different. As I sat there, waiting for the next hand, I got a call.

On the line was Julian Michalowski, the owner of Coastal, a new cannabis company in Santa Barbara. They already had a handful of stores, a mix of dreams and plans, and they wanted me to join as a consultant.

"You're the guy in marijuana retail," they said.

My reaction was guarded, skeptical.

"Do you have investors?" I asked, knowing the costs.

"Yes, we have a group that really believes in us," he said. "We've raised about $20 million."

The figure was about the same amount Wicklow and Adler were throwing around, looking to snatch up MedMen shares for pennies on the dollar.

"Why build new stores when you can take control of MedMen?" I said, telling him about the infighting at MedMen and the upcoming board meeting. I could present his offer in front of all the key decision-makers.

"Adam, if that deal's on the table, we're ready to jump."

Just like that, the game was on.

The following 10 days were a blur of activity, a marathon of meetings, calls, and strategic planning, all aimed at one goal: crafting a letter of intent that would outshine anything Adler and Wicklow could muster. The submission of our term sheet wasn't just a business maneuver; it was corporate warfare, a delicate dance of legalities and strategies designed to force the board's hand.

———

Walking into the office that I built, the office I was now barred from, felt like stepping into a ghost of my own past. There was no key card in my pocket, just a security guard who barely looked up as I approached the turnstile. I had to wait, a small indignity, and ask permission.

"Hey, can you let me in?" I hollered.

It was all a sharp reminder of how far I'd fallen. In the lobby, I noticed the media coverage and clippings that adorned the entry area walls had all been removed, my name and photo with them. I was now a phantom, haunting the corridors of my own legacy.

As I took my seat, every eye in the room flicked my way, then just as quickly looked away. It was like stepping into a courtroom where your fate had already been sealed, but the jury couldn't bear to meet your gaze.

Ben Rose, my grand executioner, sat at the head of the table and next to Jason Adler, also in attendance.

"Whatever it is you think about Gotham, whatever it is you think about Jason, I want us all to put that aside," he said. "Jason and I have been working closely post–Adam's departure as CEO. With a new outlook for the company, we've decided to partner to secure the future of this business."

"Hi, everybody. Thank you for this opportunity," Jason said. "Believe it or not, I'm excited about the prospects for this company. This is the number one brand in cannabis, undisputedly, and we just need to organize its finances to withstand the current market environment and be positioned to come out the other side crushing it."

The jargon-filled speech was not a sales pitch to the board. It was a eulogy for the company I had poured my life and soul into.

Jason laid out his proposal, a vision for MedMen completely devoid of its founding principles and mission statement, an exercise in financial engineering with the singular outcome of feeding his own greed and completing the last move in his long-term campaign.

As he spoke, I could feel the narrative being rewritten. It was a surreal experience, like watching my wife and kids lauding their new husband and father, all pretending I never existed.

But I couldn't stay silent.

"Guys, I need to get this on record," I interjected. "This deal values the company at $70 million, giving them 30 to 40 percent control. It's a stranglehold that will end with them owning everything."

I couldn't take it anymore.

"For the record, Jason Adler and Gotham Green have already made multiple loans to the business," I said. "Every single loan has been staged out where they have given us the money in a way that puts a noose around the company's neck, and then allows them to re-trade the deal at more favorable rates. This current deal . . . They are going to get the whole thing."

I looked at Ben.

"I have no idea how Ben who, representing Wicklow, with over $100 million of equity investment in already, is okay with this. Other than he and Jason having some other behind-the-scenes relationship. But that notwithstanding, the board can't proceed with this when it has a bona fide offer on the table that's far superior."

Ben interrupted me.

"Whoa, whoa, whoa, Adam, I've let you speak. I've let you speak. That will be enough, okay? There's enough Jason bashing," he said. "We all know the reason that all the previous deals haven't worked is because of you. That's why you're gone. We've let you say your piece. Jason is by far the only choice we have in the matter, and the truth is, he does very much believe in the business. I've reviewed the offer you have presented, and it's not legitimate and we do not have time to waste."

"All we know about Gotham is that they will, at every opportunity, fuck us," I said. "They could have supported the business from the beginning and saved the business months ago."

The meeting devolved quickly. My plea, my evidence of a better deal, was drowned out by the cacophony of greed and betrayal.

"Adam, we've heard what you have to say," Ben said, and moved to vote on the deal. "We are going to vote to move forward with the Gotham Green proposal. I'm going to be the first. Do we have a second?"

One hand went up.

"I have a second."

And soon it was over. The vote was a formality, a rubber stamp on the assassination of my dream, a final ice pick to my skull.

———

I disappeared into my Cadillac and lit another joint, needing to clear my head. Driving through the city, I found myself in Hollywood when I looked up and saw it—a giant, gleaming billboard for a new cannabis store. A few blocks later, another one. It was hard to believe: When I first started, getting a billboard like that wasn't even an option. Back then, cannabis couldn't touch mainstream advertising. But it was our work—my relentless commitment, the rules we rewrote, the lobbyists and political campaigns we funded, and the ability to execute inside of impossible— that paved the way for these public ads. We pulled cannabis from the shadows into the open. Now, you could buy joints in broad daylight, practically anywhere you looked. The industry I helped build had arrived, and here I was on the outside, looking in.

Instead of heading home, I found myself back in Century City, at Phil Stutz's doorstep. I called for an emergency session, and he happened to be available. Entering his condo, the weight of the world seemed to lift just a bit. I slumped into the chair across from him and told him about the board meeting. I was all ears, desperate for any nugget of advice, anything that might resemble a lifeline.

"I'm going to tell you a story about this painter," he said.

"Ok?" I replied, a bit impatient. I was here for solutions and relief—not a history lesson.

"So, he's a master artist, and he's an old man at this point, at the very end of his life," Phil said, "when he received an unexpected messenger at his studio door." I shifted uncomfortably, unsure where Phil was going with this.

"What does the messenger say? That the Vatican is going through a restoration, and his works are being painted over."

But apparently the painter was not moved.

"They are painting over your masterpieces!" the messenger said again, furious and panicked.

At this, Phil paused.

"What does the artist do? He turns to the messenger and tells him: 'Can you do me a favor and please leave? Because I'm working. Once I create something, I move on to what's next. They can do what they want!'"

Phil's condo was silent, the story hanging between us like a tangible thing. I had no idea if the story was true, but Phil's point was clear. The end of my experience with MedMen wasn't about the betrayal, the loss, the corporate chicanery. It was about creation and relishing the relentless pursuit of what's next.

"What's done is done," Phil said. "The only question that matters now is, what are you going to create next?"

EPILOGUE

I had to end the book at some point, but this story continues to unfold. In the summer of 2020, as congressional and independent investigators started to probe allegations of prosecutorial abuse and misconduct inside the Department of Justice, a whistleblower came forward and revealed that the antitrust review Barr initiated into our acquisition of PharmaCann was politically motivated.

Testifying in front of Congress, John Elias, a longtime government lawyer working for the Department of Justice's antitrust division, claimed that Attorney General Bill Barr personally disliked cannabis and ordered the antitrust attorneys to start bogus investigations into acquisitions and mergers to stymie the growth of the industry and specifically mentioned one such merger: MedMen-PharmaCann.

"Personal dislike of the industry is not a proper basis upon which to ground an antitrust investigation," Elias told Congress. He went on to suggest that Barr's actions could constitute an abuse of authority, a gross waste of funds, and gross mismanagement.

No duh, as Andrew Modlin would say. Later that year, in the face of other Trump-inspired shenanigans, Bill Barr resigned as AG. He takes his place in a long line of Washington bureaucrats who—based on fear, misinformation, or ignorance—sidelined, but only for a moment, the unstoppable momentum that will lead to the end of cannabis prohibition.

In 2021, with Barr gone, the US cannabis sector exploded. There were over 300 mergers and acquisitions that year in a market that by the end of 2021 was valued at over $25 billion.

Far from Washington, on November 22, 2021, in Santa Monica, California, a jury swiftly dismissed the baseless claims brought against me by James Parker, our former CFO. The jury not only absolved me of every count and allegation, but also held Parker accountable for his deceitful tactics, including Breach of Fiduciary Duty, Breach of Duty, Breach of Loyalty, Misappropriation of Trade Secrets, and Conversion.

Later the next year, on December 13, 2022, I prevailed in my lawsuit against MedMen. An arbitrator ruled in my favor, finding the company guilty of fraud in connection with my departure. After slogging it out, this legal victory resulted in a judgment of $3 million in my favor, along with legal fees for Nigel Burns, a legal warrior who has always had my back.

If only MedMen could pay. After struggling to find their footing as a company for years, MedMen filed for bankruptcy on April 27, 2024. Jason Adler, Ben Rose, and the cast of rotating, uninspired suits that would follow them had failed by epic proportions.

Incredibly, only a few days later, on April 30, 2024, the Department of Justice announced it would move to reclassify cannabis from Schedule I to Schedule III controlled substance in the United States, essentially decriminalizing the plant and taking the next and monumental step toward the end of prohibition.

This story, fraught with challenges and triumphs, is bigger than me. My role only covers the essence of a pivotal era, a chapter in an evolution. The narrative here is far larger, bright with possibility, and just beginning.

Acknowledgments

This story is woven from the threads of countless communications, interactions, and relationships I have been fortunate to experience on this incredible journey. As the narrative arc of this book unfolds, I want to acknowledge the forces behind its most pivotal moments.

Laura, my wife and life partner. I wouldn't have even begun this journey without her. She was my reason, and the future family she represented was my most fundamental motivation. I could never express enough gratitude for her unwavering support, patience, and love.

Andrew, my business partner. Andrew had a vision for the future of cannabis retail that unlocked the mainstreaming of weed. His genius and once-in-a-generation talents brought our business and the industry to life.

Chris Ganan, my childhood friend who connected his world with mine to create a financial pathway to the mainstreaming of our business and the industry.

CannaMoms: Moriah, Jacel, and every single CannaMom the world over. They instilled in me the mission to mainstream marijuana and, in doing so, opened my eyes to my own potential.

David Subotic: His belief and support, paired with his unique background, opened the industry's Pandora's box—access to the public markets. David was an expert in this world and guided me through MedMen being first.

Stephen Schuler and Dan Tierney: Their belief in MedMen and capitalization of our business, which at the time was on an unprecedented scale, set the stage for a permanent asset class. There is a lot of credit deserved for being first in a world full of followers.

Rick Bierman: This story only happens because of the tools I had, both in my DNA and from my life experience, to chase my dream.

Thank you to every believer, advocate, supporter, investor, and reformer who made their contribution to my journey and the mainstreaming of marijuana. A special thanks to: Axel Barnabe, Jay Brown (Los Angeles), Jay Brown (Vegas), Nigel Burns, Rob Chalmers, Nick Danias, Dan Daviau, Lou Deritis, John Jezzini, Efrem Kamen, Rob Kampia, Yelena Katchko, Kelley Crosson, Nam Le, Matthew Philbin, Anthony Quintal, Andy Rayburn, Lindsay Robinson, Steve Sisolak, Antonio Villaraigosa, Lance Washington, Herb Wesson, and Armen Yemenidjian.

Thanks to Matt Holt, Katie Dickman, and the incredible team at Ben-Bella Books for believing in my story and for their dedication to bringing this book to life with such care and craftsmanship. I'm also deeply grateful to Richard Abate, my literary agent, for making it all possible. A special thanks to Geoff Gray, the brilliant writer and storyteller, whose collaboration was the driving force behind transforming this journey into words on the page.

And to every human who ever wore the "Red Jacket" and worked at MedMen, playing their part in inviting the world to mainstream marijuana, I will be forever grateful for your contributions.

About the Author

Adam Bierman is the cofounder and former CEO of MedMen, the pioneering American cannabis company that became the first US cannabis unicorn. Under his decade of leadership, MedMen grew into the most recognized brand in the cannabis industry, expanding across five states, operating 33 retail stores, and employing more than 1,000 people.

Bierman's visionary efforts brought cannabis into the mainstream with flagship stores in iconic locations like Beverly Hills and New York's Fifth Avenue. His work helped redefine cannabis as a normalized part of culture and commerce, transforming it from a stigmatized substance into a thriving business sector.

An unconventional thinker, Bierman consistently challenges expectations. Today, he partners with disruptors and innovators, pushing boundaries and embracing the question, "Why not?"